THE
BEST
THEY COULD BE

Related Titles from Potomac Books

THE
BEST
THEY COULD BE

HOW THE CLEVELAND INDIANS BECAME THE KINGS OF BASEBALL, 1916–1920

SCOTT H. LONGERT

Potomac Books
Washington, D.C.

Library of Congress Cataloging-in-Publication Data
Longert, Scott.
   The best they could be : how the Cleveland Indians became the kings of baseball, 1916-1920 / Scott H. Longert.
      pages cm
   Includes bibliographical references and index.
   ISBN 978-1-61234-493-5 (hardcover : alk. paper)
   ISBN 978-1-61234-494-2 (electronic)
   1. Cleveland Indians (Baseball team)—History—20th century. I. Title.
   GV875.C7L68 2013
   796.357'64097713209041—dc23

                                                                    2013000217

Printed in the United States of America on acid-free paper that meets the American National Standards Institute Z39-48 Standard.

Potomac Books
22841 Quicksilver Drive
Dulles, Virginia 20166

First Edition

10 9 8 7 6 5 4 3 2 1

CONTENTS

1

A FRANCHISE IN PERIL

Though he had made the rail trip from Chicago to Cleveland many times in the last fifteen years, this December 1915 journey was anything but routine for American League president Ban Johnson. He surely had some major regrets as he traveled to Cleveland to meet with ball club owner Charlie Somers and confront him about the deteriorating financial condition of the Cleveland Indians. Somers had been a crucial asset to Johnson when the American League was just a promising idea. Johnson, as president of Minor League Baseball's Western Association, had launched a plan in 1899 to challenge the unsuspecting National League head-on. His brash idea involved building a competing league, and when he first met with Somers, he was looking for a heavy-duty financial man to start a major league franchise in Cleveland.

League Park had been empty for a year since scoundrel Frank Robison, owner of the Cleveland Spiders, had gutted the team. The 1899 Spiders were the disgrace of the National League, losing an unbelievable 134 games. The usually loyal Cleveland fans were ready to tar and feather the villainous Robison for sending away stars like Cy Young, Bobby Wallace, and Jesse Burkett to fill out the roster of his new St. Louis club. The Cleveland newspapers blasted the

1

devious owner until he left town, allowing his brother Stanley to watch over the shambles of a once-proud franchise. It came as no surprise when the league office dissolved the franchise after the 1899 season. Johnson arrived in Cleveland hoping to find the right person to share his ambitious dream. The planets must have been in perfect alignment, for Johnson found just the man he was searching for.

Thirty-one-year-old Charlie Somers happened to be one of the wealthiest men in northern Ohio. His father, Joseph, owned prime real estate and also controlled a large number of coal mines in Ohio and Pennsylvania. In the late nineteenth century and well into the twentieth, coal was the leading source of energy. An abundant supply existed in southern Ohio and throughout West Virginia and Pennsylvania. Labor could be had cheaply, and the demand for it had no bounds whatsoever. Young Charlie not only maintained his father's empire, but he expanded it greatly. However, he did have one weakness his father abhorred: Charlie Somers loved the game of baseball.

Through a great deal of luck, Johnson connected with Somers. In a short meeting at a Cleveland hotel, he convinced Somers to become a major league owner and learned, to his delight, that Somers was interested in bankrolling franchises and building ballparks in other cities as well, and he was willing to spend a fortune to see their shared dream come true. The National League had no idea it was about to go to war with a player as formidable as Charlie Somers. During the winter of 1900 the two partners in crime sneaked in and out of cities in the Midwest and Northeast, targeting prime land on which to build stadiums for their soon-to-be-thriving American League (AL). Johnson had the grand vision, while Somers had the business sense and pure guts to pour his money into the new venture. When Johnson appeared to falter in securing a Boston franchise, Somers stepped in, found a location for a ballpark, and then wired a letter of credit totaling $250,000 to a Boston bank. The park was built, but there were no takers on running the franchise. Somers, through some creative accounting, named his partner, John Kilfoyl, president of the Cleveland franchise, freeing Charlie up to own the Boston club as well.

In 1901, few men in professional baseball had the backbone and the smarts to accomplish what the son of a coal baron could. Several articles written about

Somers in later years claimed he loaned substantial amounts of money to both Connie Mack and Charles Comiskey to help them finance their AL clubs. When ballplayers jumped en masse from the National to the American League in 1902, rumor had it that Charlie Somers had set up a fund for owners to use in luring players to join the brand-new league. Nothing could slow down the newly appointed American League vice president, even his wife's threat of divorce if he continued in the less-than-respectable business of baseball. Mae Gilbert Somers was certainly not bluffing. She followed through in 1906, causing a sensation among the well-to-do set in Cleveland.

Now a bachelor, Somers enjoyed a number of stable years running the American League's new Cleveland franchise. He had excellent players, including Napoleon "Nap" Lajoie (also known as Larry), who was the premier hitter in all of baseball. Due to Lajoie's enormous popularity, the team name became the Naps. Other stars on the club included Elmer Flick, Addie Joss, and Bill Bradley. The team was competitive, usually finishing each season among the leaders. From 1906 through 1908 the Naps averaged eighty-eight wins per season. However Somers made the mistake of keeping his core players despite a decline in performance. Injuries and the retention of aging veterans resulted in several losing seasons. By 1911 Somers seemed to have righted the ship, with twenty-four-year-old Joe Jackson, his new outfielder, tearing up AL pitching.

But despite Jackson's and Lajoie's hefty batting averages, the team slipped further, and the grandstand at League Park began to sport a large number of empty seats. After many years of generating healthy profits for Cleveland baseball, attendance at League Park continued to fall. By the 1914 season it had hit an embarrassing low. The first two months of the 1915 season saw little improvement in gate receipts. Though not as hated as Frank Robison, Charlie Somers was no longer the idol of the Cleveland fans. To compound Somers's financial woes, the spring of 1915 saw his real estate dealings implode, while his coal mine empire was threatened by a recent worker strike.

The Sporting News published a May editorial asserting that the Cleveland owner had too many interests outside of baseball and should sell out. The editorial went on to say that most owners had few investments outside of baseball, allowing them full concentration on their teams. Somers could no longer oversee production at his mines, manage out-of-state real estate deals, and handle the day-to-day obligations of a major league franchise. For the first time in his long financial life, Charlie Somers was grossly underfunded and overextended.

A committee of Cleveland bankers had seized control of Somers's far-flung assets, which were losing value with each passing day. The only means of paying off creditors was to sell off as much as possible, including the Cleveland baseball franchise. As of the 1915 season the team had changed their nickname from Naps to Indians; Larry Lajoie had been given his release at the end of the 1914 season. One of the Cleveland newspapers ran a contest and announced the winning entry as the Cleveland Indians. Ban Johnson told the press he was searching for a way to allow Somers to maintain his hold on the team. The only way to accomplish this was with a large infusion of capital. Given the current situation, an investor coming forward seemed as likely as the Indians winning the pennant in 1916. According to sportswriter Henry P. Edwards of the *Cleveland Plain Dealer* there were two simple solutions. He wrote in his column, "Sell or strengthen. Such [are] the demands of the public. Somers had made his mistakes and his baseball team is a joke." The *Detroit Free Press*, a newspaper in another AL town, offered a more blunt assessment: "[Manager Lee] Fohl's outfit looks so bad that by comparison the Browns and Athletics look like pennant contenders. Cleveland in its present form is the absolute zero of major league baseball."

Somers's money troubles were made even worse by the emergence of the Federal League (FL). The addition of a third major league in 1914 gave players new leverage. They could now play two sides against each other to get the best contract they were able to negotiate. Three Cleveland pitchers, including twenty-three-game winner Cy Falkenberg, had jumped to the Feds. To stop the wholesale defections, AL and NL owners had reluctantly raised player salaries, even offering long-term deals to star players. In 1914 the team had a costly payroll of $90,000. Baseball experts of the day claimed a reasonable payroll for a second-division team should be around $50,000. Somers apparently paid close attention, cutting salaries in 1915 by 40 percent. A good portion of that total came directly from the January release of Lajoie. Truly one of the all-time greats, Lajoie had captured the imagination of Cleveland fans going all the way back to his arrival in May of 1902. A tremendous hitter and gifted infielder, Lajoie was the face of Cleveland baseball for thirteen seasons. It would have been a fine gesture for Somers to allow Larry to finish his career in Cleveland. In Major League Baseball, however, money usually wins out over sentimentality. Thus the "Great" Lajoie was sent packing, along with his three-year contract calling for $9,000 per year.

Another factor in Somers's financial collapse was a $17,000 investment in a scouting system that branched out across the United States. Somers had the progressive idea of trying to root out young talent and send promising players to certain minor league teams until they were skilled enough to join the Indians. At one point in 1914, he had nine scouts on the payroll. It is also believed Somers had an interest in several clubs, including Portland, Oregon; New Orleans; Waterbury, Connecticut; and Toledo, a belief supported by the fact that when Somers officially bowed out of Cleveland, he quietly resurfaced as the owner of the New Orleans Pelicans.

Despite the ravaging of the Indians' payroll and the release of seven scouts, Somers was teetering on the brink of collapse in August of 1915. On August 21, it was reported that he had dealt his best player, Joe Jackson, to the Chicago White Sox for $25,000 and several Chicago players, who would later turn out to be outfielder Bobby Roth and pitcher Ed Klepfer. Neither of the two would be of significant help to their new club, although Roth would eventually bang out some home runs and have several good seasons. According to the *Plain Dealer*, rumors had been flying all day on the 21st that Jackson was to be sent elsewhere. First there was a report that he was to be traded to the Washington Senators for two players and cash. Then came a story that Jackson and star shortstop Ray Chapman were both headed to the White Sox. Word leaked out that Harry Grabiner, Chicago's team secretary, had arrived in Cleveland secretly to negotiate the deal to pry "Shoeless Joe" away from the Indians. One has to wonder—if the frugal Charles Comiskey was willing to part with $25,000, what might the price have been if all the AL owners knew what was happening? At any rate, .400 hitters are a very rare commodity that should be cherished, not cast away. Maneuvering to keep his franchise afloat, Somers dug himself into an even deeper hole. If he thought attendance was pretty bad with

Jackson in the outfield, imagine how excited the fans were to see Roth and Klepfer perform.

For his part, Jackson seemed quite relieved to be a member of the Chicago White Sox. He told the newspapers, "I am perfectly satisfied. Why shouldn't I be? I am helping Charlie Somers out of some of his troubles. I was willing to go anywhere he wanted to sell me. Then I stand a chance of getting into some sweet World Series money." It is doubtful many remembered those words in 1919, when Jackson got involved with some real sweet money that would cost him his MLB career.

Though fans were shaking their heads at the loss of Jackson, they were further distressed that Somers had listened to offers for Ray Chapman. At twenty-four, Chapman had clearly established himself as Cleveland's shortstop for the long term. In 1915 he played in all 154 games, hitting a respectable .270, legging out 17 triples, and scoring 101 runs while stealing a total of 36 bases. Somers believed he needed some spin control and addressed the concerns of the Cleveland faithful. He stated, "Because of a bad financial year, I was forced to let Jackson go. It was up to me to take some radical move to relieve the pressure and this deal was the result." He added, "Now I can positively say that Chapman will remain." Somers mentioned that Frank Navin of the Tigers had offered to pay big bucks to acquire Chapman, but Cleveland's struggling owner said Chapman was to remain a fixture here in town.

The 1915 season ended with the Indians winning a grand total of fifty-seven ball games. Only one pitcher on the staff was able to get his winning percentage over .500. The team was able to avoid last place thanks to Connie Mack's Athletics' win total of forty-three, by far the worst showing in both major leagues. Manager Lee Fohl would survive the season and several more to come. However, the fall and winter of 1915–1916 would be a demoralizing time for fans of Cleveland baseball.

According to a story by *Cleveland News* sports editor Ed Bang, Somers's accumulated debt totaled a gargantuan $1.75 million, an astounding figure in the early twentieth century. His holdings included the Cleveland Indians, the Cleveland Spiders American Association baseball club, twenty coal mines in Ohio and Pennsylvania, and two substantial real estate ventures in Milwaukee and downtown Cleveland. Somers's total assets were believed to be in the neighborhood of $2.9 million, but a sizable chunk of the assets were not liquid, unable to be converted into cash. John Sherwin, president of First National Bank of Cleveland and chairman of the bankers' committee, expressed hope that he could repair the damage and allow Somers to at least keep the Cleveland franchise. Ban Johnson's December visit, however, virtually assured that Somers had run out of time as far as the American League was concerned.

A group of AL owners came forward to announce their support for their fallen colleague. Clark Griffith of Washington, Col. Jake Ruppert of New York, and Robert Hedges of the St. Louis Browns all voiced the opinion that Charlie Somers should be able to keep his club. Each owner pledged to give players to Cleveland without any upfront money. Among the names tossed around were Washington's first baseman Chick Gandil, catcher Eddie Ainsmith, and second baseman Ray Morgan. These were fine gestures, but what Somers desperately needed was money. The owners had stopped far short of mentioning the critical need. Looming large was the silence of Connie Mack and Charles Comiskey, men who owed a large debt to Somers for helping them get their franchises rolling in 1901.

Despite his earlier mandate that Somers must sell, Ban Johnson backtracked a few steps. The Federal League was about to collapse. With the competition out of the way, perhaps he could convince the AL owners to ante up in Somers's defense. He called for a special owners' meeting near the end of December to review the Cleveland situation. The meeting produced a pledge to loan Somers $100,000 to help get him through at least another season, but the committee refused to accept the pledge, stating that Somers had to get out of baseball. The Cleveland Indians were to be sold.

When the public learned that the Indians were now firmly controlled by a group of concerned bankers, speculation arose that a new local buyer would step forward and keep any outsiders from taking the franchise. Gossip circulated as to who would rescue the ball club. The first serious name to surface was entrepreneur Ben Hopkins, a huge baseball fan and in his younger days a regular visitor to spring training. As the man who built the Cleveland Belt Line Railroad, which allowed freight trains en route to the city's industrial belt to bypass downtown, he had quite a bit of money available. Hopkins and Ban Johnson met at the Hollenden Hotel in downtown Cleveland to talk about the possibilities, however, the deal went nowhere. The sale price, rumored to be between $500,000 and $600,000, possibly proved to be a bit too much for the railroad builder.

Before he left Cleveland, Ban Johnson stated, "Cleveland is such a good baseball town that I am sure that some Clevelanders will step to the front and purchase Mr. Somers holdings. Cleveland is a city of 1,000,000 people yet it has only one ball club. All it needs is a winner." Johnson believed a city as large as Cleveland could even support two baseball clubs, so one team should have no problem filling stands provided the team could win some games. With Hopkins out of the picture, local Cleveland organizations discussed forming committees to save the team. The Cleveland Athletic Club (CAC) announced their intention to buy the team. Within days another local syndicate came forward. This one was led by a former Cleveland sheriff claiming to have the money for the purchase, and Larry Lajoie was lined up to be the manager for the 1916 season. Both organizations seemed serious about buying the team. The CAC had a lot of money behind it, with many of its members among the wealthiest of Clevelanders.

In early January of 1916, a representative from the CAC met with the bankers' committee in an attempt to strike a deal. The bankers would not budge from their asking price of $560,000. The CAC countered with a lukewarm offer of $400,000, stating they would likely have to spend an additional $40,000 to buy more players. To nobody's surprise, the offer was rejected. The Lajoie backers announced they were probably going to fold as well. With this news the dark winter skies over Lake Erie got even darker.

Ban Johnson expressed his disappointment that the local syndicate had decided to withdraw. Johnson told the local papers, "I certainly had hopes that the CAC syndicate would come to the front and take the club, as I believe it would be a great investment." He then added ominously, "If Clevelanders don't want it, I will find some other purchaser." Did Johnson have some out-of-town buyers waiting to step in? He did not elaborate but advised he was traveling to Cleveland on January 7 to speak to several more potential buyers.

The next day, word circulated throughout town that Johnson planned to meet with ex–FL moguls Harry Sinclair, Ed Gwinner, and league president James Gilmore. Since the peace agreement between the major leagues and the Federal League appeared to be a done deal, Gwinner, the owner of the Federal League's Pittsburgh club, expressed an interest in buying the Cleveland Indians. Reportedly, Gwinner, who had millions, was capable of meeting the bankers' committee asking price. In addition, he seemingly had the desire to stay in baseball, regardless of the dissolution of the Federal League. As a resident of Pittsburgh, he could easily travel back and forth between the cities.

The meeting with Johnson took place on January 10, 1916. It ended without a buyer for the team. Once again the asking price proved to be a stumbling block. The pressure on the AL president had to be building. Spring training was less than two months away, and he had no ownership for the Indians. The papers began questioning the need for local ownership. The *Plain Dealer* asked, "Why so much hysteria about local capital being invested? Does the public care two street car transfers who owns the club as long as it is a winner?"

The article went on to point out a long list of owners who were not lifetime residents of the cities in which they owned a team. Charles Comiskey had transferred his St. Paul franchise to Chicago for the start of the American League. Charley Murphy, who had owned the Chicago Cubs, came from Cincinnati, while John T. Brush, the New York Giants owner, originally made Indianapolis his home. This argument did actually make a considerable amount of sense. Cleveland had established itself as a baseball town going back to the Cleveland Forest City team of the late 1860s. It was a charter member of the American League from 1901. Did it really make a tremendous difference if the owner did not make Cleveland his home?

At the end of January, Indians vice president E. S. Barnard announced plans for the 1916 spring training trip. The entire group was to arrive at the St. Charles Hotel in downtown New Orleans on the 20th. On March 1, all thirty members of the squad would be on hand, with exhibition games beginning March 5. The only snag in the plans was the lack of money to pay the train fares plus player expenses for camp. If new ownership did not come forward, the players might be working out in a gymnasium in Cleveland. Manager Lee Fohl had to be breathing a little uneasily, knowing that a new owner might want his own man to step in to manage the club.

With two weeks left until the start of spring training, word reached Cleveland that a buyer from Chicago had entered the field. The gentleman's name was not made public; however, it was known that the buyer and league president Johnson were good friends. Throughout the winter, buyers had come and gone, but this particular deal was said to be "on fire." Attorneys representing both the bankers' committee and Charlie Somers traveled to Chicago. The asking price for the team was believed to have been lowered to $500,000. In a statement released to the press, attorney George Steele of the bankers' committee said he expected negotiations to be completed within ten days.

Now that a deal seemed to be in the works, Cleveland ballplayers began to speak up about the coming season. Ray Chapman volunteered to be in New Orleans early to help teach the new recruits. Catcher Steve O'Neill wrote to Lee Fohl saying he should find a catcher to work forty games in 1916, and that he would catch the rest. Pitcher Guy Morton wrote that he had quit his winter job, which turned out to be hunting, and was ready to report early.

On February 15, the news broke that the sale of the Indians was just days away. A big-time Chicago businessman would likely be the main investor. Ban Johnson had set aside Washington first baseman Chick Gandil and Chicago catcher Tom Daly for the new owner to purchase. Johnson urged the mystery owner to consider spending a large sum on top of the purchase to acquire Frank Baker from the Philadelphia Athletics. The timing of the cryptic message coincided with the plans for Cleveland players to head south to New Orleans. It is interesting to speculate if Johnson had the Chicago buyer as his plan B all along. Plan A had failed to bring in a local man or group. Possibly Johnson had found a buyer quite some time ago but preferred to give Clevelanders a chance to step up. That did not happen, allowing Johnson to put his man in place. The AL president was a very forceful individual. He may have decided early that coddling the Cleveland locals would do little to solve his major dilemma. Maybe Johnson had his problem solved all along, though the solution appeared to have been revealed only with his mid-February announcement.

The official news the Indians were sold came the following day. Charley Murphy, the former Chicago Cubs owner, sent a representative to Cleveland to determine if League Park and its grounds were available for sale separate from the ball club. Murphy wanted the chance to purchase the park and lease it to the new Indians owner. But his envoy learned from the bankers' committee that the sale of the team had already been agreed to. Upon hearing this story Ban Johnson did confirm Cleveland had a new owner. When pressed for details Johnson refused to give up a name. Why he did this remains unclear; however, it assuredly got all four Cleveland newspapers jamming telegraph wires and phone lines to Chicago trying to get the scoop. On the morning of the 17th, the sports sections all had blazing headlines revealing that the senior partner of Dunn & McCarthy Contractors had pledged to buy the Cleveland Indians. His name was James C. Dunn.

2

"SUNNY JIM"

With all the speculation that a wealthy Clevelander or an owner from the dissolved Federal League would buy the Indians, how did a railroad contractor with no connection to organized baseball become the purchaser? Dunn and Ban Johnson had a number of mutual friends in the Chicago area and may well have known each other from the restaurants and bars both of them frequented. But that does not add up to becoming a major league owner. A very entertaining explanation appeared in Franklin "Whitey" Lewis's 1949 team history, *The Cleveland Indians*. Lewis, as sports editor of the *Cleveland Press*, surely had access to a clipping file dating back to February 1916, when some of the old Cleveland sportswriters who had known Jim Dunn were still living. The tale told by Lewis puts Ban Johnson in a popular Chicago saloon complaining about his troubles finding a buyer for the Cleveland team. Suddenly Johnson has a revelation and points to Dunn, telling him he's going to be the new owner. Dunn, shocked, stammers that he only has about $15,000 in cash available. Excitement fills the saloon as the men around them (including the bartender) shout out dollar sums they are willing to invest. Before long all the capital is raised. Still taken aback, Dunn says he knows nothing about the business of baseball. Johnson assures him he will get the right men to run the club. The story ends there, with everyone raising their glasses and drinking a toast or two to the new owner.

This may have made a great story for Franklin Lewis, but it boasts more than a little embellishment. Jim Dunn had started out in business as a fourteen-year-old messenger boy for the First National Bank of Marshalltown, Iowa. Born September 11, 1866, in nearby St. Anthony, Jim was the first child of William and Elizabeth Dunn. William, like many other mid-nineteenth-century Irish immigrants, made his way to Iowa and purchased farmland there. His marriage to Elizabeth was the second for both, eventually producing a family with nine new children to go along with Elizabeth's five. Leaving the overcrowded Dunn household, Jim quit school early to seek his fortune in banking and finance. He spent several years as a bookkeeper, meeting Henry Anson when he worked for the oil company A. E. Shorthill. Anson agreed to lend money to Dunn so the young man could start a coal contracting business. If needed, Henry's son Cap—who played first base for the White Sox and managed the team—could front Dad some money. Anson had few equals in the game. His batting skills and all-around ability made him a genuine superstar.

As he was getting his start in business, Dunn married Edith R. Forney of Marshalltown on January 14, 1888. Soon Dunn branched out to become a general contractor, selling coal, wood, and lime to various businesses in the area, taking offices in the City Bank Building with a partner, Robert A. Elzy. In 1904 Dunn got his first substantial contracting job in Marshalltown, building a sewer from State Street to the Iowa River. Sometime afterward, Dunn left Marshalltown, settling in Chicago, where railroad contracting became his main focus, eventually landing him a job in Cleveland to build part of a new railroad line for Ben Hopkins. When construction began in 1907, Dunn moved to Cleveland temporarily, renting a home on East 84th Street. When he had some downtime, Dunn attended ball games at League Park, where he got to follow the Cleveland Naps' red-hot 1908 pennant race.

During their surprise winning streak in September, Dunn noticed the large number of fans streaming into the ballpark. As a shrewd businessman he realized that there was money to be made in professional baseball. It did not hurt that while Dunn sat in the grandstand, Ed Walsh and Addie Joss hooked up in one of the greatest pitching duels ever seen. A perfect game pitched by Joss on a Friday afternoon in October with ten thousand fans on hand convinced Dunn to branch out from railroad contracting into baseball. With both the White Sox and Cubs under solid ownership, he had little opportunity to do so in Chicago. He wisely passed on any involvement with the Federal League, instead opting for a chance to acquire a proven AL or NL franchise. It would be eight years before the opportunity to own a major league franchise became available to the railroad man, and Dunn, now a millionaire, decided to enter the fray.

The Cleveland that Dunn would visit again had grown considerably since his last stay in the city. Since 1910 the population had expanded at a rate of 42 percent and would reach a figure of nearly 800,000 in the 1920 census. Downtown Cleveland had become a vibrant city with department stores and elegant restaurants and hotels all within walking distance of Public Square, as well as auto showrooms offering several makes of locally manufactured automobiles. Alexander Winton's touring cars were a work of art, custom built for each individual buyer. Other local automakers included the White Motor Company (an early innovator in steam-powered engines), Peerless, and Chandler. The Stearns Motor Sales Company offered the "Knight," with luxurious upholstery, room for seven passengers, and curtains that fit over the rear windows if privacy was desired. If an auto buyer wanted a clean, quiet ride, there were two electric car manufacturers: Baker Electrics and Rauch & Lang. Tires were in plentiful supply, with B. F. Goodrich of Akron maintaining a megastore on Euclid Avenue.

Downtown Cleveland boasted a number of first-rate department stores, including the May Company, Bailey's, and William Taylor Son & Company. For the gentlemen, B. R. Baker specialized in suits and overcoats. The city's entertainment industry was booming, with no fewer than eight theaters between downtown and the eastern suburbs. Silent films were extremely popular, along with live vaudeville shows performed daily. For the more cultured crowd, the Cleveland Museum of Art opened its doors in the spring of 1916 at a cost of $1.2 million.

Jim Dunn had the reputation of being the eternal optimist, winning him the nickname Sunny Jim. Arriving in Cleveland on a gray February day, the forty-nine-year-old Dunn needed all the optimism he could gather. Facing the press for the first time, the new owner needed to make a positive impression on the media and the fans. He said, "I will not stand for a tailender. If I thought the Cleveland club's destined to remain a second division team, I would not buy it, but I believe it can be turned into a first division team with some expenditure of money, and that is what I intend to do."

Dunn's words were exactly what a baseball-starved town needed to hear. After two years of lousy baseball, Sunny Jim talked of returning the city to the first division. He vowed to bring in much-needed talent to bolster the dormant franchise. He believed the city of Cleveland was destined to be one of the greatest in the country. As first impressions go, Dunn scored very high on Cleveland's popularity meter. Even his wife, Edith, received praise from the papers.

Ban Johnson told reporters about the great opportunity missed by Ben Hopkins and the other Cleveland money men. He stated, "I am greatly surprised that no Cleveland capitalists saw what a splendid proposition it was. I gave them all the chance there was, but they did not see fit to acquire the club, and consequently it goes to outsiders." Johnson's words sounded almost apologetic, but the fact remained that he really had given local people the option to own the team. Now a new man in town, albeit a wealthy one, had control of the team.

At this point Charlie Somers had been removed from the equation. His debt was immediately reduced to $1.2 million. Somers moved quickly to pay off his obligations. The coal strike ended, and he reopened his southern Ohio mine and resolved his real estate problems. Before the Indians claimed their first pennant, Charlie would be a millionaire again. After a second costly divorce settlement in 1919, Somers pursued wife number three, bought a huge yacht, and spent his summers boating in the waters off Lake Erie near his beach house in Sandusky, Ohio. Shed no tears for the former owner of the Cleveland Indians. He died a very wealthy man in 1934 at the age of sixty-six.

Before arriving in Cleveland to speak with reporters, James Dunn contacted Lee Fohl to let him know that his services would likely be retained. They discussed the immediate needs of the team, with Fohl recommending the purchase of first baseman Chick Gandil from Washington. The other possibility was Ivan Howard, an infielder with the St. Louis Browns. Dunn assured Fohl he would have pursued third baseman Frank Baker if he had obtained the club a week or two earlier. Baker had been sold by Connie Mack to the New York Yankees. Dunn stated he would move on and make the best of the situation. Fohl still had to convince both Dunn and Johnson of the necessity of sending his pitchers and catchers to New Orleans before the rest of the squad. A technicality had Johnson running the Cleveland team until Dunn's paperwork with the American League was finalized. Fohl pleaded that his young staff needed extra attention to work out their flaws. He argued that most other clubs had established veterans returning, while the Indians needed to look at a number of prospects before settling on a roster. Johnson bought the argument, allowing Fohl to go ahead with his spring training plans.

Within several days Jim Dunn opened his checkbook as promised. He acquired backup catcher Tom Daly from the Chicago White Sox. He then bought the contract of Ivan Howard, designating him to become the utility infielder. Dunn next turned to the Washington Senators to begin negotiations for Chick Gandil, who had compiled a lifetime .335 average at League Park. Dunn needed a veteran first baseman with some pop to his bat along with good fielding skills. Gandil had actually told Ray Chapman a few months earlier that he really wanted to play in Cleveland. He claimed that he enjoyed being in the city and liked the players as well. Part of Gandil's appeal to the Cleveland management hinged upon his 1912 performance in Washington. He joined the Senators on Memorial Day and went on a tear, leading the club to seventeen straight wins. For the season he hit .305, drove in eighty-one runs, and hustled for thirteen triples. Lee Fohl convinced his new boss that Gandil could do the same in Indian town. Fohl said, "I can point out to you where we lost twenty games last year because of mistakes at first base. With a player of the intelligence of Gandil and his mechanical ability, first base should be played as it has not been since George Stovall was in his prime." This may have been high praise indeed, yet the Cleveland club had not won anything with Stovall at first base.

Speculation arose that the Cleveland owner had made some inquiries about obtaining pitcher "Smoky" Joe Wood from the Boston Red Sox. Despite serious problems with his pitching arm, Wood had managed to win fifteen games in 1915 with an amazing earned run average of 1.49. Dunn and Fohl knew that Wood could not pitch regularly, but they were willing to give the idea some consideration. However Wood was reported to be receiving a salary of $7,500, which most likely pushed that deal to the sidelines. Wood did not play baseball in 1916, but circumstances would keep him on Cleveland's wanted list.

On February 22, Jim Dunn announced the formation of his front office. His top man was to be Bob McRoy, the former secretary of the American League. In addition to being an expert on league matters, McRoy had spent time in the front office as secretary and treasurer of the Boston Red Sox. During the 1912 World Series, McRoy handled the ticket sales plus distribution for all the Boston home games. His résumé gave Dunn an experienced executive who could advise the new owner on the many different aspects of running a baseball organization.

The sale of the Cleveland Indians became official on February 24. Jim Dunn established himself as team president, while Bob McRoy held the dual title of vice president and treasurer. Dunn also named some of his new stockholders, who included McRoy; Dunn's contracting partner, P. F. McCarthy; two brothers, Reed and Dick Lane, both Chicago attorneys; and Tom Walsh, a fellow railroad contractor from Iowa. Reed would serve as team secretary. One of several stockholders with Chicago connections turned out to be John Burns, owner of the saloon and café on the first floor of the Fisher Building, which housed the AL office in Chicago. Could there have been a shred of truth to Whitey Lewis's tale of how Dunn acquired the club? Not likely, but Johnson and Dunn probably met more than once at Burns's establishment to discuss the terms for Dunn's purchase of the Indians. As an insider, Burns likely wangled a few shares from his pals.

Since the new Cleveland front office had Chicago connections, an announcement came that April 25 would be designated James Dunn Day at League Park. Charles Comiskey planned to accompany his White Sox to the game and take part in the celebration. Traveling with Comiskey were the famed Woodland Bards, a gentleman's club with close ties to the Chicago owner. Their participation and the obligatory gifts for the new Cleveland boss ensured the day would be a memorable one for all Cleveland baseball fans.

Addressing fans at the game, Dunn again promised he would field a team they could be proud of. He cautioned fans not to expect a pennant in the first year, but a team that would battle for every game and always give the best it had. In just seven days the Cleveland owner proved to be a man of action, putting his front office into place and signing two players—Gandil and Howard—while actively pursuing several others. Dunn had taken major steps to win over the skeptical Cleveland fans. The optimism of Sunny Jim was contagious, allowing the bitter memories of the previous year to gradually disappear with the falling snow of late winter.

The purchase of Chick Gandil from Washington became official on February 26. To acquire Gandil, Dunn paid Clark Griffith $5,000. Speaking to reporters in Chicago about his latest deal, Dunn said, "The purchase of Gandil will, I believe, give us one of the fastest fielding infields in the league. Gandil is as good as any around first base; Terry Turner has only one superior at second, that is Eddie Collins; Chapman is the king of them all at short; and we are sure to show a classy third baseman from our candidates we have for the position." Dunn went on to say he had no further plans to buy any more players but would jump back in if any desirable players appeared on the market. Terry Turner had been with Cleveland since 1904, playing mostly third base and shortstop. He did have time at second base during the 1915 season, but Bill Wambsganss played the majority of games there. Ray Chapman had proved himself to be an exceptional shortstop, but there was still uncertainty about the third-base job.

A whirlwind of activity had preceded the Indians' annual spring training journey to New Orleans. Now that the ownership situation had been solidified, the players were ready to make a new start, as the rest of the team prepared to join the pitchers down south.

Much had been said about the new Cleveland infield and its possibilities. Henry Edwards, who had covered the team since its beginnings in 1901, weighed in on prospects for the outfield, infield, and pitchers. He wrote, "While the outfield is not as strong on paper because Joe Jackson had been sold, better teamwork can be expected. With all due respect to Joe Jackson, who was one of the best batters the league has known, Joe simply would not team it with his associates, and no manager could make him. If Bobby Roth continues to play the game he did here last season, Jackson will not be missed." It was probably one of the worst assessments ever made by Cleveland's veteran sportswriter. True enough, teamwork is critical to having a good defensive outfield, but a player of Shoeless Joe's caliber does not come along very often. The elite company of outfielders in Major League Baseball had only three members: Ty Cobb, Tris Speaker, and Joe Jackson. Even if Bobby Roth had a great season, the team would have still needed a Cobb or a Speaker to replace what Joe Jackson could bring.

Edwards expected Jack Graney to repeat his steady 1915 batting performance of .260, along with his better-than-average defense. Elmer Smith had been primarily a pinch-hitter the previous season, but with his ability to hit the long ball, he appeared ready to be the everyday right fielder. Comparatively speaking, the outfield of Graney, Roth, and Smith fell well short of the better AL combinations. Detroit had Cobb, Bobby Veach, and Harry Heilmann. Chicago had Happy Felsch in center field with Joe Jackson in left. The two outfielders possessed lots of power between them and were both able to hit above .300. The World Champion Boston Red Sox were very strong at all three positions. Tris Speaker could do it all from center field: hitting well over .300, bashing out doubles and triples, stealing a base, or throwing out guys trying to take an extra base.

It was all in a day's work for the amazing Speaker. If there was a ball hit deep to the alleys that Tris could not get to, it was likely that Harry Hooper or Duffy Lewis would make the play. For the Cleveland outfielders to compete with these players, they would have needed help from Graney's dog, Larry, the Indians' lively mascot.

In winding up the analysis, Edwards believed the Indians had two pitchers they could depend on, Guy Morton and Willie Mitchell. Morton debuted with Cleveland in 1914, winning one ball game while losing thirteen. He could only get better after that, and he did, posting sixteen wins in 1915 while losing the same amount. Willie Mitchell started with the old Cleveland Naps in 1909, maintaining a record average of near .500 with less than stellar support from his teammates. The remaining pitchers competing for spots in the rotation were the newly acquired Ed Klepfer; holdovers Sam Jones, Paul Carter, and Fred Coumbe; and a cast of characters including Rip Hagerman, Clarence Garrett, and Al Collamore. Two other pitchers reported to spring training with little or no fanfare. Neither Stan Coveleski nor Jim Bagby got much press coverage when they showed up in February of 1916. Reports stated that Bagby had some skills as a pinch hitter, while Coveleski had pretty fair control of his pitches. The odds of either one sticking with the varsity seemed to be remote at best.

Spring training in New Orleans got off to a smooth start. The early work put in by the pitchers kept sore arms to a minimum. Sessions began each day shortly after noon, lasting for two hours. Since lunch had to be skipped, the players loaded up on breakfast while using what remained of their $2.50 daily meal allowance for dinner. The afternoon practice kept the players away from the racetrack, disappointing the neighborhood bookies. At the end of each workout, the squad ran a lap around Heinemann Park. All handled the extra running fairly well, except for manager Fohl, who huffed and puffed his way well behind his players. Soon Mardi Gras time arrived in New Orleans, allowing the team to watch the parades from their hotel balcony. Due to the large crowds in attendance, the players were four to five per hotel room until the end of the festivities.

Ray Chapman became the number one disciple of Sunny Jim Dunn, the eternal optimist. He told interested reporters, "I cannot but believe Cleveland is going to do things this season. You can bet on it that we are going to play better ball than we did a year ago, and it is going to take some airtight work to beat us. Stranger things have happened in baseball." Chapman believed the acquisition of Chick Gandil was a steal and that Elmer Smith could be ready for a breakout season. Ray analyzed every position in the club, expressing confidence in its improvement for the coming season. He did confess to doubts about the pitching staff but had great faith in Lee Fohl's ability to develop the necessary talent. Chapman had been with Cleveland since 1912; his cheerful outlook for 1916 helped buoy the spirits of the Cleveland fans who had had almost nothing to get excited about for the past two seasons.

Lee Fohl firmly believed that aggressiveness in baseball translated into winning. He subscribed to the theory that the more a player will hustle and fight, the more likely he is to succeed. He cited Ray Chapman and Chick Gandil as measuring up to that standard. Chapman, according to the *Plain Dealer*, was "as earnest an athlete as ever wore a Cleveland uniform, and not one of the tribe enthuses more over a victory or is more despondent because of a defeat as he." Gandil may have been a scrapper, but he was a far different person from Ray Chapman. Gandil had some serious character issues that would come to the surface in just a few years. Chapman became a fan favorite during his four seasons in Cleveland, the kind that fathers took their sons to see play ball. He gave his best effort each game, each at bat, each play in the field. He had a winner's mentality, which made him one of the best all-around shortstops in the American League.

While the players worked out under the warm New Orleans sun, back home the front office moved forward at a steady pace. In early March, Bob McRoy announced a decrease in ticket prices at League Park. For the 1916 season upper-box seats would go for $1.00 instead of the customary $1.25. Jim Dunn believed no ticket at any ballpark should sell for more than a single dollar. This probably did not sit well with the other AL owners, who were not looking to giving any breaks to the fans. Dunn appeared to be a fan's owner, trying to be as fair as possible to the ticket-buying public. In addition, the practice of reserving six rows of seats just behind the boxes—the "yellow section" for Saturday, Sunday, and holiday games—was being discontinued. That meant all seats behind the boxes on the main floor were available at 75 cents for each home game.

In previous years, half the upper first-base pavilion was reserved seating for Sundays and holidays. This practice, known as "pink reserved seat tickets," was also being discontinued, allowing fans to buy any tickets they wanted on a first-come, first-served basis. McRoy advised fans if they wanted seats for Opening Day on April 12, they should send orders to the ticket office right away. The change in policy benefited both the fans and the club. Seats were cheaper and more readily available to anyone with the cash to spend. This policy gave Dunn extra money in advance sales that could be poured back into operations on a faster basis. With all the buzz the new owner had created, the chances for a sell-out crowd on Opening Day seemed a real possibility. If the team showed just a little progress after 1915, then a good year at the box office was all but assured.

As Dunn and associates counted their money, the Indians began to step up the pace of their spring training. Fohl now had the squad doing a leapfrog drill all the way around Heinemann Park. Each player had to jump over another player, repeating the exercise until they had lapped the entire park. Today most players would be calling their agents to complain, but in 1916 these players went along with the strange exercise. Somehow they all made it to the finish line without any season-ending injuries.

Intersquad games proved little except that the regulars were far superior to the substitutes and the rookies trying to catch on with the big club. Bobby Roth hit very well, though, as he reminded his teammates, he had left his favorite bat at home to prevent any damage to it until the regular season. The bat in question had come his way via Joe Jackson. Shortly after the two switched teams, Jackson met with Roth in Chicago, asking him if he liked the change in scenery. Roth said he liked it very much except for his hitting, which was going nowhere. Joe offered one of his bats to Roth, who promptly accepted. The next day Bobby had a big day at the plate, and his slump ended. From that point on Roth only used the Jackson bat, which he named Betsy, the same name used by Joe for his own trusted weapon.

The end of March served notice that serious decisions had to be made about the 1916 Cleveland Indians, especially regarding the pitching staff. With time running out, one young hurler began to assert himself. Already known as an exceptional pinch hitter, Jim Bagby showed signs of becoming a major-league-caliber pitcher. The *Plain Dealer* commented, "In Jim Bagby Fohl has obtained a better pitcher than he had expected. Until coming south, Fohl had not banked much on Jim." The primary reason Fohl discounted Bagby as a pitcher was his belief that the Pacific Coast League star needed to put on fifteen pounds to survive in Major League Baseball. Before the start of training camp, Bagby sought medical help for a problem with his throat. The doctor diagnosed a pair of bad tonsils that needed to come out. The surgery was successful, enabling Bagby to gain some needed weight, which added to his stamina. Now showing a sharp breaking curveball with better than average control, Bagby had a good shot at making the squad. He further solidified his cause by adding a fadeaway to his repertoire.

Besides Bagby, Morton, and Klepfer, no other pitcher had stepped forward yet. Stan Coveleski, the only spitball pitcher in camp, had not done much to impress anybody. Henry Edwards commented, "Coveleski is a spitball pitcher. Without the moist delivery, he could not make good in a Class B League." Not the most flattering comment, but Stan had been careful with his arm, holding back on the spitball until late in training. Soon the Indians would break camp, but Coveleski still had a few opportunities left to impress his manager.

The Cleveland Indians ended spring training by winning several exhibition games against the Chicago Cubs and Cincinnati Reds. Fohl told the newspapers he believed his team had more talent than both the Reds and Cubs. Sunny Jim's optimism had invaded the mindset of the Indians' field boss. Several days later it would have been hard for anyone in town to challenge Fohl's positive outlook. On April 8, 1916, the Cleveland Indians acquired Tris Speaker, the greatest center fielder in all of baseball. Not quite a miracle, but very close indeed.

3

THE TURNAROUND BEGINS

I n less than two months, the Cleveland fans had seen a new owner, a new attitude, and, on the eve of the 1916 season, a new center fielder who brought
with him the promise of great things to come. How in the world did Jim Dunn,
a neophyte AL owner, pull off this phenomenal deal? In a word, money. Tris
Speaker and Boston owner Joe Lannin could not agree on a suitable contract that
would please both parties. Speaker refused to report to spring training with the
Red Sox, preferring to stay home in Hubbard, Texas, until matters were straight-
ened out. Speaker had been a prime beneficiary of the FL war that had raged two
years earlier. Joe Lannin feared he could lose his star ballplayer to the "Feds." To
ensure that Tris remained in Boston, the owner dusted off his checkbook, paying
out $35,000 for two years of service. This generosity came to a halt when the
Federal League disbanded after two shaky seasons. For the 1916 season, a disgusted Speaker received a contract calling for more than a 50 percent cut in pay.
A man as proud as Speaker considered the offer to be nothing less than an insult.
Many ballplayers would have handed over their firstborn child for a contract of
$9,000. However, these players could not hit line drives all over the field, nor
could they sprint to deep center field to flag down sure doubles and triples.

The end of spring training saw no significant progress between Lannin and Speaker. This deadlock prompted Jim Dunn to confer with his associates on the possibility of bringing Speaker to Cleveland. Without hesitating, Dunn sent Bob McRoy to Boston in hopes of cutting a major deal. Negotiations went slowly as McRoy tried to put together a package large enough for Lannin to consider. According to newspaper reports, Dunn spent over $50 on long-distance telephone calls to Boston. The talks continued until Lannin saw what he wanted: a colossal amount of money. He agreed to let Speaker go for $50,000 in cash, young relief pitcher Sam Jones, and a player to be selected within the next ten days. That player turned out to be Fred Thomas, a minor league third baseman. Dunn and McRoy had pulled off the biggest deal in Cleveland baseball history. The morning of April 9 proved to be a shocker for the Indians faithful. Tris Speaker in a Cleveland uniform! Just too incredible to be true after the horrible season of a year ago.

Bob McRoy sent a telegram to Cleveland that read in part, "The cash consideration in the deal for Speaker will not be announced. Pitcher [Sam] Jones and an infielder to be picked by manager [Bill] Carrigan within ten days will be released to Boston. I can say the infielder will not be Chapman. In fact there will be no loss of playing strength by the Indians, unless it be Jones, whom we regret to lose."

McRoy put to rest any fears that to pry loose a player of Speaker's ability meant that Ray Chapman would join the Red Sox. Certainly sending away a pitcher with the potential of Sam Jones had to hurt a bit, but very few Northeast Ohio residents could raise any loud objections. McRoy went on to comment how pleased he was to figure in bringing the great Speaker to Cleveland, while giving all the credit to Jim Dunn. The amount of money spent was almost as startling as the news of the Speaker deal. The average ballplayer earned somewhere between $3,000 and 5,000 annually. Charlie Somers had sold Joe Jackson, an elite player with batting skills equal to Speaker's, for $25,000 the previous season. To acquire Speaker, Dunn spent a sum equal to 10 percent of the $500,000 purchase price that he had paid out for the Indians just two months prior.

Dunn proclaimed to the Cleveland fans that he was not finished in his attempts to bring more talent to Cleveland. He said, "I am not making any skyrocket talks about what I am going to do, and for that reason will not say what players I am after." He further elaborated on the Speaker deal. Dunn said, "Getting Speaker is a business proposition with me. When I made up my mind to buy the Cleveland club it was because I believed Cleveland was a grand baseball town if the sport were properly conducted and the fans were given a winning team." In only forty-five days Dunn had worked many hours overtime to bring good baseball back to Cleveland. Huge amounts of money had been spent to ensure that better days were ahead. No other owner in either league had stepped to the forefront like Jim Dunn. The boss of the Indians displayed a remarkable amount of courage in buying the club along with his shrewdness in knowing when to pull the trigger. Very few fans in Cleveland were surprised to hear the news that ticket sales were proceeding at a brisk pace, all thanks to Sunny Jim.

The only piece of business to complete in the Speaker deal involved getting the star outfielder's signature on a new contract. Jim Dunn expected this to be just a formality. He reasoned Speaker wanted to play ball and should be anxious to lend his signature quickly. Though Dunn expressed confidence, news arrived from Boston that Speaker had reservations about leaving the Red Sox. According to a story in the New York Times, Speaker said, "There is no need of my stating that this deal was a complete surprise to me. As I understood it, Mr. Lannin and I had practically agreed upon terms. Whether I shall go to Cleveland remains to be seen." Shortly after Bob McRoy completed the deal with Lannin, the Cleveland vice president visited Speaker at his apartment in Boston, but Tris was anything but cooperative. He refused to sign his new contract and declined to board a Cleveland train with McRoy.

The sticking point hinged on Speaker wanting a share of the $50,000 Lannin received. The papers reported Cleveland had offered a salary of $15,000, a raise of $5,000 over Lannin's proposal. Speaker figured he should get a cut of the action while believing Lannin needed to hand over the cash. The next day Speaker partly changed his stance, declaring he would leave Boston to head west but still wanted a share of the purchase price. Speaker said, "I suppose I must play in Cleveland. If you want to continue in the big show you must go where the club owners send you. I hate to leave Boston, for I like the people here. I have never played big league ball for any other team than the Red Sox." Speaker, now twenty-eight years old, had made his first appearance with the Sox in 1907. He cracked the starting lineup in 1909 and then began a streak of six consecutive .300 seasons. He helped Boston win a World Series in 1912 and once again in 1915. It's easy to understand why Speaker had little enthusiasm about leaving a championship team for a club that had struggled for a number of years. Speaker had a good life in Boston and many friends there, plus a high standard of living. To leave the East Coast and start over in Cleveland would take some adjustment.

When Speaker boarded a train leaving Boston, the newspapers mourned his passing. The *Boston Herald* wrote: HERE GOES CARRIGAN'S CHANCE TO COP AGAIN IN 1916. The headline in the *American* was even blunter: BOSTON WILL SUFFER A SEVERE LOSS. The papers believed pitcher "Smoky" Joe Wood, Speaker's close friend, would soon follow Tris to Cleveland. They were correct in that prediction, but a year off the mark.

While Tris Speaker rode the rails to Cleveland, extravagant preparations for Opening Day were nearing completion. The plans for League Park had been finalized before the Boston deal; however the arrival of Speaker enhanced the anticipation tenfold. To celebrate the new season, the Cleveland management intended to hand out ten thousand Indian headdresses with colored feathers. A twenty-piece musical band was hired to perform along with strong-voiced singers, both men and women who pledged to keep the crowd in good humor. Mayor Harry Davis gladly accepted the invitation to throw out the first ball. He added the stipulation that his catcher could only be Jim Dunn. As an added touch, the Cleveland Elks Club volunteered to bring a thirty-foot American flag to be raised before game time. The Pyle & Allen Cigar Store reported that ticket sales were simply out the door, while the stadium box office reported massive lines of ticket buyers. The combination of a fresh start for Cleveland baseball and the appearance of Tris Speaker in an Indians uniform virtually guaranteed standing room only on April 12.

All signs pointed to a glorious day for the Cleveland faithful when the season opened against the St. Louis Browns. Even the ordinarily miserable early April weather had yielded to warmer temperatures with a slight southwest breeze. All appeared to be in sync except for Tris Speaker declining to sign his contract before game time. He liked the terms of his new deal but still wanted $5,000 of his purchase price from Joe Lannin. This puzzled Jim Dunn, who thought Speaker should sign first and then worry about his extra money later. The Cleveland owner attempted to reach Lannin by phone but could not make connections. Shortly before noon Speaker advised he would play in the opener but hold off on signing.

Why he remained so obstinate about the $5,000 is open to speculation. Possibly he resented Lannin for trying to slash his salary and then selling him to a second-division ball club. The Red Sox were world champions, and their prospects to repeat were better than good. To leave this situation had to hurt, and not just in the wallet. One did not see the Washington Senators trying to unload Walter Johnson or the Tigers attempting to dump Ty Cobb. It's likely that Speaker's pride took a big hit from the move to Cleveland. Any possible way to strike back at Lannin may have appealed to him, hence the demand for the additional 5K. Once again Sunny Jim stepped up to the plate. To ensure that his mint-condition center fielder took the field with his new teammates, he wrote a check for $5,000 and handed it to Speaker. A moment later the deal became official, the contract signed and delivered. Reporters asked Dunn why he didn't hold Speaker out of the lineup and try to collect the $5,000 from Joe Lannin. Dunn stated, "Nothing doing, I am going to play fair with the Cleveland fans. I might make a big pot of money by springing Speaker on the public Thursday, but by playing him today, we will win in the end."

The pot of money did roll, at least for Speaker. Within several days an advertisement would appear in the *Cleveland News* with a full-length image of Speaker in uniform. Below the likeness was a frosty bottle of beer. The caption read: TWO PEERLESS LEADERS OF CLEVELAND: TRIS SPEAKER AND DIEBOLT WHITE SEAL BEER. The new center fielder was going to love his time in Cleveland.

With the addition of Tris Speaker to the starting lineup, Lee Fohl decided to demote Elmer Smith to utility outfielder and number-one pinch hitter. Bobby Roth moved to right field. The Indians' Opening Day lineup read:

Graney—left field
Chapman—shortstop

Roth—right field

Speaker—center field

Gandil—first base

Turner—second base

Evans—third base

O'Neill—catcher

Mitchell—pitcher

This represented a major departure from last season's lineup, with only Chapman, O'Neill, and Graney as holdovers. Gandil was making his debut in a Cleveland uniform, while twenty-year-old Joe Evans got to start at third base. Placing Roth, Speaker, and Gandil in the three, four, and five spots gave the Indians power along with production in the middle of the lineup. Jack Graney, as the lead-off hitter, had the ability to get on base, always trying to work the opposing pitcher for a walk. Ray Chapman could bunt, move runners along, and put the ball in play. This set up the big boys to knock in the runs. On paper the Indians figured to be a much-improved ball club. They probably would fall short competing with Boston, Detroit, and Chicago, but a finish in the upper division ahead of St. Louis, New York, Washington, and Connie Mack's woeful Athletics was a distinct possibility.

Opening day of 1916 revived the hopes of the long-suffering Cleveland fans. A pennant was something that went to teams like Boston or Detroit or Chicago, not to Cleveland. Fifteen seasons had gone by without a single flag for the Indians. Despite the empty feelings, over eighteen thousand fans turned out for the inaugural, the largest crowd ever for a Cleveland home opener. As the newspapers remarked, for the time Clevelanders forgot about the futile attempts by the American military to capture the elusive Mexican bandit Pancho Villa. They put aside the unpleasantness in Europe, which many believed would soon have American troops fighting overseas. Spring styles were cast aside and nobody spoke of the high cost of gasoline. Instead, they rode the bright yellow trolley cars to 66th and Lexington, which brought them to the entrance gates at League Park. The crowd all but overwhelmed peanut vendor Sammy Wyse, who nearly had his cart knocked over several times. He remarked he had not seen a wild crowd like this since the frantic pennant race of 1908. Soon the stands were bursting with fans donning the free colorful Indian headdresses handed out by the ushers. The staff of the downtown Spalding Sporting Goods store took their seats in the grandstand. Hours earlier they had turned off the lights, drawn the blinds, and posted a sign that read: DIED GRANDMOTHER – THE BOYS ARE AWAY THIS AFTERNOON. Very creative prose, but likely few shoppers believed Grandma had passed on.

The band struck up a military tune to get the crowd revved for the game. Seconds later a thunderous roar erupted from the grandstand when the Indians left the clubhouse to begin the walk to the home team dugout. The crowd applauded when Chick Gandil came into view and then let go with another ear-splitting roar when Tris Speaker walked toward them. Any misgivings that the former Red Sox outfielder had in coming to Cleveland had to be dissipating quickly.

The St. Louis Browns ambled toward their visitors' dugout without much notice, though some fans greeted manager Fielder Jones, who had frequented the grounds years before as player-manager of the Chicago White Sox. The head groundskeeper rang the infield bell, and his crew sprinted onto the field to remove the large brown canvas covering the diamond. Though clouds were hovering over the field, no rain came pouring down to spoil the party. The bell rang again and the Indians raced to the infield, wearing their spanking new white home uniforms with navy blue stripes. Blue caps with white ribbing and black socks completed the ensemble. Joe Evans picked a ground ball cleanly, firing a strike to Chick Gandil. The crowd yelled once more, despite it being only infield practice. After the Browns got their work in, the opening festivities took place at home plate. The Cleveland Elks presented the team with an enormous blue banner with the word "Indians" engraved in red letters on the front. Jim Dunn walked slowly to home plate followed by Mayor Harry Davis. A portly man with a perpetual smile, Dunn awkwardly acknowledged the cheers of the fans. Though he had been in control of the Indians for two full months, Dunn had never faced a crowd before, let alone a wildly vocal one. He watched Mayor Davis take the mound and groove one down the middle to catcher Steve O'Neill. Led by their enthusiastic mascot Larry the dog, the players and officials marched to the center-field flag pole to raise the colors for another baseball season. Moments later home umpire Billy Evans shouted the time-honored words: "Play ball!"

The game itself proved to be anticlimactic as the Browns easily whipped the Indians 6–1. The only Cleveland run came in the bottom of the first inning when lead-off hitter Jack Graney drew a base on balls off FL exile Bob Groom. Ray Chapman sacrificed Graney to second. After Bobby Roth grounded back to the mound, Tris Speaker drew another walk. Chick Gandil hit a grounder to the Browns third baseman, who threw wildly to first, allowing Graney to score the game's first run. Cleveland pitcher Willie Mitchell got in trouble early, giving up single runs in the second and third innings, including a home run by the Browns' impressive new first baseman, George Sisler. Mitchell lasted only five innings, being replaced by Jim Bagby in his first major league appearance. Probably a touch nervous, Bagby gave up two more runs before he settled down the rest of the way. The highlight of the game occurred when a stray puppy wandered onto the playing field. Larry the dog immediately dashed across the infield to intercept the intruder. The Indians' four-legged mascot had worked long and hard to secure his job, and no interloper would be allowed to steal any of the attention from him. The fans roared while Larry chased the confused trespasser around the outfield until the poor dog escaped under the left-field wall. Mission accomplished, Larry proudly jogged back to the dugout, his foe vanquished.

Despite a very disappointing loss to St. Louis, fans left the ballpark still excited about their team. They now had a front office totally committed to winning, some promising young players, and a superstar playing center field. The record crowd demonstrated to management that the Cleveland fans had every intention of supporting their club. The message was simple and to the point: put a representative team on the field and we will back it all the way.

The following day the Indians got a good pitching performance from Guy Morton, who shut out the Browns for seven innings. Using a live fastball, Morton struck out eight batters while cruising toward an apparent victory. Unfortunately he came apart in the eighth inning, allowing four runs and an eventual 4–2 defeat. A walk to light-hitting pitcher Dave Davenport opened the door for the rally. Pitching in the Federal League the previous season, Davenport had blistered the baseball for an average of .092. He struck out an amazing fifty-two times in just fifty-one games. One must keep in mind that the dead-ball era was still very much in play and that hitters were not swinging for the fences. Be that as it may, another round of timely hitting spelled defeat once again for Cleveland.

The players cleaned up after the game, had dinner, and then took the street-cars downtown for a night at the Alhambra Theatre. A crew from the Central States Film Company had been on the field for Opening Day, shooting much of the ceremony along with some of the game action. The players would all have the opportunity to see the crowd storming the entrances, the nearly filled grand-stand, individual shots of themselves in their crisp new uniforms, and the pres-entation of the Indians banner by the Cleveland Elks. No doubt the film played for quite some time to allow the fans who missed the opener a chance to at least view the highlights.

On Friday the Indians broke into the win column, topping St. Louis 3–0. An unlikely hero emerged in pitcher Ed Klepfer. In the words of Henry Edwards, "Klepfer's control was perfect. Not a pass did he issue. Rarely did he pitch three or even two balls to a batter. Strikes, strikes, strikes—those were what he per-sisted in throwing." After a first-inning walk to Ray Chapman, Bobby Roth sin-gled, Speaker walked, and then Terry Turner delivered a pop fly double to left field, scoring two. With two runs to work with, Klepfer sailed along, scattering three hits over nine innings. A few more outings like this, and the Jackson trade of the previous season might not be so one sided.

The Detroit Tigers came to town on Saturday to start a four-game series. Owner Dunn and his staff were anxious to see what kind of weekend atten-dance his team could draw. They had little to worry about, as a massive crowd of nearly twenty-four-thousand fans packed their way into League Park. An esti-mated eight thousand people were turned away at the gate. This turnout rep-resented the third-largest crowd in League Park history. Attendance numbers for the three games with the Browns and one more with Cobb and the Tigers now equaled one-third of the entire attendance for the 1915 season. Spurred on by the huge crowd, the Indians used excellent defense and clutch hitting to beat Detroit in ten innings, 4–3. The hometown fans got to see Tris Speaker at his finest. The gentleman with the prematurely gray hair pounded out three hits (one of those a double), stole a base, and then dazzled the crowd by throwing out Ralph Young at the plate in the top of the tenth inning. A double by Jack Graney scored the game winner in the bottom of the tenth.

In just five games the Cleveland club had gone a long way toward erasing the memory of the 1915 season. They demonstrated better than average defensive play, some skilled hitting, and the all-around hustle that had been lacking in seasons past. The team still had some strides to make to stay on the field with Boston or Chicago, but this ball club had a foundation to build on.

"A club, to be a winner, should have a corking good catcher, a star at either short or second, and one in center field. Give a team three such men in those positions and it is bound to be successful," said St. Louis Browns manager Fielder Jones after the opening series in Cleveland. "The Indians have such men in O'Neill, Chapman, and Speaker, and for that reason I cannot but rate them as a strong baseball club." Jones's observation rings true even today. A winning team has to be strong up the middle. The early games in April demonstrated that the Indians were indeed muscular at the three key positions. Ray Chapman had great range in direction, a strong throwing arm, and the ability to turn the double play. Steve O'Neill was a wall of granite behind home plate, able to block base runners with the best of them. Tris Speaker had no peer in center field, using speed and instinct to run down long fly balls that were headed for extra bases. Runners, particularly those on second base, always had to keep a sharp eye on Tris for fear of getting picked off when the center fielder crept up behind them to take a throw from the pitcher. The Indians had no worries up the middle, but the other five spots still needed some tinkering.

With April coming to a close, the city of Cleveland held a grand celebration in honor of Jim Dunn. The Chamber of Commerce welcomed Chicago's prestigious Woodland Bards. Upon their arrival the Bards' president, Joe Farrell, received the key to the city at a reception held at the swank Hollenden Hotel near Public Square. Many of the leading baseball officials planned to attend, among them Ban Johnson; Charles Comiskey; Garry Herrmann, owner of the Cincinnati Reds; and Charles Weeghman, late of the Federal League and new owner of the Chicago Cubs. Barney Dreyfuss, owner of the Pittsburgh Pirates, had to cancel due to a severe head cold. Nonetheless the list of attendees proved to be a most extraordinary one. After the festive luncheon concluded, a parade of automobiles would leave the Chamber of Commerce Building and then proceed east on Euclid Avenue to East 70th Street. From there the procession would turn north to Linwood Avenue, where the cars were to be parked. A squad of police officers gathered on Linwood to guard the autos while the officials and the Woodland Bards entered League Park via a private entrance. The Cleveland Chamber of Commerce bought 1,200 seats for the game. They announced a new motto at the ballpark: "As Jim Dunn put Cleveland back on the baseball map, we will keep it there."

The celebration became a complete success as the Indians beat up on the Chicago White Sox 9–2. Graney got the home team rolling in the bottom of the first with a leadoff double. Singles by Terry Turner and Bill Wamby, a fielder's choice to Speaker, a walk to Chick Gandil, and another double from Steve O'Neill accounted for five runs. Pitcher Fred Coumbe coasted through nine innings, while the Indians added four more runs along the way. Early in the contest, the Woodland Bards gathered in front of the Cleveland owner's box and serenaded him with "The Wearing of the Green." As they sang, Dunn removed his green hat and waved to the crowd of twelve thousand, which responded with animated shouts. Among the fans in attendance was Secretary of War Newton D. Baker, a former Clevelander. Despite the increased tensions between Germany and the United States, the secretary could not resist stopping home for a day to catch the Indians in action.

The euphoria that had enveloped the city streets quickly dissipated the next day when Ray Chapman went down with a knee injury. Early reports listed Chapman with a minor knee problem, but swelling developed, and a doctor's exam revealed the shortstop would be out of the lineup for three to four weeks. Bill Wamby stepped in to play shortstop, but Chapman's absence for an extended period let some of the air out of the large balloon hovering over League Park. There would be excitement for several months as the Indians put a string of victories together that kept them in the first division. They actually stood in first place on May 17 with a record of 19–9. After they beat Walter Johnson and the Senators 4–2, Jim Dunn sent a telegram to his ball club. It read, "Accept my congratulations for your glorious victory over the mighty Johnson. Have the boys smoke on me tonight." Accordingly, Lee Fohl visited the local cigar shop, buying all the boys fancy cigars compliments of their grateful owner. However, most of the other clubs in the American League were not showing any excitement about the streaking Indians. New York Yankees manager Bill Donovan derisively called them "a flash in the pan."

The Indians returned home on May 21 to a spectacular crowd of twenty-five thousand. Excursion trains and trolleys brought fans from all over northeast Ohio to see their heroes in action. A run on the concession stands before game time resulted in all peanuts being snapped up before the first pitch. A large delegation of fans came from Milan, Ohio, to honor their hometown boy Elmer Smith. Others traveled from Norwalk, Sandusky, Painesville, and Ashtabula.

With the massive crowd came a number of scalpers intent on selling tickets at a profit. Several were caught red-handed by Cleveland police and taken to Jim Dunn's office. For once the jovial owner did not have a smile on his face. Reportedly he stared down the criminals, then said, "Boys, I'm doing my best to popularize baseball in this town and place it on a higher plane. You are doing your best to neutralize my actions. Your offense is punishable by a jail penalty, but I'm going to let you go. Please don't do it again." The offenders hurried out of the office, not to be seen again until the next game that drew a big crowd.

Crime seemed to be running rampant at League Park. While the Indians were playing a June game against Boston, a young man from the neighborhood slipped into the Cleveland clubhouse and stole forty-six dollars from Ray Chapman's locker. The injured shortstop wandered into the clubhouse only to find his money gone. He alerted the park police, who somehow had an idea who the culprit was and found him sitting in the grandstand. A search produced the bills stuffed in the young man's shoe.

Criminal activity aside, things were booming at League Park. Attendance continued to be the best in quite some time. Fans traveled from miles away to see the new and improved Indians. The Electrical Workers of Cleveland bought six thousand tickets for a mid-June game. They did not come empty handed, bringing twelve klaxon horns complete with storage batteries. Jim Dunn's staff handed out several thousand megaphones with song sheets for the crowd to sing parodies about Lee Fohl and Tris Speaker set to the tunes of popular songs. Along with inspired baseball, good old American fun had returned to the ballpark. Eventually Edith Dunn got caught up in the excitement, having her husband install a ticker wire in their Chicago home. Each day she invited several friends over to watch the inning-by-inning results. Being a fan of Cleveland baseball once again became a great thing to be.

Over the course of a long season, a team must have solid pitching to keep them within striking distance. Cleveland did not yet have all the arms needed to keep up the pace. In August, Dunn tried to help the pitching staff by trading outfielder Elmer Smith to Washington in exchange for left-handed pitcher Joe Boehling. Despite the last-ditch effort, the Indians slowly faded out of contention even with terrific play from Tris Speaker and a surprising five-home-run season from the bat of Jack Graney. The Indians managed to play .500 ball for the season, winning a total of seventy-seven games. This represented a substantial improvement over the hapless squad of 1915. Cleveland fans could argue that the glass was half full.

4

LAYING THE FOUNDATION

The vast sums of money spent by Jim Dunn certainly helped turn the fortunes of the Cleveland Indians around. From day one his influence steadied the organization, allowing for progress both on and off the field. With the new ownership, emphasis shifted from the drama of cash woes and players shipped off for money to assembling the top players available while letting Lee Fohl do his level best to put a winning club on the diamond. It should be noted that the Cleveland roster already had players capable of helping the team win a championship—players who were not destined for the Hall of Fame, but who each nevertheless brought some high degree of skill necessary to build a competitive team. The men themselves came from starkly different backgrounds, one a coal miner from Pennsylvania, one who studied for the ministry like his father, and one who came directly from the campus of the University of Mississippi, where he studied medicine. Another started as a pitcher in minor league ball but made the switch to the outfield, where his defensive skills became noteworthy. These men, along with one of the game's best shortstops, gave Cleveland the core players needed to escape the lower ranks and become a legitimate pennant contender.

One of the most stable positions in the Cleveland lineup happened to be the left-field position. Jack Graney had been patrolling the outfield of League Park since the beginning of the 1910 season. John Gladstone Graney, born on June 10, 1886, was one of nine children born to James and Mary Graney. The family had roots in St. Thomas, Ontario, Canada, where the elder Graney served as a dispatcher for the Michigan Central Railroad. Like thousands of other young men in Upper Canada, Jack took to the ice and played a bit of hockey. Somewhere in his teenage years, Graney found baseball more to his liking, becoming a fair country pitcher with a lively fastball. At age twenty he started to play semipro ball with a local St. Thomas ball club. Success in Canada led to a contract with Fulton, New York, in the Empire State League. Graney did get a trial with the Chicago Cubs in 1907 but failed there, being released to Rochester of the Eastern League. He had only been in Rochester a month and a half when he was shipped out to Wilkes-Barre, Pennsylvania, of the New York State League. Graney enjoyed a good deal of success in Wilkes-Barre, resulting in a contract offer from the Cleveland Naps. The pitching staff Jack competed against had too much talent and experience for a twenty-two-year-old to win a spot with. He did manage to break camp with the Naps and actually pitch three innings before manager Lajoie loaned him to Columbus for a month; then he went on to Portland, Oregon, for the full season.

However, in his later years Jack enjoyed relating the story of how he wound up in Portland. Gordon Cobbledick of the *Plain Dealer* interviewed Graney long after his playing days. The story related that the young left-handed pitcher had a definite wild streak that prevented hitters from digging in at the plate. While pitching batting practice, Graney fired fastball after fastball in a vain attempt to impress manager Larry Lajoie. Graney said to Cobbledick, "I was in there determined to make an impression, and I made it. I wasn't content to lob the ball up there for the boys to take a good cut at it. I had to put something on it to show 'em what I had."

Unfortunately, most of the throws were nowhere near home plate. The fourth batter to step up was the Naps manager, the "Great" Lajoie. "I knew all about Lajoie, as every kid in America did," Jack later recalled. "But I was a particularly cocky kind of kid, and I had a crazy idea I could strike him out. I cut loose a fast ball, and Larry did see it and try to duck, but it hit him just above the left ear, and he went down like a load of bricks." The ball bounced all the way into the grandstand, bringing an abrupt halt to batting practice. Later that evening Jack received a summons to see Lajoie in his hotel room. Extremely nervous, he entered the room to see Lajoie holding an ice bag to his head. Handing Graney a railroad ticket to Portland, the manager explained to his young pitcher that the place for wild men was out west. A very funny story but likely concocted by the sportswriter and his subject. Graney had a very good sense of humor, which allowed him to tell yarns with the best of them.

Back in the minors, Graney pitched fairly well, winning seventeen games in 1909. However, it was his hitting that attracted the attention of the big-league club. In between starts Graney played the outfield, showing a good deal of promise as a batter and fielder. The Naps brought him back to spring training in 1910, when he won a job as the regular right fielder. This may have been due to Lajoie giving up his job as manager and returning to player-only status. Deacon McGuire had taken the job, leading the club to a dismal season of only seventy-one wins and eighty-one losses. Graney did not have an outstanding year, batting .236 with one home run and thirty-one runs batted in. On Opening Day he started in center field in place of Joe Birmingham. The recent renovation of League Park had been completed, with two concrete tiers of stands that gave the outfielders some difficulty judging fly balls. Cleveland, behind the pitching of Addie Joss, led by a run going into the ninth inning. With two men out, the St. Louis batter stroked a line drive to center field. Graney raced in to grab the last out but completely misjudged the ball, seeing it fly over his head and roll to the bleachers. While the fans called out for Graney's murder, two runs were scored, eventually winning the game for the Browns.

Graney quietly made his way to the clubhouse, feeling awful that his mistake cost Cleveland an Opening Day victory. The veteran players glared at him, not saying a word. A minute later someone slapped Jack on the back. It turned out to be none other than the game's losing pitcher, Addie Joss. He told Graney to cheer up; there would be another game tomorrow. From that moment on Graney never looked back. His major league career was firmly on track.

Jack rarely hit over .260 for a season, but he did have the knack for find-ing a way to get on base. He developed a razor-sharp eye at the plate, which enabled him to draw a large number of free passes from exasperated pitchers. His skill in the outfield improved each year, adding to his value as an everyday player. The Cleveland management thought highly of Graney, rewarding him with a generous $700 raise after his rookie season.

The all-around ability of the Cleveland outfielder eventually got the atten-tion of the fabled Ring Lardner, then covering sports for the *Chicago Tribune*. In a 1914 column, Lardner used the voice of the "Sox Bug" to compliment Graney as one of the American League's best outfielders. The Sox Bug was puzzled that whenever a discussion about the current stars (i.e., Cobb, Sam Crawford, Lajoie, Baker, and others) took place, the name of Graney never came up. The bug stated, "I don't hear nothing about the best hitter I ever seen. I'm referring to John Gladstone Graney o' Cleveland. I read in the records his average for last year was .267 and that he made 138 hits for 189 total bases; that he got eight-een two baggers, twelve triples and three homers." Later in the column the Sox Bug commented on Graney's ability as an outfielder. He said, "The rest of 'em is satisfied to catch the fly balls it's possible to reach. Graney catches the ones he can't get nowhere near." The bug went on to suggest that Cleveland should trade Joe Jackson to Chicago for some pitching, then move Joe Birmingham over to right field, allowing John Gladstone Graney to handle the rest of the outfield.

From the tone of Lardner's prose, it's clear that Graney played extremely well whenever he visited Comiskey Park. The Sox Bug lamented that all of Jack's 138 hits must have been recorded in Chicago, but a quick check of box scores proves that Graney did get some base hits outside of Comiskey Park.

After he had established himself as a major league ballplayer, Jack became something of a practical joker. In 1919 he pulled off one of his better stunts at spring training in New Orleans. The Indians were playing an exhibition against the overmatched Tulane University college team. Cleveland sandlot star George Uhle had been signed the previous winter, and manager Fohl decided to pitch him against the college boys. Uhle breezed through the lineup, allowing for the defense behind him to slack off and watch the show. When Cleveland took the field for the start of the seventh inning, the left fielder was nowhere to be seen.

Moments later Graney appeared, riding the old horse that pulled the lawn mower around the field. While everyone in the stands and on the field broke out in laughter, Jack rode the horse bareback for a while, and then man and horse galloped away behind the grandstand. He returned quickly to the field, motioning for Tris Speaker and Joe Wood to join him behind the pitcher's mound. The three outfielders lay down on the grass, urging Uhle to resume pitching. As hard as they tried, the Tulane hitters could not get the ball out of the infield. As if this was not enough, in the next inning Graney called for Larry Gardner, Ray Chapman, and Bill Wamby to join the trio for some rest and relaxation behind the mound. Only the first baseman, the catcher, and Uhle remained at their positions. Buoyed by the challenge, Uhle struck out the side to end the game and the comedy. Though no actual statistics were kept, it is believed that Jack Graney's horse was the all-time leader in major league exhibition games played by an animal.

Given his soft spot for our four-legged friends, it isn't surprising that it was Graney who, in 1913, gave the Cleveland ball club their official mascot, Larry the dog. The bull terrier was first acquired the previous year by Doc White, the Cleveland team trainer. White and the head bellhop at the Hollenden Hotel had put a wager on the outcome of the boxing match between the world champion Abe Attell and Cleveland's own hero Johnny Kilbane. The winner of the friendly bet would receive a bull terrier puppy named Prince. Kilbane fought a brilliant fight, and Doc White gained a new friend. After one year White had had enough of the feisty terrier and gave him to Graney, who renamed the dog Larry, presumably in honor of the famous second baseman Larry Lajoie.

Larry's duties as the Cleveland Indians mascot consisted of performing tricks on the playing field, chasing down foul balls, and stealing straw hats from unsuspecting fans while keeping things loose in the dugout. He traveled on the road with the team, entertaining fans all around the AL circuit. In June of 1914, Larry received the ultimate honor: an invitation to meet President Woodrow Wilson in the White House. The Naps were in Washington for a series with the Senators. Cleveland congressman Robert J. Bulkley arranged the afternoon visit between the players and the president. This appointment marked the third time the Cleveland club paid a visit to the executive mansion. In 1906 the team had stopped by for a chat with Teddy Roosevelt. Two years later they returned to the White House to meet with Teddy's successor, the very large William Taft. Apparently Taft had some fear of getting his hand squeezed by the athletes, declining to shake anybody's hand. However, President Wilson had no such reservations, extending his hand to Graney, Birmingham, Turner, and the rest. The president approached Larry and said, "So this is Larry, the mascot?" The players acknowledged it was indeed him. President Wilson added, "My daughters tell me he is a very smart dog. I am sorry I could not have been there [at the game] to see him perform." It is not known if Larry extended his paw to the chief executive, but the visit went smoothly, outside of Larry eyeing a squirrel on the White House grounds and giving chase.

The players enjoyed having Larry around even on the road trips. The little bull terrier had the time of his life serving as mascot. Newspaper photos of the Cleveland team usually had the dog posing front and center, and he also appeared with the team on baseball cards. In a 1913 Naps portrait Larry sits in the first row directly in front of his best friend Jack Graney. Larry was such a success that once in a while Graney felt he deserved to go home to Canada for a brief rest. Larry the celebrity traveled alone via steamer across Lake Erie to Port Stanley, Ontario. From there, an escort would get the dog to the interurban streetcar that went through St. Thomas. The conductor made sure to stop in front of the Graney home, where Larry jumped off the car and dashed for the front door. Few people, let alone dogs, had it so good.

Through the years, all was not a bed of roses for the excitable little mascot. In a game against Washington, an argument broke out on the field between the Senators' manager, Clark Griffith, and umpire Bill Dinneen. After several minutes Griffith somehow got hold of the game ball and started to walk away with it. Dinneen ordered the manager to toss him the ball, and the angry Griffith complied by rolling the ball slowly on the grass. This was too much for Larry, who dashed onto the field, grabbing the ball before the umpire could reach it. While the fans broke out in laughter, Larry sprinted back to the bench, sitting in front of his pal, Jack Graney. Dinneen approached the Cleveland bench to retrieve the ball, only to be driven back by a snarling Larry. After the game Clark Griffith sent a letter to Ban Johnson demanding some action to be taken against

Larry. Several days later the AL president acted, slapping Larry with an indefinite suspension. The mortified terrier packed his bags for the long ride to St. Thomas.

As his career developed, Jack Graney became a master at "waiting them out." *Baseball Magazine* marveled at his ability to work the count and draw a large number of walks from opposing pitchers. F. C. Lane, in his article about Graney, mentioned that his ability to get on base had few equals in the major leagues. The leadoff hitter had the responsibility to get to first base and work his way to scoring position while having enough base-running sense to score in a variety of ways. Graney, now nicknamed Three and Two Jack, scored 106 runs in 1916 along with 142 base hits and 102 walks. With a batting average of only .241, it seems unlikely that pitchers were afraid to throw strikes when Graney came to bat. Lane would remark, "In this more intangible field of batting power we can find no more shining example than Gladstone J. Graney. Here is a man who bats not only with his hands and arms and feet, but most important of all with his brains." Lane went on to argue that a good batter does not necessarily have to possess a high batting average. He cited the ultimate struggle of the pitcher versus the batter. Belting out triples and homers was fine, but Lane argued that batters need to harass the pitcher, wear down his strength, and exhaust his patience. Then the big hitters could tee off to put the game away.

As Graney himself told the writer, "When you hit a pitcher safely, you do not bother him a great deal unless he is trying for a no-hit game or unless there are men on bases. But if you work him for a pass, you get him up in the air. This takes his mind off his work, upsets him generally, and undermines his confidence in himself." Three and Two Jack reasoned that when pitchers lose their control, they lose their effectiveness. He believed forcing a pitcher to throw eight or nine pitches would begin to wear down his stamina. "He is burning up a lot of strength in the old soup bone and in spite of all his hard work, he fails in his object." This philosophy suited the Indians well. Their leadoff hitter got on base quite frequently, Ray Chapman, the second hitter, had great skill in laying down the bunt, and one swat from Tris Speaker was good enough to get the run across the plate.

Pitchers in the American League admired Graney's ability to wait them out. Lefty Williams of the Chicago White Sox called him the hardest man to pitch to. Invariably whenever they faced one another, the count always figured to be three and two. Williams had the dilemma of grooving one across the middle and risk an extra base hit or trying to cut the corner and hope for a strike. He knew Graney would rarely swing at a bad pitch, which forced Williams to decide upon the lesser of two evils. Williams called the Cleveland hitter one bad man to pitch to.

Jack Graney's value to the Cleveland Indians was that of a swift outfielder who covered a large amount of ground while being a leadoff hitter who got on base as well as anyone in the game. His batting average never hovered around .300, but his overall ability to play winning baseball certainly aided the Indians in moving up the standings to become a legitimate contender for a pennant. In the era before the lively ball, batting with brains had as much importance as swinging for the long ball.

With the addition of Tris Speaker, Cleveland now had an excellent defensive outfield. Right field needed to be settled, but the importance of strength up the middle was soon to become an important component in the Indians' drive to the upper division. To contend, a team needed a catcher who could command respect; a catcher who could rifle the ball to second base to cut down a runner attempting to steal; a man who blocked home plate like a concrete wall while keeping every pitch in front of him. These impressive attributes belonged to Steve O'Neill.

The son of Irish immigrants, Steve O'Neill was born in Minooka, Pennsylvania, on July 6, 1891. His parents, Michael and Mary, left their home in Galway, Ireland, and arrived in Pennsylvania in 1885. Many of the early Irish arrivals were poor farmers, driven out of their homeland by the widespread potato famine of the late 1840s, who had scraped together or borrowed just enough money to book passage to North America. Upon arrival, the men often took jobs as dockworkers or carriage drivers while the women worked as domestics for wealthy families. At the time Michael and Mary settled in Minooka, the best means of employment in the town of two thousand was the coal mines. Scranton and the surrounding communities represented the heart of anthracite coal country in the United States. If you were Irish and a male in eastern Pennsylvania, you put on the overalls and became a coal miner.

Steve O'Neill had four older brothers, all born in Ireland, who became miners along with their father. At the turn of the twentieth century, Steve left school to join the elder O'Neills in the family business. At ten years old he got a job tending to the mules that brought the coal cars to the surface. His pay for taking care of the temperamental animals was $1.45 a day. By today's standards this type of work is difficult to comprehend. Child labor laws were for the most part nonexistent, allowing young boys to take on very dangerous work at long hours without any provisions for safety. Leading animals hundreds of feet below ground and guiding them to the surface had many hazards. Chief among them was the danger of getting kicked in the face or stomach, which could cause serious injury or even death. Narrow pathways also allowed for boys to get pinned against the shaft walls by an angry mule.

After proving his worth handling the unpredictable mules, Steve got a promotion shoveling coal into the cars. For nine hours each day, he shoveled tons of the rock without any complaints, developing massive upper body strength to go along with the mental toughness necessary to survive seven years in the mines. Blocking runners at home plate and handling foul tips off the shoe tops were a walk in the park compared to the abysmal working conditions of the Minooka coal mines.

Despite the long, arduous days working underground, the O'Neill brothers found the time to play baseball. Many of the young miners used whatever daylight was left to choose sides and play until dark. "Baseball is really the miner's greatest recreation," Steve told *Baseball Magazine*. "You would suppose after spending nine hours daily in the coal dust of the mine shaft doing the hardest kind of physical work that the miner would be glad to take it easy for the few hours of daylight that remain." Not so the boys of Minooka. Every spare minute saw the locals on a makeshift field sharpening their baseball skills.

For the O'Neills, baseball became a means to escape the drudgery of the coal mines and possibly earn a decent living. John, the oldest, began playing minor league ball, eventually winding up with Utica. Local legend has it that John, a catcher, watched Hughie Jennings from nearby Pittston make it all the way to Louisville of the National League. Convinced he had enough skill to play pro ball, John put away his mining tools for good. Younger brother Mike enrolled at Villanova University, where he pitched for the varsity. In 1902 Mike played minor league ball briefly for Montreal, then signed with the St. Louis Cardinals, beating his older brother to the major leagues by one season. A story circulated that Mike persuaded the Cardinals owners to sign John in order to establish the novelty of a brother battery. The two O'Neills performed well in 1902, with Mike winning sixteen games and hitting two home runs while John split time at catcher, handling fifty-nine games. To make sure nobody could steal their signs during game time, Mike and John often spoke to each other in Gaelic.

Though the two brothers enjoyed some success in professional baseball, it was generally acknowledged that the third brother, Pat, had the most skill. However, an arm injury suffered while toiling in the mines put an end to any thoughts of a baseball career for Pat, who had been an accomplished catcher. Pat's injury killed any chance the O'Neill brothers might have had of equaling the Delahantys' record of five brothers in the major leagues. They would have to settle for second place. Despite a ruined baseball career, the setback did not hinder Pat from teaching the Minooka lads the finer points of the game. By 1907 he had enough talented kids to form a team named the Minooka Blues. Members of the squad included younger brothers Steve and Jimmy; next-door neighbor Mike McNally (New York Yankees); and an outfielder from Scranton, Charles "Chick" Shorten (Boston Red Sox). The Blues became a crack outfit, taking on and beating teams from larger communities including Wilkes-Barre and Pittston. A local sports reporter described the Blues, saying, "They look like boys, but play and think like men." When the Wilkes-Barre club watched the Blues work out, they declared them a bunch of boys not ready to compete with the older guys. Manager Pat convinced the Flatirons to play the game anyway, and it resulted in a 2–0 victory for the Minooka Blues.

On occasion (usually Sundays), some major league clubs would stop in Minooka to play exhibition ball. Blue laws were still in effect in Pennsylvania, but enterprising owners knew they could find a ball game in the small towns just outside of Scranton. Steve had the opportunity to study the ballplayers and learn some of the finer points of the catcher position. When Mike and John O'Neill were still with the St. Louis Cardinals, the players visited the family home after their exhibition game. All were guests for dinner, while Steve was chosen to be the beer runner for the evening. At regular intervals he took the empty green pitcher to a nearby saloon for a refill. This kept up most of the night, but Steve never slowed down, keeping the beer readily available for the thirsty ballplayers. Years later one of the house guests would tell the story, then add the punch line, "Even then Steve was good at handling a green pitcher."

By 1910, Mike O'Neill was still in baseball, now managing the Elmira club of the New York State League. He had three catchers on his roster, including his nineteen-year-old brother as the third stringer. Apparently Steve's older brother was impressed just enough to sign him to a contract for the princely sum of $50 monthly. After injuries to the other catchers, Steve, who had been languishing on the bench, finished the season catching twenty-eight games like a true veteran. It looked like Elmira had a promising young catcher for the 1911 season, but Athletics owner Connie Mack successfully maneuvered to transfer this highly regarded prospect to Philadelphia.

Steve celebrated his opportunity to play in the major leagues by spending another grueling winter working in the mines. He earned just enough money to keep him going until the start of spring training with the Athletics. He impressed Connie Mack from the start, so much so that the manager gave O'Neill a note to go on a shopping spree at the local sporting goods house. There he purchased a top-of-the-line catcher's mitt along with the best pair of spikes he had ever worn. Though having a good spring, he opened the season with Worcester, Massachusetts, of the New England League. There Steve blossomed, catching over 100 games while batting a respectable .282. His activities on the field were bringing him a good deal of attention, but it was an off-the-field incident that turned more than a few heads in the northeastern city. For some reason the Worcester ballplayers took regular abuse from the local tough guys, possibly a matter of who ruled the streets—the locals or the hired guns from out of town. One afternoon Steve and a friend went for a stroll away from the ballpark. Soon they were followed by a group of hooligans tossing insults and taunts at the two young men. O'Neill abruptly halted and turned around to face the unruly crowd. He stared down the toughs for a short time and then said in a calm voice, "I assume you fellows are looking for trouble. If that is what you want, it's perfectly all right with me. All I ask is that you be sports enough to fight only two at a time." After a short period of silence, the would-be assailants backed away. The incident ended the reign of terror from the locals. From that day on the Worcester ballplayers could roam the streets without any fear of confrontation.

O'Neill had a strong interest in the art of boxing. In later years he became close pals with champion featherweight Johnny Kilbane, often visiting the popular fighter at his Cleveland-area training camp and sparring for a time with highly regarded middleweight boxer Mike Gibbons. The Scranton locals loved telling the tale of a professional wrestler who came to town and went to the gym looking for a couple of victims to work out with. He asked two locals who were tossing around a basketball if they would like to wrestle him for a short time. Each man aggressively battled the wrestler for five-minute periods until they called it quits after an hour. The new man in town struggled to his feet with both ears bleeding, admitting he had gotten much more of a tussle than he expected. He asked who he had just wrestled, only to find out it was Steve O'Neill of the Cleveland Indians and brother Jim O'Neill, now playing shortstop for Washington. Toughness ran very deep in the O'Neill family. It is easy to understand why the Cleveland catcher could block runners off home plate like few men before him.

During August of the 1911 season, the Cleveland Indians bought Steve's contract from Philadelphia. Connie Mack debated the sale, but he had Ira Thomas, Jack Lapp, and several other promising recruits in the minors. Mack told the Cleveland writers, "We cannot use all the good catchers we have, and rather keep O'Neill down any longer, I let the Naps have him. He can throw like a shot and is a mighty good man in other ways, especially at the bat." Steve made a brief appearance in Cleveland at the end of the season, getting to play in nine ball games. The next year he split the catching duties with Ted Easterly, catching sixty-eight games. His hitting turned out to be a weak spot: only .228 with four doubles, no triples or home runs. In 214 at-bats he drove in a grand total of fourteen runs. What kept him in the lineup was his defense behind the plate. Cleveland's new manager, Harry Davis, had spent most of his career playing first base for the Athletics. Very likely he got a good look at O'Neill in spring training of 1911 and realized what a talent he had in the Cleveland rookie. Ted Easterly, strong with the bat, outhit Steve by a mile but could not match his defensive skills behind the plate. In 1913 Easterly was sent to the Chicago White Sox, further opening the door for the Minooka strongman. Once given the opportunity, O'Neill proved to be as reliable as any backstop in the game. Beginning in 1915, he caught over 100 games for nine straight seasons while in a Cleveland uniform. The foundation of the team began at catcher.

A list released by the American League in late August of 1911 revealed that after purchasing Steve O'Neill from Worcester and Connie Mack, Cleveland had made another acquisition: a shortstop from the Davenport, Iowa, club by the name of Ray Chapman. Within a year this purchase would pay huge dividends for the organization. Born on January 15, 1891, in Beaver Dam, Kentucky, Chapman began playing baseball at an early age. His playing field of choice lay in a grassy back lot between his grandparents' house and barn. Stories mention that Ray's grandmother Martha knit him his first baseball uniform and cap.

When he was a teenager his father, Everett, moved the family of five to Herrin, Illinois, the heart of mining country. The elder Chapman held down a job in the coal mines while working as the town constable in his free time. For a short period Ray worked underground with his father, but his developing skills as a baseball player allowed him to leave the mines behind. He first gained some notoriety when playing shortstop for the semipro Stoelzle Hardware team. Chapman did have to share the headlines with another rising star, outfielder Bobby Veach. It is not a stretch to believe the Stoelzles had their way with most of the area teams. Probably the only team that could match up to Chapman and Veach's was Pat O'Neill's Minooka Blues. What a dream game that would have been! After a stint with the local club Ray got the opportunity to play minor league ball with Springfield, Illinois, of the Three-I League. The talent Chapman faced included future major leaguers Heinie Groh and catcher Les Nunamaker honing their skills. From Springfield he went to Davenport, Iowa, hitting and fielding equally well. Scouts from Cleveland recommended Ray to Charlie Somers, who at the time still had some money to work with.

Somers bought Chapman's contract, sending Ray to Toledo, where he excelled from day one.

At the end of August 1912, Chapman, along with a young first baseman named Wheeler "Doc" Johnston, joined the Indians. Henry Edwards wrote in his column, "The best of the recruits looks to be shortstop Ray Chapman of the Toledo club. He is touted to be the best infielder in the American Association." The recruits both made their home debut on August 29. In three at-bats Ray beat out a bunt for his first hit as a Cleveland Indian. He did well in the field, handling nine chances with one error on a low throw to first base. Overall the fans were very pleased with what they saw. The fans really got their dollar's worth when Chapman raced into short left field to snag a Texas Leaguer that appeared to be falling in for a base hit. The Cleveland infield soon became one of the fastest in the American League with Johnston at first, Chapman at shortstop, and veteran Terry Turner playing third. The only slowpoke remaining in the infield was Larry Lajoie.

Chapman appeared in thirty-one games for the 1912 campaign. His stats were reasonably productive, showing a batting average of .312, six doubles and three triples in 109 at-bats with twenty-nine runs scored, nearly one per game. He stole ten bases as well, demonstrating the all-around ability he would be noted for in the years ahead. Before the season ended Chapman moved to second in the batting order, following Doc Johnston. The two newcomers greatly impressed Cleveland's faithful by stealing bases, stretching singles into doubles while causing havoc on the bases with their daredevil style. The Naps came to life in September, at one point winning nine games in a row. No doubt the enthusiasm of Chapman and Johnston woke up the other players, who would otherwise have been playing out the string and making their off-season plans.

On September 20 the Naps rallied to take an extra-inning game from the New York Yankees, scoring two runs in the bottom of the tenth to win 5–4. Chapman showed off his speed by stretching a routine single into a double. The surprised Yankee second baseman booted the throw in, allowing Chapman to race to third. The fans were taken aback by the play, which the papers called a "Ty Cobb stunt." A double by Terry Turner brought Ray home with the tying run. A passed ball and wild pitch scored Turner with the winning tally. Fans and players alike were buzzing about the base-running skills of their new shortstop. Most of them believed Chapman had little chance to take the extra base but were stunned he had the speed to get to second safely and then get to his feet and sprint to third on the error. Few members of the Naps had the quickness and judgment on the bases that Ray already had.

The season ended with a four-game road trip to St. Louis. An open date on Friday, October 4, allowed the Naps to stop in Herrin, Illinois, for a barnstorming game against the local miners. It is very likely that Chapman had a hand in arranging the exhibition game at his hometown. The papers reported that Herrin's entire population of 1,159 would attend, including women and children. A further dispatch mentioned that the town cigar maker had created a new cigar for the occasion, which would smoke fast and be strong in the pinches. He named it the "Chapman Special." The game itself had a record crowd due to school being called off. In addition most businesses shut down for the day. When Chapman came to bat in the top half of the first inning, the city attorney walked up to home plate and presented the Cleveland shortstop with an expensive watch charm, courtesy of the local Elks Club. The Naps easily won the game, with Lajoie powering out two long home runs off a pitcher from the Three-I League. This had to be quite a day for Chapman, who in just one month had demonstrated he had the goods to be a regular for the Naps. His prospects for the future appeared to be very bright.

As a ballplayer Ray Chapman had all the attributes necessary to be a top-flight performer in the big leagues. He had the skills to field his position well above the norm, the consistency to hit for a high average, enough strength to drive the baseball up the alleys, and exceptional speed on the bases. His demeanor on and off the field won him the admiration of his teammates and fans both home and away. His positive outlook energized his teammates when the going got tough. Ray nearly always had something good to say to sportswriters after a well-played game or even a difficult loss.

Henry P. Edwards covered the Cleveland baseball club from the early 1900s through the 1920s. He had the opportunity to get up close and personal with just about every athlete who wore a Blues, Naps, or Indians uniform during his lengthy tenure. He characterized Chapman as a hardworking ballplayer with a disposition that could chase away the gloom that now and then enveloped a ball club. According to Edwards, Ray had the personality to make friends and keep them. The sportswriter could not come up with a single enemy Chapman had made. He recalled that Ray had a great ability for storytelling when the Indians were on the road. Each night the shortstop would come up with anecdotes and tales from the diamond that drew a great deal of laughter from his teammates. If the occasion warranted it, particularly after a difficult loss, he would get a quartet together to break out in song and eventually cheer up everybody in the clubhouse or on the train bound for a faraway city. Edwards remarked that travelers would stop by to hear the songs and laughs, then walk away believing the Indians must have won the ball game. During spring training of 1914, Chapman broke his leg while working out in Athens, Georgia. Manager Joe Birmingham purportedly said, "More than half of my team is out of the game."

Ray Chapman served as the face of Cleveland baseball for his nine seasons there. Fans and teammates alike held him in high esteem for his winning personality. The boys in the League Park neighborhood had great regard for Ray, especially when he smuggled baseballs after home games and passed them out to every kid he saw. "Chappie" was one of the real good guys of Major League Baseball.

During the winter months, Chapman went home to Herrin, where he had a job as a sidewalk supervisor. Since that assignment left him some extra time, he put in hours at Walker's Men Store. The boys at the store liked to play a practical joke every now and then. One afternoon the owner asked Ray if he would take the trolley to nearby Johnston City to pick up his automobile, which had been left at the second Walker's Men Store. Chapman agreed to make the trip and drive the boss's car back to Herrin. The trolley arrived in Johnston City, allowing Ray to take a short walk to pick up the car. However about halfway back to Herrin, a police car pulled up and ordered the driver to stop. The police officer asked to see Chapman's driver's license, which Ray did not have. He got a stern lecture from the policeman and, then drove carefully back to the store. Very embarrassed, he told Walker what had just happened. At that point everybody in the store broke out in laughter as Ray realized he had been set up.

When Jim Dunn purchased the Indians in 1916, Chapman, as one might expect, gave very optimistic quotes to the newspapers. He heartily endorsed the acquisition of Chick Gandil and offered to report early to spring training to help the young players get established. In a period when the Indians' new management really needed some good public relations, Chapman helped provide it without any urging. The Indians were fortunate to have a spokesman with great credibility, not to mention terrific prowess at shortstop.

Along with an exceptional shortstop, a winning ball club needed a second baseman who could field and quickly turn a double play. When Ray Chapman reported to Cleveland he had the veteran Lajoie to work with. Though slowing down considerably, Larry could still take the toss and get the relay to first base. Within two years, declining skills along with a high salary hastened the departure of Lajoie to Philadelphia. In the latter stages of the 1914 season, the Naps purchased the contract of a young infielder from the Cedar Rapids club named Bill Wambsganss. The twenty-year-old spent his formative years in Fort Wayne, Indiana, but was actually born in Cleveland, Ohio, on March 19, 1894. His father, Philip, a Lutheran minister, moved the family to Indiana to accept the leadership of a church there. The younger Wambsganss attempted to join his father in the ministry, actually attending Concordia College from 1910 to 1912. However, Bill became very anxious speaking in front of groups. At times he stuttered and had problems getting a single word out. While at Concordia he played a lot of semipro baseball, which got him to thinking about a career as a major league player. After graduating from Concordia, Wambsganss stayed with the ministry plan, enrolling in a seminary in St. Louis for three years of study. It was there he met a fellow student who had played minor league ball with Cedar Rapids. After joining the seminary team, Bill got a recommendation and soon had a contract for $100 a month to play Class-D ball in Iowa. It turned out the elder Wambsganss was a baseball fan himself, which cleared the way for Bill to spend the summer exploring this new opportunity.

The next September Wambsganss returned to the seminary for another year of theological study. Second-year students had the chance to go out in the community to gain practical experience. Bill selected a faraway teaching job in Fremont, North Dakota, which lasted until Easter. This assignment allowed him the spring and summer off to join the Cedar Rapids club for another season. A coincidence, perhaps? Not a chance!

Wambsganss played very well during the 1914 season. In eighty-four games with Cedar Rapids, he batted a healthy .317. His stellar play drew the attention of a Cleveland scout, which led to a subsequent offer to join the Naps. After getting his father's blessing, Bill boarded a train for Cleveland, arriving in early August.

Being born in a Cleveland suburb gave Bill Wambsganss membership in an elite club of major league ballplayers that began with the five Delahanty brothers. Cleveland sent an impressive group of ballplayers to the major league ranks in the late nineteenth and early twentieth centuries—no fewer than three from this contingent are members of the Hall of Fame: Ed Delahanty, Rube Marquard, and Elmer Flick. Other Cleveland pros included the Naps third baseman Bill Bradley and George "Dode" Paskert, who played many years in the National League.

Bill Wambsganss had much to live up to when he joined the Naps in the latter half of the 1914 season. His debut occurred on August 8 in Cleveland, where he played the last five innings at shortstop and got his first two major league hits. The *Plain Dealer* lauded his performance, stating, "He looked after his territory in brilliant fashion, having two putouts and one assist that were of the kind that are greeted with applause, while at the bat he stung the ball with energy, making two hits, each with the bases occupied."

Printing box scores with Wambsganss's name in them proved to be a difficult assignment for the various editors. The first box score had "W'bag'nss." Next came "Wambag's" and then "Wamb'nss." Probably out of frustration the next box score in the papers listed "Wamby," which easily fit in with the other players' names. Apparently Bill understood the dilemma, easily adopting the name and keeping the shortened version the rest of his life. Speaking to *Baseball Magazine*, Wamby explained what it was like to live with such a different last name. He said, "I don't know whether it fits me or not, but I have worn it all my life and will probably carry it with me to the end. Anyway it's a name that people don't confuse it like Miller or Jones even though there seems to be ninety-six different ways of pronouncing it."

The following season Wamby split his time between playing second and third base for the Indians. He batted poorly all year, finishing with a batting average below .200. Ordinarily this anemic hitting would mean a lot of bench time, but when your team loses ninety-five ball games and finishes second to last, there are other things to worry about. Wamby played well defensively, which bought him more time in the starting lineup. In 1916 he spent a considerable amount of time playing shortstop when Ray Chapman injured his knee. He improved his batting average almost fifty points to .246 while doubling his runs batted in and runs scored. Chapman returned to shortstop in late season, prompting Wamby's permanent move to second base. From that point on the two infielders developed a rapport that led to many slick double plays in the years ahead. The arrival of Bill Wambsganss in Cleveland gave the club a classy-fielding second baseman who would make the occasional spectacular play, one of which is still talked about today.

On a warm September morning in 1912, seventeen-year-old Joseph Patton Evans registered for classes at the University of Mississippi in Oxford, with the goal of studying medicine in the bachelor of science program. Then he reported to the head football coach to try out for the varsity. Though only 5'9" and weighing below 150 pounds, he would make his mark as a hard-hitting end on offense and defense.

Joe Evans was born in Meridian, Mississippi, on May 15, 1895. As a student he excelled in the classroom but found time to play organized baseball, and by graduation time he was known as one of the best athletes in the county. At the University of Mississippi he played both varsity football and baseball. His classmates gave him the nickname "Little Joe" for obvious reasons. However, when he took the field for either sport, he played well above his physical size. The 1914 Ole Miss student yearbook gave Joe credit for the baseball team's 1914 state championship. For most of the season his batting average hung around the .450 mark with a flurry of doubles, triples, and home runs.

The 1914 Rebels varsity had the distinct advantage of being coached by none other than Brooklyn outfielder Casey Stengel. Coming off a season with injury problems and a .272 batting average, Stengel thought about leaving professional baseball to become a coach. He got in touch with his old high school coach Bill Driver, now the head football man at Mississippi. Driver told his former student he could come down to Oxford in February for free room and board while coaching the baseball squad. Stengel agreed to share his NL experience with the team, devoting much of his time to working with the infield. His methods worked well, as the Rebels had a winning season, eventually claiming the state championship. When Stengel left Ole Miss to return to Brooklyn, he received a gold-handled cane, which he kept for most of his life. In typical Casey style, he told reporters in a 1961 interview, "Yes sir, when they call me the Professor, they ain't kidding. There's a good reason."

Joe Evans established himself as one of the university's best athletes. In his sophomore season he quarterbacked the football team through a difficult schedule, highlighted by throwing two touchdown passes in a 21–0 win over LSU. In 1914 he repeated the feat by throwing for two scores against Tulane in a 20–6 victory. He had bulked up, if you will, to a hefty 160 pounds, which allowed him to run through tackles while being even more of a stalwart on defense. According to the Mississippi yearbook Evans was "a cool and crafty general of the team; a lightning quick runner; sure in defense and deadly in offense." In a very rough football game against VMI, in which fourteen men were injured in just the first quarter, "Crafty Joe" managed to keep his feet and stay in the game for all four quarters. Accounts of his performance on the field usually said Evans "played star ball" or "led the way for the red and blue."

His off-the-field performance equaled his accomplishments on the diamond and gridiron. As a sophomore he was a member of the Honor Council, which indicated that his grade average soared above his classmates. A roster of the Ole Miss Honor Council indicates that only two students were chosen from each class, except for the seniors, which had four students represented. Evans was the rare student athlete who could keep his grades high while putting in the practice time to excel in two sports. In the early part of the twentieth century, few professional athletes were college educated; some had not finished high school or even grade school. Most ballplayers did not come from families that had the resources to send their sons to school. Joe was quite a rarity in his day: a ballplayer with the intellectual skills to pursue a medical degree.

After a stellar season with the 1914 Mississippi Rebels, Evans's play at third base got the attention of local and national scouts. During the summer break he made a foolish mistake by playing for a local semipro team. It is uncertain whether he knew the risks involved, but when he reported for school in the fall, Joe found himself ineligible to play any further baseball for Ole Miss. Despite his being sidelined for the 1915 college season, the Cleveland Indians offered Evans a contract. He jumped directly to the big club, where he got an on-the-field audition for the third-base job. With Cleveland having a ghastly season, they allowed the twenty-year-old to play forty-two games, in which he batted a fair .257 with twenty-eight hits. When the season ended, Joe returned to Mississippi, where he enrolled in school to continue his studies toward a medical degree. The Indians allowed him to finish the winter quarter before he reported to spring training. There would be some minor league duty in 1916 in Portland, but Evans returned to the Indians later in the season and remained for good. A year later the players began to call him "Doc," for he now had his bachelor of science degree. He went on to medical school at Washington University in St. Louis but managed to report to spring training every year to get in shape for another season. Joe Evans did not become a marquee player for the Indians; however, he remained an important member of the team, able to step in at third base or move to the outfield when necessary.

At the close of the 1916 season, the Cleveland Indians had built a nucleus of ballplayers that would lift the team out of the lower half of the American League. With Tris Speaker, Jack Graney, Steve O'Neill, Ray Chapman, Bill Wamby, and Joe Evans, the core of the team was now in place. From the 1917 season on, they were a team to be taken seriously.

5

WAR ON THE HORIZON

While the January snow covered the shores around Lake Erie, Jim Dunn visited Cleveland to confer with his top lieutenants. The subjects of discussion were the mailing of the new contracts for the 1917 season and whether Dunn should buy a franchise for the newly proposed professional football league. Always careful before entering a new venture, the Cleveland owner wanted all the information possible before throwing his money at a risky opportunity. In the end he decided to pass on the idea, believing he could not make a profit over a ten-week season. In all fairness he did not have a crystal ball that would have allowed him to see the future, in which Cleveland fans would gladly risk freezing to death to see pro football.

Other issues were brewing that cast some legitimate doubts over the coming baseball season. Rumors floated that Dave Fultz, the thorn in the side of all major league owners, had plans for the Players Fraternity to boycott spring training. Fultz, with the aid of key ballplayers, had started the Fraternity in 1912 to protect the rights of those who played professional baseball. A former player himself and a practicing attorney, Fultz knew all too well how players rarely got a fair shake from their unscrupulous bosses. He worked diligently to bring justice to members of the Fraternity, winning a number of victories that helped improve the players' welfare. At one time the organization had a membership of over a thousand major and minor league players. Each member paid dues of eighteen dollars to cover Fultz's salary plus expenses.

Problems arose before the start of the 1917 season when Fultz brought four grievances to the attention of the owners. One was a demand that owners eliminate the clause in some players' contracts that stipulated the team could suspend an injured player without pay for an injury that required a lengthy recuperation. Ban Johnson fumed at the accusation, stating no such clause could be found in any contract. Johnson challenged Fultz to produce one, which he did. There are no recordings of the meltdown that must have occurred when Fultz called the AL president's bluff. Shortly after the incident, the owners introduced a change in player contracts that prohibited any forfeiture of salary due to an injury. This move helped relations slightly, but the other three grievances, all pertaining to minor league claims, went unresolved. At this point Fultz decided to go for the home run. He boldly asked his Fraternity members to leave their contracts unsigned and go out on strike. He believed his members would follow along, compelling the owners to concede.

The Indians had several players who belonged to the Fraternity, including their superstar, Tris Speaker. Jim Bagby, Bobby Roth, and Chick Gandil were the other members. Would these players actually defy their bosses and jeopardize their income to prove their solidarity? Most owners and sportswriters believed the strike had little or no chance of happening. They took the position that everyone in professional baseball enjoyed a fair salary and should have no complaints against their beloved owners. Henry Edwards called Dave Fultz "a danger to the game." He strongly believed Fultz had much to do with helping along the rise of the Federal League in 1914 by urging players to delay signing their contracts. This maneuver caused major league owners to hand out inflated salaries to keep their stars from jumping. Likely Edwards was not alone in his rants against the Players Fraternity leader; there seemed to be a growing desire for Dave Fultz to disappear permanently.

A date of February 20 was set as the date to strike. That coincided with the opening of training camp in Pasadena for the Chicago Cubs. In related news

Fultz announced he had applied for the Fraternity to become affiliated with the American Federation of Labor (AFL). If that happened, the owners would be at odds with the average workers who bought tickets to ball games. The onus now was squarely on the players, who had roughly one month to make an important decision.

The suspense did not last long. Speaker willingly signed his contract but added that he did not know how his fellow members stood on the strike issue. The names of other Cleveland Fraternity members were revealed, among them Ray Chapman, Jack Graney, and Stan Coveleski. For those three to honor the strike would seriously hurt the Indians' chances for the upcoming season. While the fans waited, players around the league quickly caved in. George Sisler signed his contract, telling reporters, "I shall go south to train March 3. Fultz may expel me if he wants. I do not think Fultz represents the majority wish of the Fraternity." Bob McRoy, the Indians' vice president, chimed in that he expected all his players would report to spring training on time. He claimed the only reason some of the Fraternity supported Dave Fultz was to use the possible strike as a bargaining chip for their contracts.

At the end of January Jim Dunn reported that half the team had signed their contracts, and of the holdouts only four were Fraternity members. Dunn stated, "The Cleveland club has no cause to worry about any action of the Players Fraternity. And I have paid no attention to what the Fraternity has been or has not been doing." Reports mentioned that nearly a hundred AL players had already signed their contracts. However the National Leaguers were not so quick to fold, with only forty-five prepared to cross the picket line. The unpopular Fultz did have some support after all.

Before the strike deadline, the AFL withdrew their support for the Fraternity, which ultimately ended any resolve the players had left. Fultz announced that the strike plans were being called off, releasing any supporters to sign their contracts. This was a resounding victory for the owners, effectively crippling any further opposition to their means of doing business. The Fraternity ceased all activity, quietly closing its doors. Dave Fultz left for Europe to train as a fighter pilot for the Allies. When he returned two years later, his bitter adversaries, the owners, asked him to join their ranks as president of the

International League, an offer he accepted. What strange bedfellows they must have made.

Spring training would soon begin as usual for the Indians and other clubs. However, there were ominous signs that the United States would enter World War I, which meant a formal draft would likely take place. Among the men eligible for service were the healthy, athletic, unmarried young men of professional baseball. This raised the question among league officials of what to do if the United States joined the fighting in Europe and hundreds of professional ballplayers faced the likelihood of becoming soldiers. If this scenario played out, the possibility of canceling a season or two looked very probable.

Jim Dunn returned to Cleveland after taking part in the AL meetings held in New York. He mentioned that the Boston Red Sox had made a token offer for Steve O'Neill, which he discarded quickly. Of interest to reporters was the announcement that the Indians would undergo military training while working out in New Orleans. According to Dunn, the owners had requested that Secretary of War Newton D. Baker provide officers at training camps to supervise the military drills. The Cleveland owner, who had served in the Iowa militia a few years back, wanted the players to march from their hotel to the ballpark in military formation. Manager Fohl balked at the suggestion, explaining that the hotel and playing field were two miles apart. He suggested all drilling be confined to the playing field, which was much easier on the feet.

Were the owners serious about getting players ready for military service, or was it just showmanship to appease the public while the game carried on? Marching ballplayers with rifles at the shoulder would provide excellent photo opportunities and very positive publicity for the game. However, marching up and down the outfield was a far cry from dodging mortar shells overseas. The true test would be the reaction of the American public. If support from fans followed, the owners probably could get the 1917 season played and hope the fighting came to an end before 1918.

While teams waited for their marching orders, Dunn traveled to Boston for a conference with Boston Red Sox president Harry Frazee. The visit centered on the purchase of pitcher Joe Wood. Still plagued with serious arm problems, Wood had sat out the 1916 campaign in an effort to get his right wing healthy again. For reasons he did not elaborate on, the eternal Cleveland optimist believed Wood could still pitch. Dunn negotiated with Frazee and then made arrangements with Wood to see if they could agree on a salary. Obviously the Boston front office believed their former ace was through as a pitcher. They were delighted to find the Indians willing to write a check for his services.

Wood arrived on the baseball scene in 1908 with much fanfare. Only eighteen years old, he had dazzled scouts with a fastball on par with the great Walter Johnson. He spent less than a year playing minor league ball before signing a contract with Boston. He won eleven games the following season, then ten in 1911. The victory totals were not remarkable; however, his ERA went down significantly both years while his strikeout totals steadily rose. Wood put everything together in 1912, leading all AL pitchers with thirty-four victories, an unbelievable winning percentage of .872, and a total of ten shutouts. He capped off his fabulous season with three victories in the World Series, spearheading the Red Sox to the championship. At age twenty-two, Wood had established himself as one of baseball's greatest stars.

But fame, as they say, can be fleeting. In spring training of 1913 Wood broke his right thumb while sliding into first base. He probably returned to action too quickly, changing his delivery slightly to compensate for the injured thumb. He soon developed a pain in his right arm that would not subside. He could not pitch on a regular basis ever again, even though he managed to throw effectively whenever he could take the mound. Despite the yearly decline in production, the Indians were willing to take a significant gamble in chasing after the ailing star.

Dunn's trip to Boston yielded no results, but the next week Bob McRoy traveled east to resume talks with the Boston club. Once again no deal was reached, but Frazee took time to speak with the media. He stated, "I named a price, and I guess it staggered him [McRoy]. Cleveland must desire his services very much, and if it wants him it must meet my price." Frazee elaborated further: "Grabbing Wood is a gamble. If Cleveland gets him it will obtain a lot of advertising, and if he should go there and win only the first two games, the club will get a big return on the money it spends for him now."

McRoy left for New York to visit Wood and try to find out for certain if the arm had healed sufficiently. It is doubtful the Indians wanted to sign Wood simply to boost attendance figures. They still needed pitching help. Dunn had already shown Cleveland fans his willingness to spend money to improve the ball club. Taking a gamble on a once-great pitcher with a damaged arm proved Dunn wanted to win much more than the next guy.

On February 25 came the announcement that Cleveland had purchased Wood from the Red Sox. Frazee had demanded $25,000 but, after lengthy negotiations with Bob McRoy, agreed to accept $15,000. All that remained was for Wood to travel to Cleveland and agree upon a salary.

Less than a year earlier Dunn had sent $50,000 to Boston for Tris Speaker; now he wrote a check for $15,000 more. Taking into account the $5,000 bonus paid to Speaker, the Cleveland owner had spent a total of $70,000 plus two players in exchange for Speaker and Wood. Despite the extraordinary sums paid out, Dunn remained elated. He told the Cleveland papers, "You can put it down that I am tickled to death. In the first place, I feel sure Wood will be able to show a lot of his old time stuff. If it were otherwise, I know Spoke would not have advised us so strongly to land him." Spoke advising so strongly? Put aside the fact that Wood and Speaker were very close friends and were roommates together in Boston for the eight years they played there. Surely Speaker wanted to help out his close friend. Whether or not he knew that Wood still had serious issues with his pitching arm is a matter of conjecture. Dunn went on to say that he understood Wood would have to take it easy through spring training, progressing at his own pace. He added that Wood had a lot of winning experience that could help the younger pitchers. However, paying $15,000 for a coach was just a tad too much. By his own admission, Dunn really had no idea if he had bought damaged goods. Time would tell on this one.

For his part, Wood expressed a great deal of optimism to the press. He said, "I know I am able to pitch winning ball. I could have done so last year. I asked the National Commission for permission to pitch for a semipro team last year but was turned down." He added that he expected no trouble in reaching a contract agreement and expected to arrive in New Orleans on time with the rest of the squad.

Local fans had a positive reaction to Wood's acquisition. Many had seen him pitch at League Park back in May of 1915. In a fourteen-inning battle he had gone eleven innings, allowing no runs while giving up ten scattered hits. He did not overpower the Cleveland hitters but kept them off balance with good control and an assortment of pitches. Fans believed if he could pitch like that again, it would be all to the good. Others voiced positive reactions, including Larry Lajoie, who called the Cleveland management "a pretty wise bunch in running the club."

On February 28, Wood signed a contract for one year at a figure believed to be $5,000. He assured Cleveland fans that he believed his arm would be ready in time to start the season with the other pitchers. He did mention again that playing with Tris Speaker factored heavily in his decision. Ironically, the two would indeed play together again, but not as the baseball world expected.

Spring training began with a bit of a surprise when the Cleveland newspapers revealed that Chick Gandil had been sold to the Chicago White Sox. Lee Fohl downplayed the move, saying Chick's batting eye had faded. The club had purchased a promising first baseman from Portland named Louis Guisto. Both Dunn and Fohl believed Guisto would prove to be a better talent than Gandil, thus the sale to Charles Comiskey's ball club. Fohl noted the Indians had several first basemen in camp, among them Joe Harris, whom they believed could start if Guisto faltered.

Several days into training camp, the squad witnessed the arrival of Lt. W. C. Harrison of the U.S. Coast Artillery. Harrison assumed the job of drill instructor for members of the team. The Washington Light Artillery of the New Orleans National Guard had recently returned from border duty near Mexico. They agreed to loan slightly used rifles to the team. The Indians were spurred on by Ban Johnson's announcement that $500 would be awarded to the best-drilled AL club. The winners could spend the money any way they chose, but many believed that the top drill squad would use the funds to have a special banner designed to commemorate the honor. The contest was scheduled for July with a panel of army officers to do the judging. The drill sergeant of the winning team would collect $100 in gold. Needless to say, the players received the directive with much enthusiasm.

The first drill involved forty players plus the Cleveland sportswriters who had arrived in camp. They worked for half an hour with Bill Wamby, Jim Bagby, and new pitcher Clark Dickinson serving as file sergeants. Most of the group had problems with their spikes getting caught in the dirt while attempting to pivot but eventually figured out some adjustments to get through the drill. Lieutenant Harrison announced he had made plans for bayonets and rifle belts to be shipped in from New York. Things were indeed getting serious.

March 17 marked the arrival of an overdue Tris Speaker in camp. He put on a uniform, joined the game against New Orleans, and then promptly smacked a triple. Most players required weeks of spring training to get ready to play, but Speaker just needed to pick up a bat and glove to be primed for Opening Day. Even Larry the dog reported on time to spring training, where he worked for several weeks with his partner, Jack Graney, until he rounded into shape.

While the players polished their manual-of-arms drill with their Springfield rifles, ticket sales in Cleveland were moving along briskly. Bob McRoy announced a probable sellout for the April 19 opener with Detroit. All the box seats were gone by mid-March, with grandstand seats well ahead of last year's turnout. Fans were anxious for the season to begin, resulting in a demand for tickets to the season opener in Detroit. An allotment of five hundred tickets was set aside for fans eager to travel to Michigan to get a first glimpse of the 1917 Indians. The loyal rooters expected an improved showing from the club that Dunn and company had worked so hard to deliver.

Spring training could not be complete without someone pulling off a well-orchestrated practical joke. This year's honors went to catcher Steve O'Neill. Apparently a film crew had taken some shots of the players going through their daily military drills. Several days later, O'Neill woke up before breakfast and then walked a short distance to the Newcomb Movie Theatre. He returned to the players' hotel, loudly announcing he had seen the boys on screen. He described how good everybody looked, causing all the players to dress hurriedly and dash off to the Newcomb. They all sat through a double feature of *Perils of Our Girl Reporters* and *The Masher Mashed*. Next up were the news reels, starting with a story on General Pershing, followed by high school cadets drilling. The show finished with a reel on the girls of the Red Cross preparing to assist the wounded troops. The house lights went on without any film of the

Indians' drills. At that point everybody realized they had been duped by the cagey O'Neill. Nothing like the vanity ploy to successfully complete a well-planned practical joke.

Several days after the close of spring training, President Woodrow Wilson appeared before Congress asking for a declaration of war against Germany. The president believed a policy of neutrality could no longer be maintained against a country waging submarine warfare against any and all ships sailing the North Atlantic. President Wilson appealed to the patriotism of all Americans, citing the German policy of warfare as "wanton and wholesale destruction of the lives of non-combatants, men, women, and children which have always been deemed innocent and legitimate." His address challenged all Americans, including ballplayers, to join together and support the government through the difficult times ahead.

President Wilson called for an army of 500,000 able men to fight overseas until the German army was forced into submission. A draft of unmarried men with no dependents would be instituted to raise the army. The draft covered men from all different stations, including businessmen, college students, farmers, and laborers. All eligible draftees were ordered to register as soon as possible, with a draft lottery to select those to go overseas.

When the declaration of war became public, little reaction was heard among the ballplayers. The Indians continued their drills during exhibition games, but no comments were noted in the newspapers. A number of Ohio colleges suspended athletics for the remainder of the school year, sending funds meant for sports directly to the war effort. Many student athletes announced their intentions to leave school and enlist in the army. Professional athletes expressed no such intentions, taking a wait-and-see attitude. The large question remained to be answered: should the baseball season be canceled while the United States entered the bloodbath taking place in Europe?

The first to weigh in on the subject was the vice president of the United States, Thomas R. Marshall. After receiving his annual pass from the league office, Marshall wrote to Ban Johnson, stating, "Baseball may be utilized for patriotic purposes by the thoughtful citizens at the present time. And as they see the contending clubs play to the limit of their ability for club success, may every man and woman in the grandstand be impressed with the duty of playing the game of patriotism to the end that American arms may triumph." Vice President Marshall plainly indicated that he desired to see the game continue as long as possible. He believed in the importance of the national pastime and its central place in the American way of life.

Ban Johnson remarked that baseball should cease operations if the war continued through the spring of 1918. He believed many players were eligible for the draft, which would result in teams being depleted for next year's campaign. Johnson advised reporters, "If the country is still involved in the war the following spring, no attempt will be made to begin another season, and the ballparks will remain closed until the return of more peaceful times." In typical Johnson style, he spoke for the AL owners without consulting them. Surely most were patriotic men who supported the war effort, but to assume they were more than willing to close their ballparks indefinitely seemed to be a stretch. President John Tener of the National League did not go as far as Johnson, stating he had not discussed any plans with the owners and would wait for developments over the next few months. Tener hedged on making any rash decision, which at the time was probably the best thing to do. Events in Europe would dictate how Major League Baseball would eventually respond.

While the United States government attempted to raise millions of dollars for the war effort, baseball did its best to show a patriotic front. The Indians opened the 1917 season with a road game against Detroit. The pregame activities promised to deliver as much pomp and circumstance as the fans could handle. Lee Fohl believed the coming season would be one of the hardest-fought campaigns in the history of the American League. He counted on his pitching staff to lead the way, starting with the opener in Detroit. Fohl thought that when Joe Wood worked his way into pitching shape, prospects would be bright for a run at the pennant.

Opening Day at Navin Field saw an enormous crowd of nearly twenty-six thousand spectators squeeze their way into the park. With the temperature peaking at a balmy sixty-five degrees, fans applauded the arrival of the Indians drill team, led onto the field by "Major" Tris Speaker. The squad displayed the intricate marches learned during its stay in New Orleans. The Detroit squad followed the Indians, demonstrating to the roaring fans all it, too, had learned over the previous month. No fewer than half a dozen bands stationed themselves on the playing field, offering a stirring rendition of the national anthem. Both teams lined up in drill formation, marching to the center-field flagpole. Managers Jennings and Fohl, along with Ty Cobb and Tris Speaker, raised the Stars and Stripes high above the grounds while fans removed their hats and loudly sang "The Star-Spangled Banner." Had war bonds been available at the park, they likely would have sold out.

The Indians got the season off on a positive note, scoring four runs in the top of the first and holding on for a 6–4 victory. Stan Coveleski went the distance, surviving two doubles by Ty Cobb and a home run by outfielder Bobby Veach. The Tigers committed four costly errors, which helped the visitors pile on six runs. Cheering on the Indians was a delegation of six hundred rooters from Cleveland, led to their seats by Mayor Harry Davis. Reporters speculated the number of Cleveland rooters surpassed previous totals by the Woodland Bards or even the Royal Rooters of Boston. The fans entered the park wearing their colorful headdresses to the tune of "Cleveland Will Shine Tonight." After the game, they marched to the players' hotel, serenading the victors with a host of lively songs. Each player made a brief appearance on the balcony to acknowledge the happy throng.

The next day Cleveland won again behind a great pitching performance from Jim Bagby. Both Indians wins came by way of Stan Coveleski and Bagby. Each pitcher now had a year's experience behind him, which manager Fohl hoped would bring a boatload of victories. Other than the players mentioned above, the staff included Guy Morton (injured much of the previous season), Fred Coumbe (whom nobody was sure about), and Ed Klepfer (who had not shown much to date). There was no timetable set for Joe Wood's return to the rotation, meaning the remaining four would carry the load indefinitely, if not all season. For the Cleveland Indians to contend, Coveleski and Bagby had to step forward with outstanding seasons. They both had the tools to do so, but could they deliver when needed? The Indians' season depended on it.

6

PITCHING HELP AND
THE 1917 SEASON

Lost in the intrigue of the 1915 off-season was the signing of two minor league pitchers to the Indians' roster. Both had made brief appearances in the major leagues but struggled to get a serious look from any of the teams. Neither was considered a young prospect: Jim Bagby was twenty-six, Stan Coveleski three months older. Due to the desperation of the Cleveland management, both pitchers were signed to deals for the 1916 season. The timing could not have been better for the pitchers. Both were eager to prove they had the goods to play baseball at the highest level.

Born on October 5, 1889, in tiny Barnett, Georgia, Jim Bagby spent his growing-up years in Augusta, situated roughly forty-five minutes away from his birthplace. Jim's father W. H. had opened a grocery store in the downtown area. Jim and the neighborhood boys played baseball at the sandlots behind the railroad yards in town. At the time young Bagby lagged behind the other guys. That did not last long, however, as he grew to six feet tall by high school and began to assert himself on the diamond. He played second base and center field and pitched for the Richmond Academy, one of the oldest high schools in the United States. In the summer he played amateur ball, pitching for the appropriately named Augusta Amateurs. An existing box score in the *Augusta Chronicle* has Bagby winning a game 4–1 without walking a batter. Later that summer he joined the Georgia Railroad team, leading them to a complete-game 11–3 victory over the West End Stars.

When the 1909 school year ended, Bagby joined the roster of the Second Baptist Church, which played amateur teams from the Augusta region. After throwing a one-hit shutout in late May, he started to attract attention from southern minor league clubs. Bagby signed his first professional contract in 1910 with Hattiesburg of the Coastal League. He had some difficulty there, losing eleven times in sixteen starts. He spent a brief period with Augusta and then signed again with Hattiesburg for the following season. After posting twenty-two wins, he moved up to Class-A ball with Montgomery, where his contract was purchased by the Cincinnati Reds. Bagby got in five games with the NL club, winning two in seventeen innings of pitching. He made his debut in late April during a slugfest with the St. Louis Cardinals. After two Cincinnati pitchers were shelled, Bagby took the mound, shutting down the Cards for six innings. A report sent to the *Augusta Chronicle* via the *Cincinnati Enquirer* spoke glowingly of the young pitcher. "One man stood out from the ruck like a monument on Pike's Peak. Mr. James Bagby is the gentleman's name, and it will be well for the fans to file it away for future reference, as James is quite likely to appear again soon." File it away indeed, as Bagby was sent back to Montgomery after several more appearances.

While shagging fly balls in the Montgomery outfield, Bagby broke his right forearm in a collision with another player. He sat for six weeks before he got the okay to test the arm. While experimenting with his delivery, Bagby discovered his arm had healed so well that he could throw the baseball even better than before the injury. He pitched in only twelve games that season but served as a utility player, described by the *Chronicle* as "batting the ball all over the lot."

In the very early stages of his amateur career, Bagby had attempted to emulate the American League's Eddie Cicotte by trying a knuckleball. He tested it out for a season, with mixed results. He also experimented with the fadeaway, but its velocity gave him a sore arm. When the soreness healed, Bagby discovered he could throw the fadeaway pitch at a slower speed while still maintaining a sharp break to the ball. The years of pitching in the minor leagues and all the trial and error helped him develop better-than-average control. Playing for New Orleans in 1915, Jim pitched 291 innings, won nineteen games, and posted an ERA of 2.15. His performance there earned him a shot with the Cleveland Indians.

Bagby not only won the job but bypassed a number of other candidates to win a place in the starting rotation. He benefited from a less-than-stellar group of Indians pitchers. Guy Morton was the only hurler in the rotation who had some real experience, having led the team in victories the previous year. Lee Fohl spent an inordinate amount of time during spring training trying to find more pitchers to help his pedestrian team. He studied Bagby and the other hopefuls carefully, giving each plenty of practice time to show their talent. After six long years in the minors, Jim Bagby would get his chance.

On April 25, 1916, Bagby entered a game against the St. Louis Browns in the fourth inning. He pitched shutout balls until the ninth inning, when he gave up two runs but still held on, allowing the Indians to pick up a victory. As the *Augusta Chronicle* noted at the time, Jim Bagby had come into his own.

Several years after his debut with the Indians, Bagby talked about his accomplishments to *Baseball Magazine*: "I suppose I can lay my early success as a pitcher to two things. First control and second, experimenting. Control is absolutely essential to any pitcher though not all pitchers ever master it to their satisfaction." He went on to discuss using different styles of delivery while throwing an assortment of pitches. With these tools, Bagby believed success would follow.

The 1916 season proved to be something close to a triumph for Bagby. He appeared in forty-eight games for the Indians, winning sixteen while losing seventeen. He pitched 279 innings, the best on the squad, along with a team low ERA of 2.55. He led all Cleveland starters in at least five categories, which made him the ace of the staff. Taking into account that the team finished at .500, Bagby did a fair job, winning sixteen times while keeping his earned run average below 3.00. His forty-eight games pitched left him fifth in the American League and a workhorse-in-progress. His teammates now called him "Sarge," his namesake a humorous 1914 Broadway play written by Irvin Cobb. When the Indians were in New York to play the Yankees, Cobb himself attended one of the games, eager to see what the young pitcher could do. Unfortunately the Yanks pounded Bagby, forcing an early exit. But Sarge clearly had a bright future with the Indians.

No doubt owner Dunn and manager Fohl were overjoyed to have a pitcher who could work almost as much as Bagby. Imagine their excitement when another newcomer proved he was capable of doing similar things. Not quite the iron horse the man from Georgia was, but a tireless worker nonetheless.

While Jim Bagby grew up in abundant sunshine with clear blue skies, Stan Coveleski rarely saw the sun rise or set. He was born into a family of coal miners on July 13, 1889, in Shamokin, Pennsylvania. He had four older brothers, all of whom were ballplayers. John had a lengthy minor league career, while Harry pitched for nine seasons in the major leagues, winning twenty games three years in a row for the Detroit Tigers. While Stan's future catcher, Steve O'Neill, worked the northern region of the anthracite mines, Stan picked slate in the western section. The community where the Coveleski family lived was primarily made up of Polish immigrants. They faced a great deal of prejudice, mainly due to their inability to speak English. To counter any problems with the locals, the families traveled in groups for the security of strength in numbers. The boys, like their Irish counterparts, received very little schooling, going directly to the mines at an early age. Records show that by 1900, 50 percent of the Pennsylvania coal mine workforce was Polish.

As a slate picker, Stan could earn approximately six to nine cents an hour. He recalled in later years that he chewed tobacco to keep the coal dust out of his lungs. That may have helped him slightly, but the dust gathered in his ears, which forced him to see an area doctor for treatment. When he got a few years older, Stan graduated to mule driver, which earned him more money but did little to solve his chronic ear problem. Only a permanent way out of the mines would bring him relief.

In any biographical sketch of Stan Coveleski, the reader will find that as a young boy he used any free time available to fire rocks at tin cans. Low flying birds were targets as well. After several years of practice, Stan got quite proficient at hitting his targets. Legend has it that a schoolteacher, finding Coveleski perfecting his skill at hitting the tin cans, asked him to pitch for the local school.

After five successful starts, Stan became a hot commodity in the Shamokin area. In 1908 he signed on to play for his hometown in the Atlantic League. He appeared in twelve games, winning six and losing two. During the winter of 1909, the Lancaster club offered Stan $250 a month, a huge increase from his nine-dollar salary at the coal mines. Despite the vast financial gain, Coveleski initially refused to sign, anxious about leaving home for the first time. Then the Lancaster representative offered a contract to his brother John, who promptly signed. After much thought, Stan went ahead and put his name on the dotted line and then proceeded to have an outstanding season, winning twenty-three games with an ERA of 1.95. He had three good seasons for Lancaster, which led to a trial with the Philadelphia Athletics. Stan pitched in five games but found himself buried in the rotation behind Eddie Plank, Jack Coombs, "Boardwalk" Brown, and "Chief" Bender.

Connie Mack decided to send Coveleski back to Lancaster, where he again won twenty games. In 1913, Stan must have blanched when he got the news that his contract had been sold to Spokane, Washington. One can imagine the difficulty he had traveling all the way to Spokane, when Lancaster was only a stone's throw from home. He did make the move, enjoying success in the great northwest. After two seasons in which he won a total of thirty-seven games, Portland of the Pacific Coast League bought his contract. Stan had a good fastball and curve along with excellent control, but he decided his repertoire needed another pitch. He turned to the spitball, using his tobacco juice to doctor the baseball. In an interview with *Baseball Magazine*, Coveleski said, "Somehow the spit ball seemed to be just the thing I needed. I was warned it was a difficult delivery to control but I never found it so." At the time spitballs were considered a legal pitch, much to the dismay of opposing hitters.

The new pitch helped him attract the interest of the Cleveland Indians. They signed Stan to a contract for the 1916 season, along with Bagby and a host of others. At twenty-six years of age, Stan Coveleski got his chance to play at the highest level. He appeared in forty-five games, winning fifteen and losing twelve while compiling an unimpressive ERA of 3.41. What really stood out was how calm he appeared on the mound. Henry Edwards noticed this right away, referring to the new pitcher as the Ice Box. Later Edwards would come up with another nickname, Brother Stan, but Ice Box seemed to fit perfectly. Coveleski had a steady demeanor, rarely experiencing the highs and lows that many ballplayers struggled with. He had no anxiety pitching against Ty Cobb, George Sisler, or later the full-time outfielder Babe Ruth. This trait served him well in his first season and would help him accomplish bigger and better things in the near future.

After several early-season road games in St. Louis, the Indians returned to League Park for the home opener against Detroit. Plenty of early-morning sunshine with comfortable warm temperatures helped bring another sellout crowd. The now-familiar military drills took place along with the patriotic songs that got the 22,000 fans ready for another season. A group of female fans dressed in colonial gowns brought in the traditional horseshoe of flowers for Tris Speaker and the boys. The Cleveland Advertising Club rolled in an extremely large baseball reproduced in flowers complete with purple seams.

Everything appeared to be in order, except for Stan Coveleski, who gave up four runs, including a homer by Sam Crawford, before the start of the fifth inning. The Tigers added three more to take a commanding lead of 7–1. The fans groaned at the results on the field, and then became drenched by an unexpected spring shower. The rain somehow energized the Indians, who closed the gap to 7–6 going into the ninth inning. Utility outfielder Pete Allison led off with a base hit. Ray Chapman laid down a sacrifice bunt, moving Allison to second. One of several drummer boys started to pound his bass drum, which got the crowd to its feet. Speaker swung at the first pitch and sent a long drive down the right-field line that curved foul at the last second. He topped the next pitch back to the mound, resulting in a rundown between second and third for the second out. Bill Wamby came to the plate and smacked his second double of the game, allowing the fleet Speaker to score from first base, tying the game at 7–7. Wamby's clutch hit brought new first baseman Louis Guisto to bat with a chance to send the screaming fans home happy. Guisto lined a single to left, scoring Wamby with the winning run. Nobody seemed to mind the rain showers anymore when Wamby raced across the plate.

A week later, Jim Dunn shared his early-season observations with reporters. "I have not seen St. Louis yet, but I cannot see where Detroit or Chicago has anything on the Indians. I think Cleveland has the best ball club in the west," he said. Dunn had just observed his team on the road taking three out of four games from the White Sox. Jim Bagby had pitched extremely well, while Sox killer Fred Coumbe once again showed his mastery against the Chicago team. The Windy City lived up to its name, whipping gale-like blasts around the park, causing coal and debris to fly indiscriminately and deposit rubbish in the players' eyes. Louis Guisto, a California native, received several chunks in his eye, forcing him to see an eye specialist to take care of the damage. Guisto told reporters, "They wouldn't think of making us play in such weather on the coast. I know I can't play my best in such cold as we have had here." Certainly not the wisest choice of words for a ballplayer trying to win a job in tropical Cleveland, Ohio.

At the end of April, Cleveland had a record of eight wins and nine losses, leaving them fifth in the standings. They lost an ugly game to the St. Louis Browns when Tris Speaker got thrown out of the park by umpire George Hildebrand. The man behind the plate took exception to Speaker dashing in from center field to argue a call. Moments later the umpire enraged catcher Steve O'Neill by calling a ball on a borderline pitch. Despite the Browns having a runner on second base, O'Neill, frustrated at the decision, fired the baseball in the general direction of third baseman Joe Evans. The startled Indian never moved, watching the ball sail into left field while the Browns runner scored easily. It is interesting that Lee Fohl remained on the bench during the entire ruckus. For some reason he let his players do all the protesting, unable or unwilling to protect them. Team captain Speaker did most of the arguing when called for. Possibly Fohl was comfortable sitting on the bench and letting Speaker handle the umpires. He may have believed that the captain on the field had more right to confront the umpires than the manager did. This system seemed to work for the Indians, for a time anyway.

In the latter part of May Cleveland stood in fourth place, having split thirty decisions. Very little excitement was being generated at League Park, with the exception of an inside-the-park home run by Joe Evans. In a game against Boston, the third baseman blistered a line drive to the left-field bleachers and then showed his All-Southern football speed by dashing around the bases before the relay throw to home plate. The fans expected Evans to stop at third with a triple but were astounded when the former quarterback shifted into high gear, motoring all the way in well ahead of the throw. Cleveland beat the Red Sox 7–1.

On May 19, President Wilson issued a proclamation defining the terms of the forthcoming draft of males between the ages of twenty-one and thirty. The order called for all eligible males to register with their local draft boards. The president set aside June 5 as the day for the registration to take place. Those who failed to register were subject to a misdemeanor charge and a year's imprisonment. This proclamation created a giant bureaucracy that would process millions of young men for military service. Several hundred major league ballplayers who had not reached their thirty-first birthdays were included. Now questions loomed concerning the fate of the 1917 season. If the draft boards called baseball players to active duty, could this have an adverse effect on the remaining schedule and the World Series? The coming months would tell the tale as rosters were likely to shrink on a weekly basis.

Shortly after Wilson's proclamation, Ban Johnson announced that the American League would buy $100,000 in Liberty Bonds. Each of the eight clubs would chip in $12,500 to reach the total. Military drilling at ball games increased, showing the nation that baseball would do its part to support the war effort. However, whether it would be contributing players to the armed forces was a matter yet to be determined.

While the owners waited for more news about the draft procedure, the Indians began to make some noise. In a late May home game against the New York Yankees, Cleveland trailed 5–0 going into the bottom of the ninth. Urban Shocker had been sailing along, well on his way to a four-hit shutout. Steve O'Neill led off the home half with a single. Pinch-hitter Josh Billings singled, and then the reliable Jack Graney lined a double, scoring O'Neill. Fans who were edging toward the exits now changed directions to see what might happen. Ray Chapman lashed out another single to score Billings with the second run. With Speaker at bat and two runners on, the fans scrambled back to their seats. They were rewarded when the Indians captain belted another double, scoring Graney from third. Speaker's hit drove Shocker from the mound, sending in Allan Russell to finish the game. The relief pitcher got one out, but Bill

Wamby singled Chapman home with run number four. A walk to Louis Guisto loaded the bases and sent the crowd into a frenzy. Reserve Ivan Howard came to bat, took a called strike, and then fouled a pitch off. As Russell began his next delivery, Speaker dashed for home, the front end of an audacious triple steal. The pitch bounced away from catcher Les Nunamaker, allowing Wamby to round third and sprint home with the winning run. The fans went wild, jumping up and down and cavorting around the infield. The Indians raced for the dugout with the crowd right behind them. They were unable to get away unscathed as a female fan planted herself at the dugout entrance, hugging and kissing every player she could grab. When the team reached the clubhouse, the player celebration began with yelling and dancing all around the lockers. Even Larry the dog got into the act, ripping the pant legs off a very excited Bob McRoy. This was a truly amazing comeback, which shook the team out of its lethargic play and sparked them on to a competitive season.

The following afternoon a crowd of 15,000 entered the grounds to witness the Cleveland debut of pitcher Joe Wood. The former Boston star had been working out for three months, trying to get his arm ready for a starting assignment. His pal Tris Speaker told reporters, "Joe is ready. If he were not, we would not be starting him tomorrow. We have every confidence in him, and if he delivers as we expect, well, just look out for us." Wood, with the fans behind him, went eight innings, allowing four runs on eleven hits. Taking into account that he had not pitched since September of 1915, it goes in the book as a very good performance. The Yankees did not score until the fifth inning, while most of their hits were of the infield variety. Wood threw mostly curve balls and off-speed pitches, mixing it up enough to keep the Yankee hitters from getting comfortable. The fastball was used on occasion, giving fans another glimpse of the famous smoke that Wood could deliver. The Indians did lose the game 4–3, but the result did not dampen the enthusiasm for the fine exhibition of pitching. If Smoky Joe took the mound every five days, the money invested by Jim Dunn would be well spent. Lee Fohl announced he was totally satisfied with his pitcher's outing, while umpire Billy Evans called Wood's performance phenomenal. Evans went on to predict many more wins for Joe Wood. Evans's quotes were very commonplace in an era when umpires spoke more to the press than the players.

Five days later a brief announcement stated that Wood was scratched from his next start. A timetable for a return was not mentioned. The old arm problems had returned, causing speculation that Joe's comeback had already ended. He tried again several times later in the season with disappointing results. It is likely Wood attempted every means available to get his pitching arm back to where it was in 1912. However, the arm had nothing left, a major disappointment surely for Wood and for the Indians. The club still had to find a dependable starter behind Jim Bagby and Stan Coveleski. That would not happen in 1917.

As the Fourth of July approached, Cleveland barely held on to fourth place with a record of 37–36. From that point on they would play at a torrid pace, winning fifty-one of their remaining eighty-two games. This feat represented Cleveland's best finish since 1908, when the Naps fell short of the pennant by a half game. Chiefly responsible for the extraordinary surge was the hitting and all-around play of Ray Chapman, the usual hitting of Tris Speaker, and excellent pitching down the stretch. Chapman did everything well, batting over .300, stealing fifty-two bases, scoring ninety-eight runs, and leading AL shortstops in assists and putouts. The claim that the Indians had the best shortstop in baseball would generate little argument from anyone in the game. The sports pages were filled with descriptions of spectacular plays Chapman made on a regular basis. Near the end of the season he led the Indians to their tenth win in a row, defeating the Philadelphia Athletics. In the first inning he walked, stole second, advanced to third on a fly ball, and then stole home for the game's first run. In the eighth inning Chapman doubled, stole third, and then scored on a ground out by Tris Speaker. A few days later the Indians shortstop appeared in Boston for a benefit staged for the late sportswriter Tim Murnane. He entered a competition to determine which ballplayer could circle the bases the fastest. Chapman flew around the infield, winning first place with a time of fourteen seconds. At twenty-six years of age, Chapman had reached his baseball prime.

Speaker hit .351 for the year along with his stellar play in the outfield. However, on August 14 a fastball from Chicago's Dave Danforth hit Speaker square on the right temple, knocking him unconscious for several minutes. A doctor rushed in from the stands to examine the injured player. After several anxious minutes Speaker opened his eyes, staggered to his feet, and tried to jog to first base. His teammates turned him around, guiding him to the clubhouse, where he waited for the Cleveland team doctor, Morrison Castle. The Cleveland physician had seen a lot of injuries in his years administering to the players, but he told reporters in a chilling tone, "About an inch lower and it might have been all up with Spoke." For several days the Indians center fielder stayed out of the lineup, suffering from headaches and nausea. His right pupil became dilated, causing him to wear sunglasses when outside. Speaker did not return to the lineup for ten days, but when he did he resumed banging out singles and doubles like nothing had happened.

Of Cleveland's eighty-eight wins, half were provided by Jim Bagby and Stan Coveleski. They pitched in an astounding ninety-eight games, and both had ERAs below 2.00 while between them they threw seventeen shutouts. Their numbers compared very favorably with the top pitching combinations in the American League, including Boston's Babe Ruth and Carl Mays, along with champion White Sox stars Eddie Cicotte and Lefty Williams. Had the Indians been able to develop a third starting pitcher, they may have been able to bring home the pennant. The best they could do was Ed Klepfer, the holdover from the Joe Jackson trade. In the latter part of the season when the Indians rallied, Klepfer came on strong, finishing with a career high of thirteen wins. Unfortunately that became the high point for Klepfer. His number came up with the selective service, and the following year found him in the trenches of the French countryside, dodging bullets from German soldiers.

Once again Jim Dunn did everything he could to make his team a contender. He paid out big money to bring Joe Wood to Cleveland even though nobody really knew if there was any life remaining in his right arm. Dunn admitted his mistake in trading Elmer Smith the previous season, buying Smith's contract from Washington to bring the popular slugger back home. In limited playing time Smith banged out three home runs, but once again Uncle Sam came to call, sending him to France along with Klepfer. Cleveland led the American League in players drafted and sent overseas. Along with Klepfer and Smith, part-time first basemen Joe Harris and Louis Guisto traded in baseball uniforms for army khaki, both winding up in Europe for the duration of the war. Despite the losses of personnel plus the prospect of more players going overseas in 1918, Jim Dunn remained confident that a pennant was just around the corner.

7

A TROUBLED TIME

Like the other baseball owners, Jim Dunn had serious issues to face before the start of the 1918 season. The war in Europe raged on, taking an alarming number of ballplayers from the major league rosters. It remained unclear what effect the conflict would have on the upcoming baseball season. Certainly a long, drawn-out war could mean more players trading bats for bayonets. Owners could not say with any certainty whether the 1918 schedule faced cancelation or at the very least some games being eliminated.

On Sunday December 2, while Dunn mulled over the all the possibilities, he learned of the untimely death of his vice president, Bob McRoy. The newspapers reported that McRoy had suffered a severe nervous breakdown during the closing days of the 1917 baseball season. Apparently the Indians executive got much too close to the game, agonizing over every wild pitch, every error made, and every loss chalked up by his ball club, often muttering to himself during the action for Graney to move in a few steps or for Bagby to keep his pitches down. The day after McRoy's funeral, Henry Edwards wrote, "Although identified with the executive or financial end of baseball, Robert McRoy was a real fan. He was the worst kind of fan, belonging to the class that roots inwardly and loses himself so completely in the game as to forget his surroundings entirely. When he was witnessing a close game he did not want to say a word nor be spoken to." This overwrought intensity helped bring about the mental collapse that led to a long stay in the Sacred Heart Sanitarium in Milwaukee. While there McRoy suffered from undisclosed complications that resulted in his death at the young age of thirty-five. The burial took place in his hometown of Chicago with Ban Johnson, Jim Dunn, Garry Herrmann, and Charles Comiskey acting as pallbearers.

When the news broke, Cleveland fans were eerily reminded of a similar circumstance just several years earlier. John Kilfoyl, the savvy financial partner in the 1901 Cleveland franchise, developed into a rabid fan who agonized over every Naps loss. During the frantic pennant race of 1908, Kilfoyl became so wrapped up in the tense battle that it took him several hours to compose himself after each game. The cumulative effect on his mental state was so damaging that at season's end, Kilfoyl reluctantly sold all his stock to Somers and got out of baseball. His health problems continued, bringing on a premature death in 1913. Now four years later Bob McRoy went down the same road, and it ultimately cost him his life as well.

Dunn quietly replaced his vice president with business manager E. S. Barnard. The Cleveland owner decided to stay within the organization by promoting Barnard, who had been with the franchise dating back to the Lajoie era. The forty-three-year-old Barnard proved to be a capable replacement, staying behind the scenes to watch over the business end as well as player transactions. It may have served the Indians well that Barnard gave much of his attention to the front office rather than the daily box scores.

Before the end of December, the AL and NL owners attempted to come together on a number of proposals for the wartime 1918 season. Ban Johnson, anticipating a drop in attendance, called for a 140-game schedule plus a limit of eighteen players per club. The NL owners wanted the 154-game schedule to remain, along with a player limit of twenty-two per squad. A shortened spring training of two or three weeks was proposed. The owners even introduced a revolutionary measure to cut players' meal money from $3 to $2.50 a day, which would save them a few pennies. Other considerations brought forth included

only one Pullman car per railroad trip, which meant players would have to sleep
in upper berths. For years the players had enjoyed a second Pullman car that
allowed everybody to sleep in the more comfortable lower berths. In Cleveland
for a visit, Ray Chapman commented on the upper-berth situation. He stated,
"I'd like to hear any member of the Cleveland Indians put up a kick on the
accommodations this year. If some of us have to take upper berths, we should
be tickled to death to get them instead of standing ankle deep in mud in the
trenches. I don't care what they put me up against, I'll not make a kick."

Another idea was to issue war contracts for all players. This translated to
paying salaries monthly as long as the season continued. If the war forced baseball into a stoppage, player's salaries would cease accordingly. The owners
seemed to be very concerned with making sacrifices in tune with the war effort.
However, much of the cost cutting would likely affect the quality of play on the
field. Less time in spring training opened the door for player injuries. Wartime
contracts left those squad members not eligible for the draft in limbo regarding
employment. The upcoming season posed uncharted difficulties for all involved
in Major League Baseball.

In his annual December state of the ball club address, Jim Dunn assured the
Cleveland fans he would field a strong team for the 1918 campaign. He
acknowledged the war in Europe would have a large impact on baseball in general, but Sunny Jim was prepared to go forward with his best effort. He revealed
to fans that he had made a seemingly fair offer for pitcher Joe Bush of the
Philadelphia Athletics, but the price was too high. Dunn said, "I was disappointed in not being able to make the Cleveland fans a present of Joe Bush, but
I was not born yesterday. They say a sucker is born every minute, and if I had
paid $35,000 for Joe Bush, I would have elected myself to that class." He let the
fans know he was not "resting on his oars" but would continue to explore any
options to better the ball club. Dunn concluded his address by stating he supported any decision to come out of Washington, even if it meant no baseball in
1918. It is refreshing to note that the Cleveland owner did not dance around the
issues but was prepared to take a financial bath if necessary. In just three years,
Dunn had become a top-flight owner. He fully understood the inner workings
of running a professional franchise while having a strong grasp of the current

issues facing the game. He spent money when warranted but knew when he was being hoodwinked by his fellow owners. The chance for a pennant no longer appeared to be something reserved for other AL franchises.

In that long period from the December baseball meetings to the start of spring training, reporters filled their columns with any insight they could conjure up. In a late-January column Henry Edwards speculated that the Indians had failed to win a pennant thus far because no Cleveland pitcher had ever won thirty games in a season. He reasoned that Jack Coombs had won thirty for the world champion Athletics in 1910, while Joe Wood recorded thirty-four wins in 1912 for World Series victors the Boston Red Sox. The best a Cleveland pitcher had done since 1901 was Addie Joss with twenty-seven victories in 1907. Though Edwards had no ability to see the future, his theory would soon be proven correct.

After conferring with Lee Fohl, E. S. Barnard announced a spring training date of March 18 in New Orleans. The players had two weeks to take off the extra pounds and then break camp on April 2 to meet the New York Giants in a series of exhibitions games. The two clubs would travel throughout the south for a week, gradually turning north for Kentucky and Indiana. The barnstorming would conclude on April 14 at Indianapolis, just in time for the opening of the season two days later. To fortify the pitching staff, Dunn purchased Johnny Enzmann from the Newark Internationals plus ten-year veteran Bob Groom from the St. Louis Browns. Though he had a dismal 8–19 record in 1917, Groom had maintained an ERA of 2.94 with four shutouts and a no hitter. Dunn believed the right-hander could pile up a lot of innings while taking some of the pressure off Bagby and Coveleski.

Everything appeared to be in order for the start of training camp when Jim Bagby announced he was holding out for more money. The newspapers reported that Bagby had earned $3,000 for the 1917 season plus a bonus in the range of $500 to $1,000. His contract for the upcoming season did not include a raise, which provoked the Indians' foremost pitcher to hold out for more. Dunn liked to reward his players with bonuses for a productive year. However, Bagby decided he wanted to get his money up front rather than hope for a bonus at season's end. He wrote a letter to the *Plain Dealer* stating his case. Bagby said,

"I do not claim it an honor to be a hold out, but at the same time I do think when a man has reached the height of his ambition, he is entitled to receive his reward."

The timing of Bagby's announcement could not have been worse. The likelihood of a shortened season with a brief spring training meant pitchers had to take great care to get ready for the season. Any days missed could have an impact, particularly if you were being counted on to lead the staff. Bagby had turned in a terrific performance in 1917. He was among the AL leaders in five different categories, including wins, saves, shutouts, and games pitched. This is an instance where Dunn should have come through with a fair raise in pay. Dangling a carrot in front of certain players worked well enough, but for your best pitcher this strategy reeked of old-fashioned penny pinching. Bagby had more than demonstrated that he had the ability during the previous season. He wanted a salary increase rather than a verbal promise of money. In this particular scenario, Jim Dunn had made an error.

Player reaction to Bagby's holdout was mixed. Several were openly disappointed because of the newly instituted sharing of World Series revenue. Now the second- and third-place finishers would share in the gate receipts from the Fall Classic. Several players believed the Indians were in a favorable position to claim one of the top three spots, thus getting extra money at season's end. Every day that Bagby missed potentially cost each team member a few good suits and a pocket watch. One player commented anonymously that owner Dunn treated everybody fairly: "Jim Dunn treated Bagby splendidly last season. He treated us all fairly for that matter, but Jim drew a handsome bonus while some of the rest of us did not. We feel sure that Mr. Dunn will do the right thing by us and why shouldn't Jim [Bagby] have that same confidence in him?"

Whether the player that spoke happened to be a bench player or a starter indicated the strong faith in the Cleveland ownership. It is difficult to determine if the quote was close to the truth. In Bagby's case, his salary of $3,000 appeared to be less than fair considering Speaker earned five times as much while Joe Wood got $5,000 for a few scattered outings throughout the summer. Regardless, the Indians needed their ace right-hander in camp as soon as possible.

At the end of March, Bagby telegraphed the newspapers that he was on his way to Cleveland to meet with Dunn. The two men conferred at the Hollenden Hotel to carve out a deal. The next morning the Indians management released a statement that an agreement had been reached and their ace pitcher had already left for New Orleans. No terms were released but the new contract was somewhere between the old salary of $3,000 and Bagby's demand of $10,000. By now Opening Day loomed just two weeks ahead.

While the Indians' squad hurried through spring training, Major League Baseball continued to implement restrictions for the upcoming season. Players would be expected to use streetcars for city travel rather than the more comfortable taxicabs. Fireproof suitcases were being built for train trips instead of the more roomy steamer trunks. Players now had to carry their own uniforms plus equipment. The league anticipated slower train service due to wartime transportation demands.

Not all the belt tightening and restrictions affected the players. The U.S. government initiated a war tax to be collected from every individual game ticket sold. A tax of approximately 10 percent would be added for each level of ticket pricing at all major league parks. To make things easier for the ticket takers and the fans, the Indians announced pricing as follows:

Bleacher seats: 27 cents plus war tax of 3 cents = 30 cents

Pavilion seats: 50 cents plus war tax of 5 cents = 55 cents

Grandstand seats: 77 cents plus war tax of 8 cents = 85 cents

Reserved and box seats: $1.00 plus war tax of 10 cents = $1.10

In this manner, the changing of pennies could be avoided altogether. Those who carried free passes into the game now had to pay a flat ten cents per pass. Even the ladies, who were previously admitted free on their special day, had to spend the ten cents to get a seat. The new ruling did not exempt schoolchildren and newsboys, but Jim Dunn assured parents he would cover the war tax himself for each child with a free ticket. In the past, Dunn had been very kind to children, distributing thousands of passes to students and newsboys throughout greater Cleveland. Based on previous totals, he stood to cover about $1,600 in taxes himself. In addition, any boy or girl who brought in a ball hit over the outfield fences would still be allowed free admission in exchange for the baseball. The government agreed this longtime tradition should continue without any penalty.

Despite the condensed spring training, the Indians managed to find time for the annual practical joke. In this instance, the target would be Steve O'Neill due to his boasts of long-range prowess on the golf course. A northeast Ohio doctor who was working out with the team arranged for a contest to determine which player could drive a golf ball the farthest. With the assistance of Ray Chapman and Tris Speaker, players mapped out the prank precisely. Among the players, only Chapman volunteered to challenge O'Neill at the long drive championship. Wagers were set, and then the two competitors lined up by home plate for one drive each. Chapman walloped a drive off the tee that cleared the center-field fence. O'Neill then took several practice swings, determined to launch the golf ball even farther over the fence. While the players stood in silence, O'Neill let go with a mighty swing, only to see the ball explode into hundreds of pieces. The instigators had fashioned a ball made of plaster of Paris, which broke up on contact. The boys had outdone themselves; now it was time to concentrate on the regular season ahead.

For the first time in many years, dark clouds and a torrent of rain engulfed League Park, spoiling Opening Day. The very next day, the rain came again, forcing another postponement. The weather cleared just enough to get the opener in on Thursday, April 18. Stan Coveleski had his spitball dancing in the light showers, coasting to a 6–2 victory. The Indians trailed by a run for six innings and then exploded for five more in the bottom of the seventh. Bobby Roth ignited the crowd of eleven thousand by lining a triple to left field with the bases loaded. Coveleski set the Tigers down in the eighth and ninth innings to start the season on a winning note. Four days later, Coveleski won again, beating the St. Louis Browns 8–1. Ray Chapman scored three runs, while Bobby Roth had another good day at the plate, banging out three hits while picking up three more runs batted in.

The Indians left town for a series with Detroit. However, the flu bug swept through the team, sidelining pitchers Johnny Enzmann and Bob Groom. Joe

Wood came down with the illness, and it appeared that he too would have to remain in Cleveland. The next day, both Bill Wamby and Guy Morton had severe attacks of the influenza, leaving at least five players unfit for duty. On the trip to Detroit, Jack Graney, Terry Turner, and Ray Chapman became ill, leaving the team in desperate straits. The Cleveland management got busy on the telephones, trying to locate replacements in hopes of fielding enough players to take the field and avoid a forfeit. On April 25 the Indians led off the first inning with the following patched-together lineup:

> Eddie Onslow—left field
> Al Halt—shortstop
> Tris Speaker—center field
> Bobby Roth—right field
> Rip Williams—first base
> Gus Getz—third base
> Herman Schaefer—second base
> Steve O'Neill—catcher
> Fred Coumbe—pitcher

That Cleveland was able to find enough players in such a short time is a testament to the skill of the front office. Eddie Onslow had last played in the American League back in 1913. Al Halt had played two seasons with Brooklyn of the Federal League, while Rip Williams had seen service with Washington as a catcher and first baseman. Williams was thirty-six years old and did not play in the majors in 1917. Gus Getz had belonged to Cincinnati the previous season but only played in seven games. He did have big league experience, starting with the Boston Braves of the National League in 1909. That brings us to the number seven hitter, Herman "Germany" Schaefer, the former clown prince of baseball. The forty-year-old had delighted baseball fans for many years with his antics on the diamond, whether it was stealing first base or sliding into each base after hitting a home run. Schaefer had not played since a brief appearance with Newark of the Federal League in 1916. The Indians signed the onetime Detroit Tiger to be a coach for the season but had no intention of using him as a substitute.

However, drastic times call for drastic action, and Schaefer played nine innings at second base. To the surprise of everybody attending the game, the sandlot Indians won by a score of 8–4. Fred Coumbe went the distance and drove in four runs with two singles and two sacrifice flies. The flabbergasted Detroit Tigers found themselves down 7–0 before they scored a run.

The next day saw more of the same with Halt, Getz, and Williams still in the starting lineup. However, Lee Fohl decided on a very significant move, replacing Eddie Onslow with Joe Wood in left field. Joe had recovered from the flu. Whether this was desperation or a shrewd appraisal is not known, but the move paid dividends as the former pitcher played flawless defense while contributing a double in four at-bats. The Indians, behind the rock-solid pitching of Stan Coveleski and a clutch home run by recovered flu patient Ray Chapman, prevailed 3–2 in twelve innings.

The team moved on to St. Louis for their next series. On May 2, Wood filled in for an ailing Tris Speaker. In the sixth inning, with two Browns on the bases and two out, Joe made a fine running grab of a line drive to deep left center field. He followed that with a double to left, scoring the go-ahead run in the seventh. One inning later while in left field (Speaker had entered the game in center), Wood flagged down a long drive over his head just steps from the outfield fence. St. Louis kept the pressure on with a double by Jack Tobin. The next hitter dropped a single in short left field. Wood came in on the run, picked up the ball on one hop, and fired a strike to catcher Steve O'Neill. Tobin was out, the game saved, Cleveland winning 3–2. Because of the flu epidemic that swept through the Indians' locker room, Joe Wood got a chance to help the club in a most unintended way. He no longer could pitch like Smoky Joe, but he could hit and play the outfield. It is likely by this time he knew his pitching days were over. Being a top-notch athlete, Wood tried his best in spring training to convert himself to another position. Box scores show Wood in the outfield during intersquad games. This probably took place due to a lack of bodies for two full teams, but Joe may very well have been using the opportunity to judge fly balls and hit the cutoff man. Maybe Lee Fohl noticed this or maybe he did not; however an outbreak of flu proved to be a fortunate opportunity for Joe Wood the all-around ballplayer.

The winning ways continued for the Indians with another victory over the Browns. Bob Groom staggered through six-plus innings, while hard-hitting left fielder Joe Wood pounded out two doubles with two RBIs. The Cleveland outfield now had a fourth option with either Jack Graney or Joe Wood playing in left field. Tris Speaker was the game's best center fielder, while Bobby Roth, for the moment, was holding his own in right field.

While Cleveland was rolling along, Ban Johnson offered some pessimistic observations on the 1918 season. Speaking to reporters, Johnson said, "The war cannot but hurt us this year. Some clubs are likely to lose money. Conditions are not normal, and as the weather has been antagonistic in many cities, we have suffered already." Johnson went on to discuss how the players lost through enlistments and through the draft had hurt the game. He hoped for an exciting pennant race to keep fans interested along with money flowing to the ball clubs. He did take a moment to give praise to the Indians, stating, "Personally, I like the Cleveland club. It has some splendid pitchers, a wonderful catcher, and some of the stars of the game in other positions. Speaker is such a great player that I take great pleasure in watching him regardless of whether Cleveland wins or loses."

Johnson did have the great pleasure of traveling to Washington to see the Indians and Senators play the first-ever Sunday game in the capital city. More than seventeen thousand people turned out to see the historic contest. Many legislators attended the game, along with foreign officials and several thousand American soldiers. They witnessed a great pitchers' battle between Stan Coveleski and the Senators' Doc Ayers. For eleven innings neither pitcher yielded a single run. In the bottom of the twelfth, a single, a bad pick-off throw to first by Coveleski, and a two-out single brought in the game's only run. Despite the loss, the spitballing right-hander was on his way to an exceptional season. While Bagby struggled to get into pitching shape, his counterpart excelled from Opening Day until the end of the season. For the time being, Coveleski carried the entire pitching staff.

Several days later the Indians were in Boston to face Carl Mays and the Red Sox. In the eighth inning, with Cleveland trailing 9–1, Speaker stepped into the batter's box. Mays let go with a high hard one that slammed into the top of

Speaker's head. The force of the blow caused the baseball to career all the way to the grandstand. Speaker somehow stayed on his feet, beginning an unsteady jog to first base. He abruptly stopped and yelled to Mays, "You are a dirty player to pull a trick like that." Mays shouted back that it was an accident, but Speaker took several steps toward the mound, hollering, "I worked on the same team long enough with you to know your methods, and I have half a mind to go right out there and give you some of your own medicine!" At that point both benches came charging out to get between the mound and the incensed Speaker. Apparently no serious punches were thrown, allowing umpire Bill Dinneen to break up the scuffle and restart the game.

Speaker, as a former member of the Red Sox, knew Carl Mays very well from the one season they played together. From center field he got a bird's-eye view of Mays's pitching style. Though obviously furious from being hit on the head, Speaker knew from observation that Mays liked to pitch inside. If his control veered off just slightly, even a few inches, a serious injury could result. Records show that during the 1917 season, Mays beaned fourteen hitters. The entire Cleveland pitching staff totaled just eighteen hit batsmen in the same period. The difference here is obvious. Mays worked the ball inside with little fear of plunking his opponent. As a result he hit a large number of batters, well above the norm for other pitchers. Certainly many other pitchers threw inside to move back hitters, but not with the regularity of Carl Mays. His numbers are well out of proportion with the other hurlers of the American League. For comparison's sake, the four starting pitchers of the Chicago White Sox, including Eddie Cicotte and Lefty Williams, hit a total of twenty-five batters for the 1917 season. That averages out to approximately six per pitcher. Stan Coveleski and his spitball hit just one batter all season. It is difficult to state that Mays deliberately threw at batters; however, he did have a penchant for keeping them away from the plate, much more so than any other pitcher of his era. That being said, Spoke was fortunate to walk away with just a bad bruise on the cranium. Two years later another Cleveland ballplayer would not be so lucky.

8

WORK OR FIGHT

When Ban Johnson spoke pessimistically about the 1918 season, he may have known a bit more than what he was letting on. On May 23, 1918, Provost Marshal Gen. Enoch Crowder issued his work-or-fight order, which basically ordered men of draft age to either work in the war industry or take a boat overseas to join the fighting. This measure was aimed at what the public called slackers—men who had avoided the draft and were not contributing to the fighting in Europe. The order noted that men who were racetrack attendants, waiters, elevator operators, hotel workers, and even fortune tellers were now subject to more rigorous employment. The U.S. government believed the work-or-fight order would solve the labor problem for farmers, shipbuilders, munitions makers, and all industries that needed help to keep pace with the demands of the War Department. General Crowder's order went on to state, "This regulation provides that after July 1st any registrant who is found by a local board to be a habitual idler shall be summoned before the board and given a chance to explain and in the absence of a satisfactory explanation to be inducted into the military service of the United States."

This announcement had to shake baseball owners to the very core of their wallets. The language said nothing about professional baseball, but no doubt

97

Secretary of War Baker would weigh in on the subject in a matter of days. The designated date of July 1 implied a shortened season, one that would cost the owners and players a great deal of money. Certainly everybody involved in baseball had to walk a fine line when commenting on the order. To say baseball should continue would not be the most prudent thing for an owner or player to say publicly. They needed to be very patriotic, supporting the work-or-fight order even if it meant a large financial loss. The only avenue that could be pursued centered on the idea that the American people needed baseball as an outlet to cope with the very serious business of conducting a war in Europe. If the American public demanded to see a baseball game after a long day in the industrial army, why not provide it? This in itself might contribute to the war effort by helping boost the morale of a tense and anxious public. The days ahead would gauge the attitude of the government and the American people regarding the importance of baseball in wartime.

Secretary Baker did not wait long to give a statement to the newspapers. He said, "The war department does not desire to disrupt the playing of baseball and prevent the completion of the schedule by the American and National Leagues. No ruling as to whether baseball players or persons engaged in any other sport come under the regulations regarding idlers and nonessential pursuits will be made until a specific case has been appealed to the provost marshal general's office." Baker did not flatly state baseball would go on until season's end but left the door open for negotiations with the owners on a solution. Ban Johnson and NL president John Tener both indicated that ballparks would soon close, due to the fact that 90 percent of the ballplayers were within draft age. According to reports, the Boston Red Sox stood to lose their entire roster, while Detroit had only three players over the age limit. If the order had to be enforced to the letter, the baseball season was in serious jeopardy.

Rumors soon surfaced that the work-or-fight order did not include professional baseball players. Word circulated that the provost marshal general's office had decided to exclude any and all ballplayers from the new directive. However, General Crowder announced that the original order had not changed and that a ruling would likely come from President Wilson after July 1. It was anticipated that the first ballplayer to be called before his draft board would probably file an appeal to challenge the new regulation. This scenario meant the White House had the final say on the fate of the major league players.

In the period before judgment day, baseball continued as usual. The Indians were in New York to battle the Yankees. Cleveland trailed 2–1 in the seventh inning when Joe Wood blasted a home run to the left-field seats. Behind Stan Coveleski, the game went all the way to the nineteenth inning, when Wood clouted another home run to put the Indians in the lead 3–2. Coveleski set the Yankees down in the bottom of the inning to win the marathon ball game. What made this performance truly remarkable was that in his previous two starts, the right-hander had gone twelve and thirteen innings, respectively. Coveleski accomplished this in a period of just ten days. He pitched forty-four innings for an average of a little over fourteen innings per last three starts. The pitch counts are unknown; however, it is probable he threw in the neighborhood of five hundred pitches. By current standards, that number of pitches is unheard of. Coveleski did all this without a whimper. He came from the school that taught simply taking the ball every three or four days and pitching until the game is over.

With Jack Graney out with a sore arm and Bobby Roth recently suspended for failure to obey training rules, Joe Wood made the most of his opportunities in the outfield. Shortly after his two-home-run performance against the Yankees, the papers revealed Wood had been playing all season without a contract. Due to his inability to pitch during the 1917 season, the Indians did not offer him a contract the following winter. In March Wood sent a wire to the Cleveland office advising Dunn and Barnard that he would report to spring training at his own expense. He worked hard at getting his arm in shape, but fate intervened when the regular season began and the Indians' roster was devastated by illness. According to the *Plain Dealer*, in the April game against Detroit, Wood had become frustrated at the outfield misplays by last-minute substitute Eddie Onslow. He approached Lee Fohl and said, "For the love of Mike, Lee, put me out there in left field before the game is lost!" Fohl obliged, and Cleveland found a new outfielder for the season and beyond.

When the team returned to Cleveland, Jim Dunn sought out his new slugger and summoned him to the office to work out a contract. Reportedly, Wood told Dunn to draw up a contract with whatever amount he thought fair, and it would be signed promptly. Playing nearly three months of baseball without a signed deal was quite risky, to say the least. However, in Joe Wood's case there was really little to lose. Whether he knew he could play the outfield and launch baseballs to deep left field is unclear, but his situation remains rare in the long history of professional baseball. Very few men could make the switch from pitcher to outfielder and be proficient there. To be able to accomplish this virtually overnight during a championship season is extremely unusual. Joe Wood happened to be an exception.

Despite the pitching of Stan Coveleski and the inspired play of the Indians batters, there were still some bumps in the road ahead. Word leaked out that Bobby Roth's suspension was actually due to a shouting match with manager Fohl. The two had been having some difficulties that resulted in a major blowup in the clubhouse. From then on, Roth's days with the Indians were numbered.

Even the usually well-mannered fans at League Park got completely out of control during a June game against the Red Sox. Umpire Clarence Owens nearly lost his life when he tossed Ray Chapman for arguing a close call at second. Chapman went to the bench but continued the argument from his seated position. Owens then ordered the Cleveland shortstop to the clubhouse, which started a near riot. Pop bottles began to fly onto the field, while threats were shouted from all points in the stands. It did not help the precarious situation that the Indians lost the game 2–0. Owens attempted to leave the field, but hundreds of fans surrounded the exits. A police escort helped Owens get outside the grounds, where Jim Dunn waited with his automobile. As upset as the fans were, nobody had the courage to approach the stylish car of the Cleveland owner, which allowed the besieged umpire to arrive at his hotel safely.

The season of uncertainty carried into the early part of June. The Indians were holding on to third place, four games behind the league-leading Boston Red Sox. While most of the lineup was set, there was a definite lack of production from the first-base position. Joe Harris, the holdover from last year, had already been drafted into the army, along with his backup, Louis Guisto. Several players with major league experience were tried at the position. They were all found wanting. That prompted Jim Dunn to send his chief scout Jack McAllister to Milwaukee for a look at an old friend: Wheeler "Doc" Johnston. Out of the big leagues for one full season, Doc had been tearing up the American Association with a batting average of .382. McAllister liked what he saw and advised Dunn to buy Johnston's contract.

This would be Johnston's second go-around with Cleveland, having played for the club from 1912–1914. He started with the Naps at the same time as Ray Chapman. Both impressed the fans with their hustle and determination; however, it was Chapman who had the staying power. Doc never hit as well as expected but did play good defense along with some decent ability to run the bases. He did not endear himself to the Cleveland management and fans by constantly flirting with the Federal League during the winter of 1914. After he played two mediocre seasons as a starter, the Indians decided to look elsewhere, shipping Johnston to the Pittsburgh Pirates. He played well in the 1915 season, banging out five home runs while stealing twenty-six bases. However, Johnston flopped again in 1916, causing the Pirates to sell him to Birmingham. At age twenty-nine, it seemed the Tennessee native had come to the end of the road. Still, he somehow rejuvenated himself after being demoted to Milwaukee of the American Association. His stellar hitting and base stealing brought him back to Cleveland for the latter months of 1918. Johnston's return to the Indians would solidify the first-base position for several years.

With Johnston now in the lineup, Cleveland came from behind to beat Philadelphia 6–3. Trailing 3–1 in the home half of the seventh inning, Cleveland loaded the bases with two men out. Joe Wood once again came through with a two-run single, which tied the score. That brought to the plate the other Joe (Evans), who lined a shot up the gap to left center field. The fans rose to their feet while Evans dashed around the bases for a three-run homer. Several days later the medical school student knocked in two more runs with a triple to help the Indians to a 4–3 victory over Chicago.

The addition of Doc Johnston ignited a hitting spree by the Cleveland batters. Joe Wood and third baseman Joe Evans were already stroking the ball well, but now the entire lineup started raining base hits all over the diamond. In a game against Detroit, the Indians swatted sixteen hits for a 13–4 romp over the Detroit Tigers. Led by Bill Wamby's four hits, the team exploded for ten runs in the eighth inning. That win put them within seven percentage points of first place. Cleveland was playing with a sense of urgency, knowing the season could come to an end at any time.

On July 3, the Boston draft board summoned fourteen members of the Boston Braves to appear at a hearing to determine their eligibility for the draft. The newspapers speculated that if the Boston players were ordered into the army, local draft boards in all the major league cities would follow suit. The Boston proceedings might have a domino effect throughout professional baseball. The White House did not release any official statement regarding the Boston situation, nor did Secretary of War Newton Baker. While things got sorted out, baseball continued as usual.

Several days later, Bill Wamby received notice from the draft board in Fort Wayne, Indiana, to report to Camp Taylor in Louisville on July 25. This news put a damper on the fans' recent celebration as the Indians vaulted into first place. Wamby could keep on playing all the way until the 24th, but his loss was a jolt to the Indians' pennant hopes. The likely candidate to play second base was thirty-seven-year-old Terry Turner, who had been warming the bench most of the season. This did not thrill the Cleveland fans who had been following Wamby in his best season to date. Always a good infielder, Wamby had been hitting around .300 while being one of the most consistent performers on the squad.

While players were being called one by one to their draft boards, Tris Speaker announced he would enter the navy in an attempt to join the aviation corps. His goal was to get an officer's commission, but he planned to enter the service whether or not he received his wings. The army had attempted to recruit him as an artillery officer, but the guardian of center field wanted only to serve in the navy. Speaker explained his decision to curious reporters. He stated, "I prefer the naval section as I want to get even with the German submarines for the cowardly deeds they have committed in sinking unarmed liners and hospital ships without warning. I know of no branch of the service in which I can get quicker and more emphatic results than by operating a seaplane." Speaker further advised he was prepared to enter the service immediately if the baseball season ended before the scheduled completion date. If baseball continued through

September, Spoke would play it out then go dive bombing over the North Atlantic. His draft board in Hubbard, Texas, had given Speaker a deferral owing to his age of thirty, which left him less than a year away from crossing the age limit for military service. Despite the prospect of his name not being called, the patriotic Speaker wanted to do his part for the Allies in Europe.

The speculation on the fate of the baseball season ended on July 18, when Secretary Baker informed the public that baseball was now classified as a nonessential occupation. The decision came after an appeal by Eddie Ainsmith, still the catcher for the Washington Senators. The draft board heard the appeal in Washington and then sent the case to Secretary Baker for a ruling. After some deliberation, the secretary upheld the board decision, quoting part of paragraph C, section 12, of the work-or-fight order. The document read, "Persons including ushers and other attendants engaged and occupied in and the connection with games, sports, amusements, etc." Secretary Baker added, "Obviously baseball players are persons occupied in a sport, so that the ruling of the local and district boards must be sustained as plainly correct." Baker did not have any objections to players outside the draft-age limits (twenty-one to thirty) continuing with their teams, stating that there was no certainty baseball would be disrupted by the order.

Baker went on to explain that Ainsmith's appeal did not challenge the language of the work-or-fight order but questioned the wisdom of declaring baseball a nonessential occupation. There were three parts to the appeal, the first claiming baseball was a very large business with heavy investments in properties. The order, as it read, would cause the properties to become useless and completely disrupt the game and/or destroy it. The second point focused on the high degree of specialized training and skill possessed by professional baseball players. The argument maintained that the skills acquired by the athletes would not transfer to any other occupation, thus lowering their standard of living. The final point centered on the fact that baseball was the national game of the United States and that its citizens relied on it for wholesome recreation outside the workplace. The emotional damage that might be inflicted on the public by canceling the baseball season would do more harm than giving exemptions to the ballplayers.

The appeal contained some valid points, which Secretary Baker did not choose to dispute. However, he asserted that in normal times baseball had its place in society, but these were not normal times. Baker said, "The stress of intensive occupation in industry and commerce in America in normal times is such as to give the highest importance and social value to outdoor recreation. But the times are not normal; the demands of the army and of the country are such that we must all make sacrifices, and the non-productive employment of able bodied persons cannot be justified." The United States government had spoken—baseball was going to war.

The Cleveland players were very surprised by the ultimate verdict. They did expect to do their part for Uncle Sam but thought the season would continue through September. Tris Speaker, acting as the Indians' representative, advised his teammates to sit tight and do nothing until an official announcement came forth declaring the season canceled. Speaker believed the team should wait it out in Cleveland. They would remain at home before their next road trip pending a decision from the front office. Speaker mentioned he would go home to Texas for a short visit, then report to the navy for duty if the season was indeed over. Ray Chapman announced he would enlist in the navy immediately if baseball was done for the year. The rest of the players were not so anxious to head overseas. Most of them planned to do their service in the war industry. Steve O'Neill and Stan Coveleski were willing to go back to the brutal coal mines, while others were ready to start work in the Cleveland-area factories. Guy Morton was content to go home to Alabama to wait for his name to be called.

As one would expect, the major league officials had much to say about Secretary Baker's edict. Garry Herrmann, chairman of the National Baseball Commission, quickly responded to the government's order. He applauded the ruling, claiming the full support of major league baseball. According to the Cincinnati Reds owner, "Baseball was loyal and patriotic and will continue to be so." His, and presumably the other owners', main concern revolved around the procedure for ending the season. Herrmann suggested the owners would meet in the next few days to sort things out. When one reads the statement, it quickly comes to mind that nowhere did it say the league intended to close their parks as soon as possible. That lack of decisiveness literally left the gates open for the interim. While the meetings went on, what would be the harm in playing a few more games, possibly extending the schedule a week or two more?

The tone of Herrmann's statement suggests that a delaying tactic was being attempted. The owners may have been genuine patriots, but the notion that gate receipts were done for the year could not have gone over well with them. A statement from John Tener echoed the sentiments of Garry Herrmann. After stating that baseball was willing to make the necessary sacrifices, Tener went on to say, "We feel, however, some provision should be made that would give us time to determine whether or not the clubs can proceed under the suggestion made by Secretary Baker or whether we will close out our business entirely. We will request the war department to make its ruling more definite as it concerns this point." Clearly the officials of Major League Baseball wanted to somehow comply with the work-or-fight order but still play out the season. This meant converting to an over-thirty league. Rosters would have to be filled with retired players and the large complement of ex–major leaguers still hanging on in minor league cities. Whether any fan wanted to see a group of old-timers shuffling around the diamond for several months was another matter.

The hope for a united front from the owners was dashed by a telegram from Jim Dunn. Truly his own man, the Cleveland owner wired the newspapers a short and snappy message. It read, "We will play a double header in Cleveland Sunday with Philadelphia and then close the ballpark for balance of the season in compliance with Secretary Baker's ruling." Dunn had advised reporters several days earlier that if Baker declared baseball nonessential, he would close League Park rather than field a team below the standard of Major League Baseball. He added that his players had told him they did not care to remain on the diamond and catch abuse from "leather-lunged" fans about their lack of support for the war effort. They wanted to contribute, and their boss agreed with them.

At this point Dunn was the sole owner to speak out for canceling the remainder of the season. His team still had a legitimate chance for the pennant, something Dunn wanted very badly. In spite of this, he had no qualms about complying totally with the recent order. Sunny Jim's behavior must have mortified his fellow owners, who had made no such statements.

While the players waited around for something to happen, the owners moved, with or without the support of Dunn, to save the season. Ban Johnson called for an emergency owners' meeting in Cleveland. The NL owners met as well to attempt to find a way to circumvent Secretary Baker's decision. Whatever resolution they made, they had to walk a very fine line between being a loyal American and a capitalist about to lose a tremendous amount of money. It is doubtful the public would have had much sympathy for a small group of middle-aged men who earned an incomprehensible amount of money compared to the average person on the street. Thousands of young men were quietly doing their duty in France, facing death at any given moment. They did not retain lawyers to challenge their draft status or prepare appeals on their own behalf. These men left their families and jobs behind to fight a horrific world war thousands of miles away. Persuading the government and the general public to support ballplayers staying out of the fight was a daunting task for the worried owners.

In accordance with Jim Dunn's statement, the Indians met in Philadelphia on July 21 for an apparently season-ending doubleheader. Over eleven thousand fans turned out on a sweltering hot Sunday afternoon. Aware that the season teetered on the brink, fans scrambled for foul balls, refusing to return them to the befuddled ushers. On most occasions, fans cheerfully tossed errant baseballs back to the attendants chasing them. Not today—some fans stuffed baseballs in their shirts, to the laughter of fellow attendees. Umpires were forced to open a new box of baseballs, a true rarity that fans were delighted to see. Cleveland took the first game 3–2 behind Stan Coveleski and then played to a 5–5 tie in the second, the game ending because the Athletics had to catch a train back to Philadelphia.

Most fans were philosophical about the likely closing of the season. One fan stated, "It's all right. It's good and proper. I like the game and all that, but if the government needs these players as soldiers or workers, why, it's all right." Another remarked, "It seems to me rather raw that the government did the thing so suddenly. I am for it, of course, but why didn't they give the leagues some notice of what was coming?" An additional fan answered that comment by saying the work-or-fight order was notice enough. Fans would miss the game but understood the needs of the government outweighed the needs of Major League Baseball.

The owners sought a last-minute audience with General Crowder and Secretary Baker to present their arguments for baseball to continue. The National Commission—composed of Ban Johnson, John Tener, and Garry Herrmann—proposed a trip to Washington for a July 23 meeting with the two men who held the fate of baseball in their hands. Clark Griffith, the Washington owner, had made a hometown appeal for the owners. Herrmann convinced his congressman, the dashing and popular Nick Longworth, to meet with General Crowder to speak on behalf of the baseball magnates. The general expressed his surprise that no representative of the national game had requested a meeting with him since his decree of May 23. Regardless, Crowder told Longworth he would agree to meet with Johnson and his crew on the designated date.

Some owners criticized Johnson for waiting too long to take any action. Johnson responded promptly, "It was not for me to tell the secretary of war or provost general what to do." This did not pacify the owners, particularly Boston's Harry Frazee, who declared he would accompany the National Commission to make certain the arguments were aggressively stated. In the meantime, Johnson announced that scheduled games should continue until the result of the meeting in Washington. Jim Dunn did not move from his previous assertion that League Park, for all intents and purposes, was now closed. He told curious reporters his decision stood unless General Crowder modified his position. If Crowder agreed to reconsider, Dunn might allow the Indians to resume action with a series against the Yankees. Clearly Dunn would not be going to Washington to plead for leniency.

Early reports intimated that Johnson, Tener, and Herrmann were only trying to seek an extension of the season rather than fight for a complete 154 games plus a World Series. A thirty- or sixty-day extension would allow owners to collect enough gate receipts to pay the bills for a good while. An extension of sixty days would take the season to September 23, which meant canceling two weeks of the schedule at most. This strategy was sensible, as it acknowledged the season would end early and put baseball in willing compliance with General Crowder's order.

Faced with the uncertainty of the moment, the Cleveland players decided to remain in town and go through some lively workouts. Bill Wamby had his trunk packed for his departure to Camp Taylor, but the balance of the roster was available to play out the string. Lee Fohl remarked that Stan Coveleski stood ready to start game 1 if the New York series went ahead. Fohl was happy that his squad got three days off to rest and attend to the minor aches and pains they had accumulated over the season. He had some optimism that an extension would be granted, allowing the Indians to chase the Red Sox for the pennant. Despite the improbability of a complete season, the Indians were in good position to close the gap on first-place Boston. At this point, the only obstacle in their path was the U.S. government.

The day of decision came and went without any final verdict. The National Commission did prepare a brief for their meeting with General Crowder, but Secretary Baker did not attend because of matters more serious than the game of baseball. Baker did indicate he would study the brief in the evening and then confer with Crowder. The papers described the document as identifying Major League Baseball as a $10 million to $15 million industry that was the premier outdoor sport of the American people. For that reason alone, it was vital to the morale of the country. The brief maintained that the game was even now of great interest to the soldiers fighting overseas, who could maintain an interest in their favorite team. The thinking there was that baseball helped the soldiers relax and take their mind off the fighting. The brief's final argument was that the number of players eligible for service constituted a very small number, which lent to some latitude in the final decision. The meeting with Crowder lasted over an hour, during which Johnson and his minions pleaded for an extension, even if the arguments presented were dismissed. Whether the National Commission had scored any points would not be revealed until Baker conferred with his general.

Two days later Secretary Baker rendered his final decision. He took into account that baseball was indeed different from any other industry in the country in that its employees were scattered around various cities throughout the northern and midwestern states. However, he stressed that it would be unfair to exempt ballplayers from the service when most classes of Americans did not have any options but to work or fight. Thus the baseball season would end September 1. Though Baker's memorandum covered all the points presented, it did not make any mention of the World Series. Now the American and National League owners had another dilemma to wrestle with. They could end the season voluntarily some ten days early to allow the championship games to be played before the September 1 deadline. The other course of action was to petition for special dispensation to allow the pennant winners to continue with the championship series after September 1. Ending the season ten days early would not sit well with the players who stood to get their salaries cut off prematurely, as opposed to the pennant-winning teams. Some players had already jumped to the steelyard teams, where they did some essential work while playing for the yard's baseball team. Sending ballplayers packing August 20 instead of September 1 just might deplete the ranks even further.

Within several days, Ban Johnson announced that he favored ending the baseball season on August 20 and then playing the World Series to completion by September 1. He sent a bulletin to all AL owners asking for their approval. To no one's surprise, the first to respond backed the plan. Jim Dunn wired his support, stating, "Whether this will be the result of the vote I do not know. I have heard nothing from the other club owners in regard to this question, and it must be remembered that the National League owners must agree before the plan can be adopted." One obstacle to approving the plan was in the scheduling. Most of the eastern team owners did not want to pay the expenses for any more western swings, while their western team counterparts did not want to travel east. This translated into a revamping of the late-August schedule. As an example, Cleveland had only three games remaining with close neighbor Detroit. A change in schedule might add two or three more games with the Tigers while canceling the remaining games with Chicago. All these plans were being tossed around in an attempt to bring the season to a close in the most efficient manner. However, the decision makers were owners of big league clubs, where money triumphs over efficiency.

The next day Frank Navin of the Tigers sided with Johnson and Dunn, but Charles Comiskey opposed the plan, citing the large crowds he was drawing at his Chicago ballpark. Clark Griffith voiced his sentiments to Comiskey, asking for the schedule to be ended on September 1. The NL owners decided to meet later in the week to discuss the matter, although Cincinnati's Garry Herrmann spoke out for canceling the World Series altogether.

While the owners fought over dollars and cents, the Indians continued to play excellent baseball. Boston came to town for a four-game series, leading Cleveland by a healthy margin of five-and-a-half games. A sweep by the home-town club would place them just a game and a half out of first place. Anything less than three out of four would probably end their chances for a first-place finish. In the 1918 season, whenever a win was needed, Stan Coveleski got the call. Once again he got the job done, scattering six hits in a 6–3 victory. Carl Mays pitched fairly well, but his own wild pitches and a throwing error by catcher Wally Schang accounted for three of the Indians runs, which proved to make the difference. Things got even more interesting when Jim Bagby stopped the Red Sox with three hits in a 5–1 win. With the game tied 1–1, Cleveland erupted with four runs in the bottom of the fifth inning to give Bagby a lead he easily held. Ray Chapman sparked the rally with a bases-loaded double, scoring two runs. He was followed by Tris Speaker with another two-bagger to plate an additional two. The Cleveland squad, fully grasping the precariousness of the regular season, played with a great sense of urgency. The big-time players stepped up: Speaker, Chapman, and the two aces of the mound, Coveleski and Bagby. This improbable season, played against the backdrop of a world war, actually had a pennant race going on. It is a tribute to the players, especially those who were poised to enter the military, that they could focus on the business at hand while providing fans with excitement right up to the end.

The Indians' strong resolve abated somewhat when Ban Johnson announced that the regular season would finish on Labor Day, with a World Series to follow. Johnson had attempted to stand firm on his plan of ending the season August 20 and then scheduling the World Series to conclude on September 1. He called a meeting of the AL owners in Cleveland, where he expected the majority to side with him. However, he found support from only Jim Dunn and Frank Navin. To force Johnson's hand, the National League sent Barney Dreyfuss from Pittsburgh as their delegate. Dreyfuss reaffirmed the National League's plan to play out the season through September 2 (the actual date of Labor Day) and then stage the World Series beginning September 4. Dreyfuss passed along the message that if Johnson did not comply, there would be no World Series played. Faced with no alternative, Johnson had to reluctantly fall in line with the dissenters, something he would be seeing a lot of in the days ahead.

The Boston series concluded with a Sunday doubleheader. Babe Ruth pitched a gem in the first game, going twelve innings for a 2–1 win. Taking the mound with only one day's rest, Stan Coveleski faced Joe Bush in the nightcap. Rain interrupted the contest after six innings, but the Indians, behind their tireless hurler, squeezed out a 2–0 victory. The Red Sox had to battle to avoid a sweep but now had the Indians breathing down their necks. There were still plenty of games left on the schedule, allowing Cleveland to put the pressure on the league leaders.

The Washington Senators came to League Park, where Jim Bagby and Harry Harper each threw shutout ball through nine innings. In the top of the tenth, the Senators had runners on first and third with two outs. Joe Judge batted a hard ground ball past the pitcher's mound that appeared to be on its way to center field. Joe Wood, now playing second base, raced behind the bag, grabbed the ball, and in one motion flipped it to Ray Chapman for the force play at second. As it happens so many times in baseball, the man who made the great play to end an inning led off the next half. Wood stepped to the plate, lining a shot to the left-field wall for a triple. After a walk, backup catcher Chet Thomas batted for Terry Turner and hit safely to right field, ending the extra-inning game. By this time most Cleveland fans had forgotten that Joe Wood had ever been a pitcher. His hitting and solid defense in the outfield plus his ability to play second in Bill Wamby's absence really made a difference in the 1918 fortunes of the Cleveland Indians.

A pared-down Chicago squad was next to visit the hometown team. The White Sox had already lost veterans Joe Jackson and Lefty Williams to the shipyards; Happy Felsch was apparently working in Milwaukee, while Swede Risberg had gone home to California to enlist in the navy. This should have been an opportunity for the Indians to gain some ground, but they inexplicably lost the first two games of the series. They did bounce back in the finale, pounding Chicago 11–2. Steve O'Neill had a double and a triple, and Ray Chapman had two doubles, while Tris Speaker and Jack Graney had one double apiece. The Cleveland fans had a big laugh when pitcher Guy Morton lined a single to right field. John "Shano" Collins grabbed the ball on one hop and then fired a rope to first base to retire the slow-moving Morton. Another blunder occurred when the White Sox third baseman, a recent minor leaguer, jogged off the field with two outs made. Terry Turner, standing on second, took off for third while the Chicago players yelled for the rookie to get back on the field. Despite all the fun, the Indians had blown a great opportunity at home to close the gap with Boston, which had just dropped three games in a row. Now the Indians had to leave town for their final eastern swing of the season. They would stop in New York first and then arrive in Boston for the looming showdown. After visiting Fenway Park, there were games at Washington and Philadelphia. To win the pennant under these conditions was a formidable task, to say the least.

While the team was traveling east, a letter to Steve O'Neill from former teammate Ed Klepfer lent some perspective to the season. Now on the front lines in France, Klepfer wrote about charging out of the trenches under heavy fire from the German Army. He said, "Steve, I have been over the top and come back without being hit. You know how it feels when you are up at the bat and Walter Johnson buzzes one of his fast ones by your ears. Well that's how it feels when the Germans are trying to pick you off. It's sure a great sensation—that of being fired at by someone you know means it." The war had reached all the way across the Atlantic to the Cleveland players. While they dodged fastballs and errant curves, at least one of their teammates was risking his life with every charge over open ground. Klepfer was not the only Indian there. Elmer Smith and backup first basemen Joe Harris and Louis Guisto were somewhere in the fight. Their thoughts were mainly on staying alive; baseball for them was something light-years away.

Before the Cleveland players reached New York, news came that Lee Fohl had suspended outfielder Bobby Roth for the remainder of the season. There likely had been another blowup between manager and player, which meant Roth's playing days in Cleveland were essentially over. Whatever happened must have been of epic proportions for Roth to be suspended while the pennant was still within reach. The emergence of Joe Wood as an outfielder with good power probably weighed into Fohl's decision. He could go with Graney, Speaker, and Wood for the remainder of the schedule, knowing each could do the job very well. Terry Turner would have to fill in at second as best as he could. For insurance, Dunn signed veteran outfielder Bob Bescher, recently with the St. Louis Cardinals. If needed, the thirty-four-year-old Bescher provided experience, and he would sit quietly on the bench. Bobby Roth did have some moments as a member of the Indians, but in no way did he have the ability of Joe Jackson. The 1915 trade authorized by a distressed Charlie Somers had put the team into free fall until Jim Dunn stunned the baseball world by acquiring Tris Speaker. Roth happened to be an innocent bystander in the debacle, unable to replace a once-in-a-lifetime talent like Shoeless Joe.

The East Coast swing got off to a promising start as the Indians trounced New York 7–2. The visitors pounded out fifteen hits, including Joe Wood's fifth home run of the year. Wood, making a strong bid for comeback-of-the-year honors (if they had the award) drilled an opposite-field shot into the right-field stands of the Polo Grounds. For his effort he received six pairs of socks from a local hosiery shop. Jim Bagby went the distance for the win while aiding the offense with three singles. Ray Chapman had three hits and a stolen base, scoring on the front end of a double steal attempt when the Yankees threw the ball away. Old-timer Terry Turner lashed out four hits, including a double and a triple.

Cleveland dropped the second game of the series but came back the following day with an easy 12–4 win. The *Plain Dealer* credited the win to Ray Chapman's getting the goat of Yankee pitcher Joe Finneran. A refugee from the Federal League, Finneran had not pitched in the major leagues since a brief appearance with the Philadelphia Phillies in 1913. In the bottom of the third inning, Chapman committed a rare error, allowing the New York pitcher to reach first. A sacrifice moved Finneran to second base, where Indians pitcher Fred Coumbe tried to pick him off. The usually affable Chapman decided to stir things up by taking the throw and planting a hard tag on the opposing pitcher. Heated words were exchanged, and a fight nearly ensued. When the inning ended, Chapman yelled to Finneran he would be bunting his next at-bat. He said, "I dare you to cover the bag, for if you do I will send you to the hospital for the rest of the season!" True to his word, Chapman laid down a bunt, but Finneran had trouble getting off the mound and somehow was late in covering first base. Chapman crossed the bag, shouting, "I knew you were too yellow to cover ahead of me!" Once again fists were about to fly, but umpire Bill Dinneen got between the two and restored order on the field. After Tris Speaker flied out, Chapman stole second, continuing to harass Finneran from behind the mound. Apparently the Yankee pitcher lost what was left of his concentration, giving up a double to Joe Wood, which opened the floodgates to a seven-run inning. Either Chapman had some inside knowledge of Joe Finneran or was in a bad mood, but the Cleveland paper believed his behavior won the game. At this point in the season, the Indians still trailed the Red Sox by two games. They would take a victory any way they could get it.

The Cleveland club arrived in Boston late on Saturday, August 17, to prepare for the crucial series with the Red Sox. Only three games were scheduled, but for the Indians to close the gap on the leaders, winning at least two games was essential. The team rested all day Sunday, taking advantage of a rare off day. This would be their last chance in the shortened season to play Boston straight up. Monday's game brought an energetic crowd of over fifteen thousand at Fenway Park, the largest of the year. Nobody scored until the top of the fourth, when Jack Graney led off with a triple to deep right center field. After one out, Tris Speaker stroked a double to score Graney. The Red Sox answered in the bottom of the inning with two infield singles and a single to left by Hack Miller. Graney threw wildly to the plate, allowing two runs to score.

Inexperience cost the Indians dearly. Joe Wood, due to some lineup shuffling, found himself playing first base. When Miller singled, Joe stood at first, watching the throw from Graney get away from O'Neill. While the catcher chased after the ball, nobody covered the plate, which an experienced first baseman would have done. Stuffy McInnis came all the way around from first to score the second tally. Wood had proven himself able to play outfield, second base, and now first, however, the on-the-job training resulted in a key mistake at the worst possible time.

The Indians wasted an opportunity in the seventh when Wood lofted a double off the scoreboard. Bob Bescher then hit a twisting line drive to deep right field. Wood took off from second, believing the ball was in there for extra bases. He should have respected the defensive abilities of his former teammate Harry Hooper. After a long run, Hooper made an outstanding grab and then tossed the ball to second for an easy double play. Had Wood waited on second, he could have moved to third after the catch. Joe Evans grounded out to second, which may well have driven in Wood with the tying run. As it was, the Indians failed to score a run they very much needed.

In the top of the eighth, manager Fohl decided to pinch-hit Jim Bagby for starting pitcher Guy Morton. Bagby grounded out and then took the mound for the bottom of the eighth. He gave up a single to old friend Hooper, and then a double by Amos Strunk and an intentional pass to Babe Ruth loaded the bases. Once again Stuffy McInnis was the man of the hour, poking a base hit to left field to drive in two runs. Cleveland got a run in the ninth inning but went down by a score of 4–2. Boston now stretched their lead to three games over the Indians, giving them a comfortable margin and some momentum for the remaining two games.

With their backs to the wall, Cleveland prepared for game number two of the series. They faced an old teammate, Sam Jones, who went to the Red Sox in the Speaker deal of 1916. Jones was having his finest season as a major league pitcher. He continued his excellent work, throwing a two-hit shutout and winning 6–0. The usually reliable Stan Coveleski allowed four runs in the third inning, giving the Red Sox and Jones all they needed for the victory. The Indians put on a shift for Babe Ruth, playing Wood and Speaker in right field, while Turner and Johnston stood twenty feet on the outfield grass in short right. Despite the tactic, Ruth still doubled down the right-field line.

After totaling just two runs in the last eighteen innings, the Indians showed some life by scoring eight runs in an easy 8–4 win in the series finale. Apparently the Boston outfielders had some difficulty with the sun, resulting in some routine fly balls dropping for hits. Jim Bagby pitched well enough to get the win, moving Cleveland to three games behind the Red Sox.

Losing two out of three to Boston seriously damaged the Indians' hopes for a pennant. They needed to have a strong road trip to remain in the chase, but the team showed signs of fatigue and uninspired play during the first six games away from home. Ray Chapman had only one hit in fifteen at-bats. Stan

Coveleski pitched poorly in the second game against Boston. Wild throws from the outfield hurt, including two errors by Jack Graney along with one from Tris Speaker. To win the pennant, they needed to play flawless baseball, but from the results on the field it appeared they had just run out of gas. They did post a win against Washington the next day, but Boston kept pace. On August 21, the Senators pounded Jim Bagby for seven runs in the first inning, coasting to a 7–1 win. Though eleven days remained in the season, the Indians did not resemble a team peaking at just the right time. They were unable to gain any ground on Boston when the first-place club lost a rare game.

Jim Dunn tried a ploy to help his fading team by trying to schedule two extra games with Detroit before September 1. The remaining Cleveland schedule had two open dates on it, allowing Dunn to attempt the extra games, which were originally to be played in September. The petition failed when an objection was filed with the league office. No doubt Boston had filed the protest, but the culprit's name went temporarily undetected. Dunn had some grounds for taking a stab at the additional games due to an imbalance in the abbreviated schedule. Boston enjoyed the advantage of playing fifteen more home games than Cleveland. Dunn reasoned that due to the lopsided scheduling, his club should have two more games at League Park to partially even things up. Though he was unsuccessful, he certainly got points for a very creative effort.

Thus the season ended with the Indians in second place, duplicating the efforts of the old Cleveland Naps of 1908. They had come a long way under the leadership of Jim Dunn, but fans were disappointed in having to wait until next season or until the war ended for another chance at the elusive pennant. Still there was much to be encouraged about. Stan Coveleski had a phenomenal year, with a total of twenty-two wins and an ERA of 1.82. Only Walter Johnson was ahead of him in those two categories. Coveleski surpassed Jim Bagby as the ace of the staff, doing his best to keep the team in contention for the entire season. Ray Chapman hit only .267 for the year but led the American League in runs scored and walks. Chapman and Speaker were among the league leaders in stolen bases, while the latter was fourth in hitting with an average of .318. Joe Evans had his best season to date, batting .263 while swatting out seven triples.

The major surprise of the season was the emergence of Joe Wood as an everyday player. Few expected him to contribute much, but he proved otherwise, establishing himself as an outfielder who could hit for power while fielding his position with above-average skill. His five home runs got him third place in the American League, behind such luminaries as Babe Ruth and Frank Baker. His two home runs against the Yankees helped Coveleski to his amazing nineteen-inning win. Wood's arm would never let him pitch again, but his skill as a batter and fielder allowed him to stay in Major League Baseball for a number of years to come.

When Jim Dunn permitted his players to depart on August 31, he had no concern that the owners in both leagues intended to play ball on September 1. Dunn complied with Secretary Baker's orders by ending the season as directed, allowing his team to report on time to their essential jobs or military service. He presented watches to Speaker and Morton, who were off to the fight, while Ray Chapman got a silver identification case for joining the navy. Bill Wamby received his watch via the mail at Camp Taylor. The next day Boston owner Harry Frazee blasted Dunn for his actions, calling for a stiff punishment in the form of a heavy fine. Frazee said, "At the next American League meeting, six clubs are going to ask why Cleveland did not play two games at St. Louis. It was the greatest violation of the league constitution in the history of the league." Frazee insisted Dunn had set a bad precedent for baseball that should never be repeated. While demonstrating his venom to the press, Frazee admitted he was the one who submitted the objection to Dunn's request of playing the two games with Detroit. It is unclear why Frazee had all this animosity toward Jim Dunn. The Red Sox had the trip to the World Series, not the Indians. Perhaps Frazee was miffed because he let Joe Wood go to Cleveland only to see him emerge as a valuable member of the team. Whatever his reasoning, there was little chance that Dunn would receive any kind of fine for being extra patriotic.

The 1918 season proved to be a most unusual one for Major League Baseball. America's first entrance into a world war brought new challenges never before faced by the country, or by professional baseball, which had been gliding along undisturbed since the late nineteenth century. Now the game had been temporarily suspended, with its immediate future uncertain. The war could drag on for years, keeping ballplayers working for the government or digging trenches in the south of France. Nobody knew for sure if the players fighting in Europe could come back home and still maintain their skills at a major-league level. Writing about the unprecedented baseball season, Henry Edwards stated, "When the game is restored, there will be new faces, new stars, and a new enthusiasm born of the victory which the Allies will inflict upon the Germans." In terms of the Cleveland Indians, he could not have been more correct.

9

DUNN KEEPS HIS PROMISE

T he autumn of 1918 brought good news to the United States and its allies. A strong American-backed offensive launched in August had driven the German army steadily back. The United States was now sending nearly ten thousand fresh troops to France on a daily basis. Enemy casualties were staggering, renewing hope for an ending to the war. In late October, telegrams from Germany were received at the White House asking for cease-fire terms. President Wilson responded firmly, demanding that the German ruler, Kaiser Wilhelm II, abdicate immediately, with a new government to be formed. After some debate, the German leader fled the country, and on November 11, a cease-fire took place. Americans rejoiced, knowing that their daily lives would soon return to normal and that their boys overseas would eventually be coming home. Among the soldiers returning stateside were baseball players, eager to exchange their rifles and ammunition for a bat and glove. Implicit in all the celebrating was the acknowledgment that baseball would resume in time for the 1919 season.

For the past three Novembers, Jim Dunn had announced that Lee Fohl would remain as the manager of the Cleveland Indians. This winter the team

owner made no such statement. Rumors surfaced in December that Dunn had
been considering making a change in leadership. Only one name came to the
forefront: Tris Speaker. The team had been clearly rising under Fohl, finishing
third in 1917 and second in the abbreviated 1918 campaign. Possibly Dunn
believed they should have won the pennant by now. He had spent vast sums of
money to bring in players not just for improved play but to capture the elusive
flag for the city of Cleveland.

In the first days of the New Year, Dunn called a conference in Cleveland
with Speaker, Fohl, and business manager E. S. Barnard. Speaker being called to
town all the way from Texas fueled more speculation that a shake-up could be
taking place. However, the next day Dunn put the fires out, announcing that
Fohl would return as manager for the upcoming season. Dunn extolled the
virtues of his skipper, saying to the press, "There has never been any real doubt
in my own mind as to whom I would appoint manager. I am not so sure that Lee
would not have landed the pennant for Cleveland if the season had gone on to
October 1 and we had been permitted to play that last long series at home. We
certainly had a great chance to cop." Dunn added that Speaker was brought to
Cleveland to consult on trading possibilities concerning Bobby Roth. According
to Dunn, virtually every AL club had inquired about acquiring the right fielder
for the 1919 season.

For his part, Speaker reportedly told Fohl he heartily approved of the way
Lee had handled the club in the past and had great confidence his leadership
would continue in the future. Dunn told interested reporters that Tris saw no
benefit in managing the team himself. Dunn added that Spoke was too valuable a player to be saddled with all the worries that go along with managing.
Still, the delay in rehiring Fohl plus the January conference with Speaker
attending had to stir up some doubt in the Cleveland fans. At any rate, Lee
Fohl now understood that second-place finishes did not give him any measure of job security.

With the manager situation taken care of, plans were made to solidify the
Indians for the upcoming season. Dunn had the benefit of eight players returning from overseas to compete for positions on the squad. Some were of minor
league caliber, but several had a chance to make an impact on the current squad.

The two first basemen, Joe Harris and Louis Guisto, were due back in the States shortly, but there was one other player who figured to be a key component in the hunt for the pennant. That player was Elmer Smith.

Born on September 21, 1892, Elmer was one of six children raised by George and Mary Smith in Sandusky, Ohio, located a short train ride to the west of Cuyahoga County. A year after Elmer was born, the family moved to nearby Milan, Ohio, where his father had a sheep farm. From his early years, the left-handed Smith had ambitions to be a ballplayer. For practice he used the large sheep barn as a target for his whistling line drives. Like so many of his fellow major leaguers Smith played high school baseball, football, and basketball, and then moved on to semipro teams in and around Milan. At age eighteen, he got a chance to play for the Kalamazoo club of the South Michigan League. He did not hit well there, which led to his release in the early part of the season. Smith returned to Milan, where he took a job digging potatoes for a local company. He played baseball on Saturdays, batting cleanup for one of the semipro clubs. During the winter months, his mother became seriously ill, obliging Elmer to stay in town and sit out the entire 1913 baseball season. After the death of Mary Smith, Elmer signed with the Duluth White Sox, which was managed by Darby O'Brien, a native Clevelander. After Smith belted thirteen home runs and hit .287, O'Brien contacted Charlie Somers, who bought Smith's contract.

Elmer reported to the Toledo club in August and finished the season there. In 1914 he was loaned to Waterbury, Connecticut, where he fine-tuned his game under the tutelage of none other than Lee Fohl. Smith batted .332 there, getting a promotion to the Cleveland roster at the end of the season. He earned a starting job for the atrocious Indians of 1915, showing some potential by hitting three home runs with twelve triples. By now he was the most popular celebrity in Milan, where fans gave him a gold watch and cheered him on during trips to League Park. As a major league ballplayer, Smith had all the local pitchers lining up to throw to him during the off-season. As was his custom, he aimed for the barn, where he launched cannon shots off the wooden walls, disturbing the startled sheep on a regular basis.

In 1916, Jim Dunn traded Smith to Washington for some much-needed pitching help. Acquiring Joe Boehling for the hard-hitting Smith raised some eyebrows throughout the Midwest. The *Kalamazoo Gazette* sportswriter, who was familiar with Smith, wrote, "Baseball critics down east can't quite figure out how V. P. Bob McRoy came to a point where he could trade Elmer Smith for Joe Boehling. They are all strong for Smith east of the Alleghenies and they figure that [Washington manager Clark] Griffith got the best of the deal." The trade turned out to be a dud; the pitching help did not materialize, while Smith pined for a return to Cleveland. A year later Dunn owned up to his mistake, paying some $4,000 to bring Smith back to Cleveland. He did not play regularly but drilled several home runs in clutch situations, which set him up for more playing time in 1918. However, the war in Europe interrupted his plans, sending Smith and the 83rd Division to France. He managed to stay healthy there, even playing some baseball when he was not in the trenches.

Several months after the Germans surrendered, Sgt. Elmer Smith received his orders to return stateside. He arrived in New York, where he undertook the mandatory delousing treatment and then, with a clean bill of health, traveled west to Ohio's Camp Sherman for receipt of his military discharge. He moved on to Cleveland to greet friends and teammates, telling them, "It was a great old war, but I can safely say I prefer baseball and can scarcely wait until I am at the training camp taking a wallop at the little leather apple once more." With Bobby Roth on the trading block, Smith would assuredly get all the wallops he wanted.

In early January of 1919, Jim Dunn and Lee Fohl made preparations for the AL meetings in January. High on their list was finding a veteran infielder, likely a third baseman, along with a pitcher to complement Coveleski and Bagby. The Cleveland front office believed they could land a quality player or two in exchange for outfielder Roth. Fohl, who couldn't wait to see Roth gone, spent much time praising his outfielder's all-around ability. He mentioned Roth's knack for stealing bases, citing his stealing home six times in 1917. At no time did Fohl mention the two suspensions he handed Roth, including the season-ending one in 1918 when the Indians had a chance to overtake Boston.

Talks heated up a week later when Connie Mack expressed a willingness to trade veteran third baseman Larry Gardner, pitcher Elmer Myers, and outfielder Charlie Jamieson for Roth and possibly Joe Evans. The only potential drawback to the deal centered on Gardner and Jamieson being left-handed batters. The Indians already had lefty hitters in Graney, Speaker, Smith, and Doc Johnston. Two more would give them an overload of left-handed bats. However the chance to bring in a highly talented ballplayer like Larry Gardner, along with a potentially good outfielder in Jamieson, was simply too good to resist. Throw in a pitcher who had some major league experience, and it appeared this deal was a major fleecing of Connie Mack. Cleveland fans surely were buzzing with the idea that another former Boston Red Sox with no fewer than three World Series appearances might be coming to League Park.

William Lawrence Gardner arrived in the major leagues by way of tiny Enosburg Falls, Vermont. Larry was the third and last child born to Delbert and Nettie Gardner on May 13, 1886. His birthplace lies in the upper northwest part of the state, a short distance from the Canadian border. The elder Gardner owned a grocery store in the business district, which supported the family of five.

As would be expected, Gardner excelled for the Enosburg Falls High School baseball team. He pitched, fielded, and hit like a phenom, clearly way ahead of his teammates and rivals. After graduation he played semipro ball in the Franklin County League. Once again he stood out against the older, more experienced players, a number of them from the University of Vermont. Whether or not that happened to be the driving influence, Larry enrolled in the university for the 1905 year. While the freshman third baseman gathered a great deal of attention, another Vermont newcomer made headlines as well. Ray Collins, a left-handed pitcher from Colchester, Vermont, immediately established himself as the ace of the staff. Despite all his natural ability, Gardner had a poor defensive season, committing errors on a regular basis. He would get better—a lot better—and by his junior year as captain of the squad, he batted over .300, leading the Vermonters to a 15–8 record.

After three seasons as a collegian, major league scouts began to call on Captain Gardner. Reportedly, Connie Mack offered a contract for $300 a month plus a signing bonus. Mack presented the contract while Larry was still playing with the varsity. When Gardner questioned the legality of signing a professional deal while playing collegiate baseball, Mack allegedly assured him nobody would find out. Sage advice from the honorable Philadelphia owner. Gardner did the right thing and waited until the end of the season, signing with the Boston Red Sox. Ironically, Cleveland got into the competition late, offering Boston $3,000 for the rights to Gardner. The Naps wanted to bring him to spring training and then, if all worked out, sign him to a deal. However, neither Boston nor their young prospect was interested.

Gardner played briefly for the big club his first two seasons, but a teammate's injury in 1910 forced him into the role as the regular Boston second baseman. Although he had little experience on the right side of the diamond, he performed well enough to keep the job and remain a starter for all his years in Boston. Two seasons later he would move to his permanent spot at third base. In World Series play, both in 1912 and 1916, he delivered in crunch time. In the 1912 epic struggle with the New York Giants, his sacrifice fly in the tenth inning won the championship for Boston. Four years later, he delivered two home runs against Brooklyn, the second a three-run shot off Rube Marquard in game 4, which swung the momentum and the series to the Red Sox.

It took ten years, but Connie Mack finally got his third baseman, trading for Gardner in 1918. As much as Mack liked the former Boston star, he apparently liked Bobby Roth even better. This information got the undivided attention of Jim Dunn, who began taking steps to steal Gardner away for his Cleveland Indians.

Though not considered a major part of the deal, outfielder Charlie Jamieson would eventually get his chance to prove his worth. A product of Paterson, New Jersey, Charlie delighted his parents when he began playing semipro ball with the hometown Lafayettes. Dad had played some pro baseball years before, teaming up with a very young John McGraw. The elder Jamieson played third base and caught from time to time. Mom was a big fan of the game, encouraging her son to leave his job in the textile mills to try his luck at professional baseball. At age seventeen, Charlie was playing in a hotel circuit when Buffalo of the International League offered $250 a month for the 1912 season. Jamieson pitched for a while with some success but soon found himself in the outfield on a regular basis. A strong throwing arm and good speed on the bases convinced his manager to leave Jamieson in the outfield permanently. In 1915 Buffalo sold his contract to Clark Griffith, sending Jamieson to the Washington Senators.

Two years later, Connie Mack acquired the young outfielder on waivers. After a poor season at bat in 1918, Mack believed Jamieson would not amount to much and thus put him on the trading block.

While eager fans waited for Dunn to pull the trigger, a minor deal took place that brought catcher Les Nunamaker to the Indians in exchange for seldom-used backstop Josh Billings. Nunamaker had years of experience, starting with Boston and then on to New York and St. Louis. The new catcher stood well over six feet tall while weighing in at nearly two hundred pounds. He would serve as a capable backup to Steve O'Neill. It did not hurt that Les had been close pals with Speaker and Wood during his time with Boston. No doubt Speaker had given his thumbs up for another member of the Boston connection.

A month after the discussions with Connie Mack, the Cleveland front office announced that Bobby Roth would be dealt to the Athletics. The arrival of Larry Gardner was assured, but terms had to be worked out with the remaining players. A possible three-way deal being discussed with Boston contributed further to the delay. After more talking, the trade became official on March 1. The Indians received Larry Gardner, Elmer Myers, and Charlie Jamieson for Bobby Roth. This deal would become one of the great trades in the Jim Dunn era, second only to the acquisition of Tris Speaker. With Elmer Smith back in camp, plus the emergence of Joe Wood as an outfielder, Cleveland could easily afford to part with Roth and his poor attitude. They now had a quality third baseman to solidify their infield, a pitcher who might become their third starter, and an outfielder with exceptional speed and strong defense. Trading Gardner for Roth straight up would have been an excellent move for the Indians; receiving two additional players from the confused Mack turned out to be a lopsided deal for the home team. Connie Mack and his Athletics were in one of their noncompetitive phases, having finished last in the American League the previous four seasons. Making ridiculous trades was business as usual for Philadelphia.

Now that Dunn and company were finished with their very shrewd trades, plans were revealed for an early March departure for spring training in New Orleans. Most of the players were in fairly good shape when workouts began. First baseman Doc Johnston looked best of all despite a near fatal bout with the flu during the winter. Ray Chapman put on a clinic at batting practice, stroking line drives to all parts of the outfield. Jim Bagby showed some good form, a strong contrast from the hold-out of last spring. Maybe, just maybe, this could be the year the pennant belonged to Cleveland.

The late arrival of Tris Speaker to camp came as no surprise to anyone. The tardy arrival of Jack Graney, however, was not expected by the management. His roommate of six years, shortstop Chapman, claimed to have won a bet, putting money on the line that Graney would miss the reporting date. Chapman said, "He never was on time for anything except his wedding, and he would have been late then if it were not for me. If we had an engagement to go to the show, Jack generally would start to shave and fix himself up at 8 and we would arrive at the theatre at the start of the second or third act."

The 1919 season began a week later than usual, enough time for owners and returning servicemen to prepare for the upcoming campaign. Due to the late start, a shorter schedule of 140 games was agreed upon by both leagues. Returning fans were guaranteed to see improved play with greater competition between teams. All the uncertainty of the past two seasons had disappeared, leaving everybody associated with the national pastime fully concentrated on the business at hand. Prosperity in business and baseball looked to be just around the corner, setting the stage for good times once again. Americans were ready to enjoy themselves, and baseball was primed to deliver.

The Cleveland Rooters Club, led by Mayor Davis, had taken 250 reservations for the Detroit road opener with another 100 expected before departure. For the reasonable price of $15, each person received round-trip boat fare to Detroit, a berth, and three meals at the Hotel Statler. The only caveat was the chance of a rainout, which meant a return to Cleveland without seeing the game.

The Indians arrived in Detroit on April 22, ready for another pursuit of the top spot in the American League. Lee Fohl had announced his starting lineup as follows:

Graney—left field
Chapman—shortstop
Speaker—center field

Smith or Wood—right field
Wamby—second base
Gardner—third base
Johnston—first base
O'Neill—catcher
Coveleski—pitcher

The previous day the team attended a breakfast thrown by the Chicago Automobile Club. After some words by Jim Dunn, each of the players walked to the podium and made a few remarks. To a man they came across as a confident bunch, not just using player-speak about doing their best to help the team, but honestly displaying a cool optimism that impressed the Cleveland reporters. Several players mentioned that if a team was to finish ahead of the Indians this season, that team would be the pennant winner. Dunn casually mentioned to his boys he would see them in St. Louis this summer. His contracting company had won a big job there excavating and grading the site for a giant new General Electric plant. Dunn anticipated a big summer for himself and his ball club.

Opening Day arrived with frigid temperatures in the thirties along with rain and occasional wet snow. The Cleveland Rooters went home disappointed with the cancelation of the initial game. Thursday had much the same weather, causing another postponement. Friday had no rain or snow but high winds and arctic temperatures. However, Frank Navin, the Tigers' owner, insisted the game be played, allowing him to honor as many rain checks as possible and thus leaving him with fewer to honor on Saturday. Saturday games were his best money maker, and the fewer rain checks used that day, the higher the gate and concession receipts. This convoluted logic allowed for a game to be played with high wind gusts and chilling temperatures. Henry Edwards noted that approximately eight thousand fans braved the weather, but by the ninth inning fewer than two thousand were still in the seats. Edwards related that many of the fans who remained to the end were wounded soldiers from the military hospital who had to wait for transportation back to the complex. Detroit managed to score four times to beat the Indians 4–2. One of the runs was scored when Ty Cobb lifted a pop fly to short left field. Ray Chapman was circling around the outfield grass when a gust of wind blew the ball back to the infield. Chapman took a step forward and then slipped on the wet grass while the baseball fell for a hit. Jack Graney chased a fly ball to left center only to watch it curve behind him and drop for another run-scoring hit.

The weather on Saturday proved to be more tolerable. Jim Bagby pitched well throughout, allowing only one run in a 3–1 victory. A double by Tris Speaker scored a run, and a perfectly executed squeeze play by Ray Chapman was enough to register the season's first win. The Indians moved on to St. Louis, and the cold, rainy weather followed. They were able to play two games, both of which they won before heading back to Cleveland for the May 1 home opener.

Cleveland fans could always rely on the front office at League Park to provide an Opening Day extravaganza. Now that World War I had ended, fans bought tickets at a record pace to be a part of the variety show produced at the ballpark. No fewer than three bands were scheduled to perform, including the much-admired Dodge Brothers from Detroit, along with the personal band of Gen. John Pershing, the commander of the American forces overseas. The military band came courtesy of the Victory Loan Committee of Cleveland. Tens of thousands of war bonds were sold in northeast Ohio, which gave the committee some clout to bring in the general's band. The concessions were loaded with hot dogs, peanuts, chewing gum, lemonade, soda pop, cigars, and scorecards, all for the benefit of the Cleveland rooters.

Around noon, fans and some of the marching band were expected to gather in the downtown area to get the party going. No doubt many fans left work a half day early to congregate at the restaurants and sandwich shops on Euclid Avenue. Most were probably unaware of another march being held near Public Square. May 1 was the designated date for a parade by socialists, union workers, and communists to demonstrate their loyalty and support to their leader, Eugene V. Debs. On June 13 of the previous year, Debs, the longtime union organizer and political candidate, gave a speech in Canton, Ohio, protesting the military draft. Police arrived to arrest him, and on November 18 he was convicted of sedition and received a sentence of ten years in prison. President Wilson had introduced the Sedition Act in 1918, prohibiting any disloyal or profane language about the United States, the flag, or the armed forces. Debs knew the consequences of his speech but went ahead regardless. His jail term had begun in mid-April, which led to the May 1 march. Union leaders were nearly always subject to harassment by the government, but speaking out against the war proved to be a dangerous undertaking.

While the Detroit and Cleveland players took their pregame practice, all hell broke loose in the downtown area. The socialist marchers carried American and red flags with them as they walked down to the intersection of East Ninth Street and Superior Avenue. In a matter of minutes, soldiers arrived and attempted to seize the red flags, symbols of the Socialist Party. Fighting broke out between the groups. A short time later, hundreds of police officers arrived on horseback, swinging their nightsticks at the marchers. Members of the Victory Loan Committee joined the riot, beating on the protestors until bodies fell to the ground. Thousands of spectators took part in the slaughter, along with a tank and several transport vehicles provided by the loan committee. When the riot ended, 125 marchers were arrested, many of them with severe injuries. One marcher was shot to death by a policeman under very murky circumstances. The riot ended in time for the spectators with baseball tickets to board the eastern streetcars and travel to 66th and Lexington for the game.

Whether or not the organizers of the march deliberately planned the protest to coincide with opening day is unclear. It was certain that there would be thousands of people milling about downtown, as well as extra police and veterans of World War I anxious to see a baseball game again. Possibly the organizers sought maximum exposure for the march, and staging it before the opener guaranteed them an audience, albeit a hostile one. They got not only their spectators but also a bloody thrashing that received national headlines. If the protestors had any notion of interrupting the game, their plans fell far short of the mark.

Though the weather cooperated, the Detroit Tigers did not, pounding Stan Coveleski for six runs in the first inning en route to an 8–1 win. The Indians never challenged, scoring their only run in the bottom of the first. Ty Cobb led the way for the visitors with two hits and two runs scored.

Cleveland did not play well early on in the season. After a 4–1 defeat handed down by the White Sox, the Indians charged that Eddie Cicotte had used the shine ball throughout the game. This trick pitch sailed on the hitters, causing a flurry of harmless fly balls. The newspapers reported that only four or five ground balls were hit the entire game. Several game balls were impounded by the players and sent to the American League office. Lee Fohl spoke to reporters after the game. Fohl remarked, "It looks as if the only way to combat such a style of pitching is to encourage other pitchers to do likewise and spread the evil until real action is taken against it. If Cicotte can get away with it, others may."

In spite of lackluster hitting and a number of costly errors, the Indians managed to claw their way into second place. Some of the ballplayers were becoming aggravated that the Cleveland fans were turning nasty toward the hometown boys. Unaccustomed boos and catcalls were coming out of the stands, which the players clearly heard. Joe Wood spoke up on behalf of his teammates, saying, "What I cannot understand is that although we are second place the crowd is after us if we make an error. I'll admit that we have made our share, but we are in second place, and I argue that any club that is doing as well as that does not deserve the treatment we are receiving."

Wood had a good point, but he failed to understand that the Cleveland fans were starving for a pennant. They had been waiting nineteen years, and the ticket-buying public was growing increasingly frustrated. Wood had seen two pennants during his tenure in Boston; Cleveland fans had seen none. Jim Dunn had brought in the Boston triumvirate and paid cash for Elmer Smith and Doc Johnston, all in an effort to carry home a pennant. For the local rooters to be grumbling was understandable.

A trip to Chicago at the end of May resulted in fireworks reminiscent of the Fourth of July. In the top of the eighth inning with Cleveland trailing 5–2, Tris Speaker slashed a hard ground ball to Chick Gandil. The first baseman knocked down the ball, grabbed it, and raced to the bag to beat Speaker. In an effort to get there first, the center fielder slid in hard, nearly spiking Gandil in the foot. Words were exchanged between the two while Speaker walked back to the Indians' dugout. Elmer Smith ended the inning by flying out, but Gandil waited at first base for Speaker to run by him on his jog to the outfield. According to

Ray Chapman, ca. 1916. An outstanding shortstop, Chapman remains the only major league player to be killed by a pitched ball. He was having a career season when an errant pitch by Carl Mays ended his life. *THE NATIONAL BASEBALL HALL OF FAME LIBRARY, COOPERSTOWN, NEW YORK*

Lee Fohl, ca. 1918. Fohl was in his fifth season as manager when a crushing defeat to Babe Ruth and the Boston Red Sox cost him his job. Fohl resurfaced as the manager of the St. Louis Browns in 1921. *FROM THE AUTHOR'S COLLECTION*

Tris Speaker, 1918. Standing at attention, this naval officer longed to fly planes over the Atlantic and bomb the German submarines. The war ended before Speaker got his chance. *FROM THE AUTHOR'S COLLECTION*

Joe Evans, 1920. Dr. Joe had a terrific season during the pennant chase, batting .349 with part-time duties in left field. One of the few ballplayers to graduate from medical school, Evans had a private practice for thirty-three years until his death in 1953. *FROM THE AUTHOR'S COLLECTION*

James C. Dunn, ca. 1916. A newcomer to the baseball business, Dunn took a struggling franchise and brought home the first pennant and World Series in Cleveland baseball history. A popular figure, Dunn spent a great deal of money to build his team. *FROM THE AUTHOR'S COLLECTION*

World Series Crowd Scene, League Park, October 1920. Fans gather while waiting for the gates to open. This scene was repeated at each game played in Cleveland.
THE CLEVELAND PRESS COLLECTION, CLEVELAND STATE UNIVERSITY LIBRARY

Cleveland Indians, 1920. One of the greatest teams ever assembled in Cleveland, with three Hall of Famers in Tris Speaker, Stan Coveleski, and Joe Sewell, plus one of the game's best shortstops, Ray Chapman. *FROM THE AUTHOR'S COLLECTION*

Jack Graney. The senior member of the Indians, Graney played fourteen years in Cleveland. In the 1930s he started broadcasting the Indians games on radio and became a stellar announcer for over twenty years. *FROM THE AUTHOR'S COLLECTION*

LEFT: Elmer Smith, 1920. In game 5 of the World Series, Elmer Smith homered with the bases full, giving Cleveland a 4–0 advantage. This was the first grand slam in World Series history. *FROM THE AUTHOR'S COLLECTION.*

BELOW: Tris Speaker crosses home plate with the only run of game 6 of the World Series. One game later, the Indians became world champions. *FROM THE AUTHOR'S COLLECTION*

Joe Sewell, 1920. Sewell got the difficult assignment of replacing the late Ray Chapman during a heated pennant race. There were a few false starts, but Sewell proved to be the man for the job. He had a stellar career that led to a place in the Hall of Fame. THE NATIONAL BASEBALL HALL OF FAME LIBRARY, COOPERSTOWN, NEW YORK

Jim Bagby, October 10, 1920. Bagby had a career season in 1920, winning thirty-one games. Always a fine hitter, Bagby launched a three-run homer in game 5 of the World Series. His complete-game victory gave Cleveland a three-games-to-two lead.

FROM THE AUTHOR'S COLLECTION

Charlie Jamieson, ca. 1920. A dependable hitter and outfielder, Jamieson bested Jack Graney for the left field job. Jamieson batted .319 for the 1920 season and hit .333 in the World Series. He would be a fixture in the Cleveland outfield for the next ten years.

FROM THE AUTHOR'S COLLECTION

Walter "Duster" Mails, 1920. A late-season acquisition, Mails pitched brilliantly, winning seven games without a loss. In the World Series, Mails pitched fifteen innings without allowing a single run. He got a full share of the Indians' World Series receipts.

FROM THE AUTHOR'S COLLECTION

Brooklyn's Ed Konetchy attempts to score from third base on a fly ball to Charlie Jamieson in game 5 of the World Series. Indians catcher Steve O'Neill waits to apply the tag. Home runs by Elmer Smith and Jim Bagby led Cleveland to an 8–1 victory. *Western Reserve Historical Society, Cleveland, Ohio*

Game Six at Cleveland. Larry Gardner hustles to beat the relay throw to first. The baseball can be seen to the left of first baseman Ed Konetchy. The Indians, behind the great pitching of Walter Mails, won the game 1–0. They now led the series four games to two. *Western Reserve Historical Society, Cleveland, Ohio*

reports, Gandil let fly with a torrent of four-letter words that shocked the ladies in the crowd. Speaker raced back to the infield with both fists clenched. When he confronted Gandil, the ex-Indian threw a punch, and the fight was on. Umpire Tommy Connolly got between the belligerents but was shoved aside by the livid Speaker. Punches flew, and Gandil hit the ground, where his team-mates stepped in to end the brawl. However, Speaker had a lot more fight left in him. Despite hundreds of Chicago fans who had taken spots on the field, Tris broke away and threw another punch, sending Gandil down once again. This time players from both teams stepped back while Speaker dove on top of the dazed Gandil, pounding away. After a few minutes, the Cleveland players pulled Speaker off the prostrate Gandil, dragging Spoke to the dugout. The players sprang into action because they noticed several firemen who had grabbed bats off the Chicago bench making their way toward the melee. Both Gandil and Speaker were seen bleeding from the mouth, while Gandil's shirt had been nearly ripped off his back. When the players returned to their positions, all seemed calm on the playing field. However the fun and excitement just would not end. Jack Graney had argued all afternoon about Eddie Cicotte's alleged shine ball. When he arrived in left field the Chicago fans greeted him with some very intense booing. Graney must have said something colorful back or made a derisive gesture. The left fielder's action caused an immediate aerial barrage of pop bottles that sailed in his direction. Reports indicated at least twenty bottles were heaved at the antagonistic Graney before ushers and police stepped in.

The Indians failed to score in the ninth inning, losing the game 5–2. When the game ended fans turned their attention to the visitors' dugout, where Speaker would make the attempt to reach the clubhouse safely. A police offi-cer led the party through the infield, while Chicago manager Kid Gleason walked closely with the Indians' squad. A mob of Chicago fans gathered on the field, but none attacked the players, watching silently as they passed by. Some of the folks in the stands commented on the fight and the profane language used by Gandil. One naval officer told the *Plain Dealer*, "I was glad I did not have a lady with me. Had one been with me I would have been forced to leave my seat, for Gandil made a megaphone of his hands and let loose with a tor-

333

rent of vile abuse." Umpire Connolly stated that Gandil had it coming due to the horrid language and that he threw the first punch. Then the umpire admitted his regret that the fight took place on the field in front of a large crowd that included many ladies and children.

Henry Edwards visited both clubhouses to gather his post-fight analysis. He reported that Speaker had a good-sized bruise on the right side of his face, along with spike wounds on his right ankle and left arm. Gandil looked much worse, with a cut lip and forehead and an eye that was nearly closed. Speaker explained his reasons for fighting, stating the vile names were too much for him to walk away from. Speaker told Edwards, "He called me names that no man could stand for, and when I started for center field, I made up my mind to challenge him to a battle beneath the stands after the game. I thought he had too much sense to start anything on the ball field and both hands were at my side when he whipped his left over and hit me on the cheek." Speaker apologized for fighting in public but believed he had to defend himself when Gandil threw the first punch.

As expected, Ban Johnson suspended both Gandil and Speaker immediately. The suspension lasted one week, with Tris receiving a $50 fine along with a letter of admonishment from Johnson. The message from the AL president expressed surprise that Speaker would allow himself to set such a poor example on the field. Johnson added, "Being a player and also a man of more than usual intelligence, I am astonished that you would do anything to bring the game discredit." It is not known if Gandil received the identical fine, but 1919 would be a banner year for the White Sox first baseman, one he would not live down for the rest of his life.

The *Plain Dealer* published a limerick the next day in an anonymous column titled "Our Daily Alarm." It read:

> *There is a first baseman named Chic,*
> *Who's said to be feeling quite sick,*
> *He's feeling some weaker*
> *Since he poked our Tris Speaker,*
> *Who totes in his right a good kick.*

The Indians ended the month of May with a record of eighteen wins versus eleven losses, leaving them five games behind Chicago. They moved on to St. Louis, where they defeated the Browns in an unusual contest. In the third inning, St. Louis loaded the bases with nobody out. Wally Gerber lofted a sacrifice fly to Joe Wood, scoring George Sisler. Ray Chapman cut off the throw home, trapping Baby Doll Jacobson between second and third. While the rundown occurred, Tod Sloan tried to move up from first second base. Bill Wamby alertly raced to the bag, tagging out Sloan and then whirling around to chase Jacobson back to third. After several throws back and forth, Wamby tagged the slow-moving Jacobson for out number three. The Indians trotted off the field, having completed a very bizarre triple play, as triple plays go. With Cleveland leading 4–3 in the top of the eighth, Steve O'Neill was intentionally walked with a man aboard. That brought up pitcher George Uhle, who drove the next pitch deep into the outfield. Both runs scored while Uhle pulled up at third with a stand-up triple. Cleveland won the game 6–3, with Bill Wamby getting some advance practice at making putouts of startled base runners.

Fighting and unruly behavior seemed to follow the Indians wherever they played. When they defeated the Washington Senators at the nation's capital, several ugly outbursts occurred. Clark Griffith argued a call by umpire Dick Nallin, who promptly threw Griffith out of the game. Fans showered the playing field with seat cushions, followed by the customary pop bottles. When those ran out, flat-shaped bottles that were not filled with soda landed on the diamond. In the days just before Prohibition, Washington fans let the world know there were still ways to purchase alcohol, even in the shadow of the White House. George McBride, the Senators' shortstop, leaned out of the dugout, motioning for the fans to calm down. A bottle came flying, hit the dugout, and shattered into several pieces that struck McBride in the face. Seeing their player covered with blood, the fans stopped throwing bottles, and the game continued.

Jim Babgy outpitched Walter Johnson, and Ray Chapman's two-run single made the difference in the 3–2 win. With the game completed, umpire Nallin attempted to reach the tunnel to the dressing rooms but had his path blocked by an angry mob. One fan stepped forward and swung at the umpire. The wild punch grazed his shoulder but nearly clipped Steve O'Neill, who was standing by Nallin. Police came racing in to get between O'Neill and the fan, now retreating backwards to escape the burly catcher. No further injuries were recorded, but this was a narrow escape for fans and players.

In late June, Cleveland had won five in a row, launching them into a first-place tie with Chicago. Reserve first baseman Joe Harris returned to the team just weeks after his tour of duty in France. Larry Gardner had started to hit and drive in runs at a steady pace. The Indians' chances looked bright until Ray Chapman injured his back and was thought to be out of the lineup for at least a month. Without their star shortstop, the team fell out of first place, landing in third behind Boston and New York.

Expectations for a pennant were increasing every day in the city of Cleveland. Both fans and sportswriters vented their frustrations with every loss. After an unsuccessful road trip, the newspapers claimed the team had lost confidence in themselves. A shake-up of the batting order was suggested, largely due to the prolonged slump of Tris Speaker. Some wanted Spoke to lead off, with Elmer Smith and Doc Johnston moving up in the order. The pitchers were criticized as well as the hitters. Manager Fohl began to feel the pressure from the fans and writers. He knew his boys could play better, but he could not seem to do anything to light a fire underneath them. As is usually the case, when the team falters, all eyes turn toward the man in charge.

It all came to a swift conclusion on July 18 at League Park. The Indians were tied 3–3 with the Red Sox when they loaded the bases in the bottom of the eighth inning. Pinch-hitter Joe Harris slashed a triple to center field, clearing the bases. The throw from Harry Hooper got away, allowing Harris to sprint home with the fourth run. The players rushed out of the dugout to congratulate Harris for giving them a 7–3 advantage. Heading into the ninth inning, happy fans walked for the exits, convinced the game was over. Elmer Myers, pitching in relief, got the first batter to ground out. More fans got up and started for the exits. However, the Red Sox were far from done. A walk and a double put runners at second and third base. Bill Lamar, the Boston center fielder, grounded out to Doc Johnston, scoring a run but putting the Sox down to their last out. Try as he might, Myers could not finish the game off, walking Oscar Vitt and then Harry Hooper. That brought the winning run to the plate in the form of

George Herman Ruth. The Babe had already homered in the fourth inning to
put Boston in the lead 2–1. Lee Fohl jogged out of the dugout, waving to the
bullpen for Fred Coumbe to replace Myers. Fohl instructed Coumbe to keep the
ball low and walk in a run if necessary. Fred took his windup, delivering a high
fastball that Ruth nearly fell down trying to reach. Steve O'Neill raced to the
mound to urgently remind his pitcher to keep the ball low. Coumbe this time
threw a poorly located change-up well within the Babe's reach. The Cleveland
fans, their jaws slack, watched as the mighty Ruth launched the ball high over
the right-field wall for a grand-slam home run. The baseball nearly cleared
Lexington Avenue, leaving spectators and players alike gaping at the spot where
the ball had left the park. Ruth trotted around the bases, with four more runs
batted in giving him a total of six of the eight Red Sox runs. The Indians put two
runners aboard in the bottom of the ninth but failed to score, giving Boston an
amazing 8–7 win.

While the players showered and dressed, Lee Fohl slowly walked upstairs
to Jim Dunn's office. Fohl held himself responsible for the ugly loss and much
more. He told Dunn, "I have failed to win the confidence of the fans although
I have done my best to make the club a winner. If the fans think you should
have someone else running the team, I think I should step aside." Dunn
accepted the resignation, at no time trying to convince Fohl to change his mind.
Dunn praised his former manager to the press, stating Fohl was a big man for
stepping down when he believed a change would help the ball club. The
Cleveland owner denied he had asked Fohl to resign, claiming it was all the
latter's decision. Dunn announced he would pay Fohl's salary in full for the
remainder of the season, a gesture he did not have to make.

From most accounts it did appear that Fohl resigned of his own accord.
However, years later in an interview, Fohl would state he was looking for a way
out as manager of the Indians. The tape-measure homer by Babe Ruth gave him
the means to do it. Fohl maintained that Dunn was under a lot of pressure from
the Cleveland fans to appoint Tris Speaker as manager. According to Fohl, the
change in managers was a mutual decision.

Baseball Magazine defended the former manager, citing him as hardworking and deserving of success. The article, released just after Fohl's departure,

pointed out that the Cleveland franchise was in terrible shape when Fohl took the job in 1915. Since that time he had guided the club to the upper division, just missing the pennant in 1918. The magazine did a lengthy interview with Fohl, giving him the opportunity to answer criticism thrown his way by various baseball writers. The article leaves little doubt that the former Cleveland manager had deep-seated problems with the local sportswriters and the fans. It is clear the writers' assessments bothered him to the breaking point. He explained at length why he used the sacrifice play so frequently and defended his handling of the pitching staff. When one adds up all the obstacles Fohl dealt with, it is not difficult to understand why he wanted out. The team owner would no longer be satisfied with good baseball. He wanted to win it all. The team leader, Tris Speaker, had a say in management decisions, as shown by Dunn's decision to bring Tris to his February meeting with Fohl. The only thing that could have kept the manager above any criticism was a pennant in 1918. That did not happen, setting in motion the cries for a new manager in 1919. After the debacle with Ruth and the Red Sox, someone had to take the fall. In Fohl's case, just being a good manager did not earn him enough credits to keep his job.

Fohl went on to manage George Sisler and the St. Louis Browns for three seasons, finishing second in 1922. After leaving St. Louis, he managed the Red Sox for three years and then spent time leading Toronto of the International League before retiring from baseball altogether. Fohl and his family remained in Cleveland, where he ran several gas stations and then worked at a suburban golf course for seventeen years. He died in 1965 at the age of eighty-eight. Lee Fohl is long forgotten in the annals of professional baseball, but he deserves a pat on the back for helping build the Cleveland Indians into a pennant contender.

Jim Dunn wasted little time finding a new manager. In this situation, there was only one person to consider: A man with an intense desire to win. A man who had aggression in his blood and could let it show at any moment. A man who hated to lose at anything. Dunn did not hesitate to hire the people's choice, Tris Speaker.

10

LIGHTNING STRIKES

Whether or not Tris Speaker wanted to manage the Indians was a moot point. He had stated back in February that he did not care for the job, citing the increased demands on a manager. Due to the abrupt departure of Lee Fohl, Speaker really had no choice in the matter. Dunn wanted him, the fans wanted him, and it was already late July. Where could they find another manager at that juncture in the season? Speaker accepted the post and then went about trying to right the course of his ball club. He told the curious reporters, "I contemplate no changes. We will go along with the same lineup and keep it until something happens that may make it necessary to shift. We will make the hardest kind of effort to win the pennant."

As sometimes happens with a change in managers, the Indians started to play better baseball. They took three straight from the Athletics and then hammered Detroit 9–1. Cleveland scored four runs in the fourth inning, thrilling the fans with another triple steal. Manager Speaker took his lead-off from third base when he noticed the Tigers' pitcher paying little attention to him. He edged further off the bag and then dashed for the plate on the next pitch. As he slid across safely, Elmer Smith advanced to third while Bill Wamby took second base, completing the triple steal. Jim Bagby coasted to victory, despite allowing thirteen hits.

By the end of July, Speaker and his boys had fought their way back to second place. Although pleased with the play of his team, Spoke believed they could do better. He told reporters, "I am satisfied with results as far as we have gone since I took over the management. Don't take it from my words that I am satisfied to continue going along and just doing a little better than breaking even, for I am not. The best word I can send home is that the boys are on their toes and eager to give battle for first place."

Throughout August the Cleveland club played winning baseball. Tris Speaker's aggressive style gained positive results from his players. They took chances on the field and while at bat. Taking the extra base became the standard. The change in managers proved to be the remedy needed. Had the switch taken place earlier in the season, the Indians might have been challenging the White Sox for first place. As it stood they were playing with a good deal of enthusiasm, which pleased the fans, especially those who wanted Speaker to run the club.

The Philadelphia Athletics came to town on the 25th for a meeting at League Park. Newly acquired Ray Caldwell was standing on the mound for Cleveland. A ten-year veteran of the American League, Caldwell had had a disappointing summer with Boston and found himself out on the street. Stories of the unemployed pitcher having too much fondness for the nightlife had been circulating around for years. Be that as it may, Jim Dunn and likely Speaker decided to take a chance on Caldwell, signing him on August 19 for the remainder of the season. Despite threatening skies, fans arrived at the ballpark, anxious to see if the new pitcher could help.

Caldwell got off to a great start, not allowing a run until the fifth inning. The Indians had pushed two runs across in the fourth, taking advantage of a couple of walks along with several scratch hits. The tight ball game continued into the top of the ninth when ominous dark clouds began to form over the park. After Caldwell got the first two hitters, a tremendous crash of thunder startled everybody on the grounds. A second later a colossal bolt of lightning hit the field, jolting all the players in their spiked shoes. Luckily, the men were only slightly affected by the bolt, except for Caldwell, who ended up flat on his back near the pitcher's mound. He lay motionless for several minutes and then got to his feet without any help. Incredibly, he felt well enough to continue with the game, getting the last hitter Joe Dugan to ground out to Larry Gardner. Within moments heavy rain began to fall, chasing the players to the clubhouse before any more blasts of lightning hit the ground. Ray Caldwell had made one of the most auspicious debuts by a pitcher in a Cleveland ballpark. He performed extremely well, allowing one run on four hits. He survived a lightning strike on the pitcher's mound, a feat that had not been seen before. Certainly the fans must have thought he was done for, lying on the ground without moving. Not only did he rise from the dead, but he actually had the resolve to finish the game. One thing is for sure: nobody would ever question the inner strength of Ray Caldwell.

While the Indians continued to make progress under their new leader, the front office received a most uncomfortable summons. The State Supreme Court of New York ordered Ban Johnson to appear and testify regarding the nature and extent of his alleged interests in the Cleveland club. This action stemmed from Johnson's July 31 suspension of Boston pitcher Carl Mays. In the middle of the month, Mays deserted the Red Sox, refusing to play for the club anymore and walking away from a three-year contract. Owner Harry Frazee elected to trade Mays, sending him to the Yankees for the sum of $40,000 plus three players. Johnson believed the Red Sox should have suspended Mays themselves and forced him to honor his contract. Obviously Frazee and the New York owners were furious with Johnson, and retaliated by forcing the AL president to appear in a New York court. The Boston and New York owners had recently obtained a temporary injunction against the suspension of Mays, allowing him to pitch for the Yankees. That was not enough for the trio. They wanted a knockdown, drag-out fight with the league president.

When Johnson made his court appearance, little doubt existed that Frazee and Yankee owners Jacob Ruppert and Tillinghast Huston were intent on injuring the league boss. The main issue concerned Johnson's authority to suspend Carl Mays, but the accusation that Johnson owned stock in the Cleveland club went far beyond the suspension controversy. A growing animosity festered between the upstart owners and the longtime "czar" of baseball. It appeared that Johnson's iron grip on the American League was weakening. Frazee and his cohorts were relatively new to baseball and did not have any special allegiance to Johnson. This had been evident in 1918 when the league president announced that the schedule would end on August 20 and the World Series would begin on September 1. He must have been surprised when Charles Comiskey and Clark Griffith, who had been with Johnson from the very beginning of the American League, opposed his plan. They sided with the outspoken Harry Frazee, which assuredly confused and angered the league president. Now he found himself in court, compelled to answer the charges against him.

Those who attended the hearing were greatly surprised when Ban Johnson testified that he did indeed hold stock in the Cleveland Indians. His investment of $100,000 in 1916 was in the form of a loan to Jim Dunn. Johnson received stock in the club, which Dunn had been buying back on a yearly basis. At present Dunn had paid back $42,000, which left Johnson with stock worth $58,000. That represented a little over 10 percent ownership of the team. The lawyers for Frazee, Huston, and Ruppert demanded that the charter of the Cleveland baseball club be introduced, but Johnson's attorney successfully argued against it. It became clear that the owners were trying to prove that the suspension of Mays was retaliation for the Yankees acquiring a quality pitcher who might push them to the top of the American League. Since Johnson held a large block of shares in the Indians, a conflict of interest was inferred. Allegedly, the league president had a vested interest in the Cleveland Indians and was acting on their behalf in trying to keep Mays out of New York. The question arose of whether Johnson knew other clubs were attempting to deal for Mays, the Indians among them. Whatever teams were in contention for the talented pitcher eventually lost out to the Yankees. If the Indians were among those attempting to deal for Mays, might Johnson not have undue influence? Johnson's lawyers objected to the line of questioning, an objection the presiding judge sustained.

How could the president of the American League own stock in one of his teams? At one point Johnson had 20 percent ownership in the Cleveland Indians. Were other club owners aware of this and okay with it? Did Johnson do this to save the Cleveland franchise with no other motives involved? It seems remarkable that a situation like this could have occurred and continued for a three-year period. If Jim Dunn lacked the total capital needed to buy the Indians, could he not have secured a loan from a disinterested party? Surely Dunn, as a very successful contractor with many tangible assets, could have found a bank to loan him all the funds needed. Instead he accepted a huge loan from Ban Johnson. It is possible that it was a selfless act and that Johnson had nothing to do with the business decisions of the Cleveland front office. Still it is a very questionable way to conduct business on any level. For their part, Frazee, Ruppert, and Huston did considerable damage to Johnson's reputation. Now the general public as well as owners from both leagues could openly question Johnson's actions.

The Boston and New York owners took other measures to discredit the league president. An unsuccessful attempt was made to bring Jim Dunn and E. S. Barnard to court for testimony on their relationship with Johnson, along with efforts to reveal the contents of the Indians stockholders' notes from previous meetings. The relationship between Johnson and the Cleveland Indians would never be fully revealed, but the power and influence of the president would soon be severely curtailed.

In early September, the Indians traveled to Chicago to battle with the first-place White Sox. Cleveland trailed the leaders by a distant six-and-a-half games but was poised to make a run down the stretch. Tris Speaker called for a 7:45 a.m. meeting to rally his troops. Speaker said, "I suppose you fellows are surprised to have to come to a meeting before you have had your coffee. I think we still have a chance for the flag, but that chance depends upon what we do in the three games with Chicago. If we can take three straight from the Sox, we have a great chance to finish first." Try as they might, the Indians could not win three straight from Chicago, dropping the first game 9–1. They came back a day later to trounce the White Sox, 11–2. Home runs by Joe Wood and Jim Bagby and triples from Wood, Graney, and Speaker led the way. However, it was a case of too little too late.

The Indians moved on to the Polo Grounds for a series with the Yankees. Ray Caldwell continued to do amazing things, dazzling the large crowd by throwing a no-hitter, the final score 3–0. Caldwell, who had fully recovered

142 THE BEST THEY COULD BE

from his bout with lightning, allowed only one base on balls in pitching to twenty-nine batters. The only other Yankee to reach first base did so via an error by Bill Wamby. A crowd of fifteen thousand stood on their feet, cheering Caldwell when the last batter grounded out to Ray Chapman. The only runs needed were delivered by Joe Harris, who smacked a two-run homer in the top of the first inning. The blow by Harris was most appropriate as the New Yorkers were honoring Gen. John Pershing for his leadership during World War I. It seemed fitting for one of his former soldiers to provide the fireworks for the day. As the season came to a close, the Indians finished on a high note, reeling off ten straight victories. They had closed the gap with Chicago, but it was not enough to overtake the league champions.

On September 25, Cleveland played a meaningless game with the Tigers. Tris Speaker elected to start Elmer Myers, who got in trouble from the outset. He gave up four runs in the first two innings, but Speaker never made a move to change pitchers. The Tigers scored twice more in the fifth, but still Myers remained in the game. Detroit won the contest 9–5, touching up the Indians pitcher for eighteen hits. An article describing the game remarked on the quality of play: "It did not seem like a real championship game at that. With nothing really at stake, pitchers Boland and Myers did not appear to exert themselves and the batsmen simply hit the apple with vigor to unfrequented sections of the park. The best thing about the contest was its brevity. It started at 3:07 and ended at 4:13 thus making the shortest game played by either Detroit or Cleveland in several years."

The article went on to mention that none of the players argued with the umpires at any time, and the Cleveland infield was guilty of loose work. Ray Chapman did not play, being replaced by Harry Lunte who made two throwing errors. First baseman Joe Harris contributed an additional error, giving the Indians three for the day. Despite the Tigers having sixteen singles, the Cleveland infield was not able to turn any double plays.

It is interesting that Tris Speaker allowed Elmer Myers to pitch a complete game. By normal standards, Myers should have been replaced by the fifth inning, when Detroit scored their fifth and sixth runs. Cleary, Myers had nothing on the ball and needed to come out. For whatever reason, the usually competitive Speaker had little interest in trying to get a win that day. Maybe he wanted his other pitchers to have a day off. The club had second place wrapped up, which meant each player had a share of World Series money coming. A victory did not change anything, but professional ballplayers were paid to win. By allowing his pitcher to remain in the game while giving up nine runs and eighteen hits, Speaker did not give his team any chance for a victory. This type of questionable behavior by Speaker would resurface years later, causing him much anguish.

Another season came to an end with another second-place finish. The Indians played first-class baseball under Speaker, winning thirty-nine out of sixty games for a percentage of .650. Had they performed at that pace for an entire season, they would have nosed out Chicago, which finished at .629. A good number of positives could be taken from the season, but the fact remained that they fell short once again. Would some fine-tuning be enough for a championship, or should an overhaul take place during the off-season? Jim Dunn and his new manager had some thinking to do over the winter.

While Dunn assessed the future of his ball club, his players scattered to different locations around the country. Most members of the team needed to work a second job to supplement their rather flimsy salaries. If a player happened to be single he might have enough extra money to ride out the winter. Those with a wife and small children had little choice but to work. Manager Speaker, who had plenty of dough, traveled to Chicago, where he would observe the World Series as a correspondent for the *Plain Dealer*. Jim Bagby went home to try and set up an auto dealership with cars manufactured in Cleveland. Joe Wood, Steve O'Neill, Stan Coveleski, and others bought land in rural New Jersey, where they planned to build a hunting camp. Larry Gardner went home to Enosburg Falls, Vermont, to work in his auto repair garage. Staying in town were Bill Wamby, Jack Graney, Elmer Smith, and Ray Chapman. Wamby and Smith had not decided what type of work to pursue, but Graney would do the labor at a radiator shop where he had part ownership. Joe Evans left for St. Louis, where he began his internship at a local hospital. Within a year he would receive his license to practice medicine. Dr. Joe had chosen the field of obstetrics, ready to bring babies into the world for many years ahead. If nothing else, the 1920 Cleveland Indians could boast a full-fledged medical doctor traveling with the team.

Before the start of the 1919 World Series, Speaker filed a report on the pitching strengths of both Chicago and Cincinnati. He believed the Reds had more quality hurlers than the White Sox, but he gave the nod to Chicago. Spoke thought Eddie Cicotte and Lefty Williams could win enough games between them to take the series. He had confidence that, if needed, Dickie Kerr would be able to win a game or two, putting Chicago over the top.

Speaker predicted the White Sox would win the World Series in seven or eight games. He listed six reasons for his prediction; among them, the Sox were smarter and stronger, plus they hit better, while having superior outfielders in Joe Jackson and Happy Felsch. He believed Eddie Cicotte was the best pitcher in the American League, which in itself would lead Chicago to victory.

Imagine the surprise when in game 1 Cincinnati battered the White Sox 9–1. Speaker's report to the *Plain Dealer* expressed his astonishment at what he had seen. He wrote, "If the Cicotte who pitched against Cincinnati today looked like the Cicotte who beat us so often during the American League campaign, then I better quit center fielding and go to pitching myself. If the White Sox played smart ball today I shall recruit the Indians for next season from some place over in Europe where they never saw our national game played." Speaker went on to list a number of instances where the White Sox fell down, but his disbelief toward the way the Reds freely hit Cicotte stood out in his writing. He cited the fourth inning, where Cincinnati put five runs on the board after two were out. Speaker said, "It is almost beyond comprehension to believe any National League club could make five runs off Eddie Cicotte, the best pitcher in the American League, after two were out." He mentioned a key play in the fourth when Reds outfielder Earle Neale hit a bouncer past the pitcher's mound. Eddie Collins raced to cover second base for the final out, but shortstop Swede Risberg was slow getting to the ball and merely knocked it down. Then the floodgates opened.

In game 2, Speaker noted the unusual wildness of Lefty Williams as the reason for the 4–2 Cincinnati win. With two Reds on base, Williams tried to throw a high fastball past shortstop Larry Kopf, a good fastball hitter. The result was a three-base hit that helped put the game away. Speaker believed that Williams just did not have much control over his pitches, which led to the key mistake. Even in a Chicago victory, the Cleveland manager had negative things to say. While he lauded the pitching performance of Dickie Kerr in game 7, he labeled the players behind him a "bunch of bushers." This had something to do with the three errors the Sox committed.

Speaker did not submit a report for game 8, when Cincinnati won the World Series with a 10–5 victory. Henry Edwards filed the story without any comments from Speaker. No one knows why he decided not to write anything about the final game. Perhaps he was too disgusted at what he saw and chose not to say anything further. One can speculate that Speaker may have figured things out, which would have given him a good reason for declining to write the final report. As an astute observer of the game, he very well knew the strengths and weaknesses of both teams. He had played against Chicago numerous times, so he had a pretty fair notion of what the Chicago pitchers were capable of. His early columns expressed a great deal of bewilderment at the effort of certain Chicago players. Possibly he put two and two together and came to a very dark conclusion that some of the White Sox players were not playing to win. If so, it makes sense that he chose to walk off the job before finishing.

There would be many questions to answer in the 1920 season, about much more than who would claim the pennant or lead the league in batting. The Indians were on track to finally achieve the ultimate victory, but it would be overshadowed by much larger concerns about the integrity of the game itself.

11
THE RACE BEGINS

The fall and winter months leading up to 1920 did not yield much excitement in terms of the upcoming baseball season. The biggest news concerned the marriage of Ray Chapman and Kathleen Marie Daly on October 29. The bride's father happened to be Martin Daly, the top executive at the East Ohio Gas Company. The couple was wed in the Daly family home, an elegant dwelling at Euclid Avenue and 127th Street. After the ceremony, the wedding party moved to the Knights of Columbus Hall for an evening of lively dancing. Tris Speaker traveled from his off-season home in Hubbard, Texas, to serve as Chapman's best man. The wedding was a joyous event that marked a new chapter in the life of the Cleveland shortstop. After an extended honeymoon in Florida, Ray would start a new job as secretary and treasurer of the Pioneer Brass Company in downtown Cleveland. Chapman emphatically stated that he would temporarily leave his new job on March 1 to report for spring training. He told reporters he planned to be the Indians shortstop for as long as the club wanted him.

At age twenty-eight, Chapman was one of the few ballplayers seriously looking ahead to when his playing days were through. He probably landed the upper-management job at Pioneer Brass through his father-in-law's connections. Instead of going back to Kentucky in the off-seasons, Chapman decided to make Cleveland his year-round home. If all went well, he would complete the transition from ballplayer to family man to respected member of the Cleveland business community. Ray Chapman's future in and out of baseball looked very bright.

The AL owners set an early December date for the start of their annual winter meetings. Jim Dunn was interested in acquiring a quality starter who could perform on the same level as Jim Bagby and Stan Coveleski. Ideally, he wanted to bring in a left-hander to complement his two star pitchers. In no particular order, the best lefties in the league were Dickie Kerr and Lefty Williams of the White Sox, Dutch Leonard of Detroit, and Herb Pennock of Boston. No word existed that any of these pitchers were available; however, Dunn had his checkbook handy just in case. At various times during the 1919 season, Dunn offered $50,000 to the Senators for Walter Johnson and $15,000 to St. Louis for Allen Sothoron, and he then attempted to buy Scott Perry from the Athletics. If any of the owners needed money for their franchises, Dunn had the funds to contribute. Unfortunately for the Cleveland owner, his colleagues knew one more quality pitcher would likely give the pennant to Cleveland, and thus no deals were made.

The franchise leaders were all in agreement about extending the 1920 season to 154 games. They had acted prematurely a year ago when the schedule was cut to 140 games, partly due to their fear of poor attendance. The hangover they had anticipated from the war years did not occur. Fans and ex-soldiers flocked to the ballparks, showing that their interest in the game had not diminished in spite of all the misery a world war can bring.

Speaking of wars, the American League owners were seeking to end the hostilities between Ban Johnson and the owners of the Chicago, New York, and Boston franchises. Frazee, Huston, and Ruppert strongly opposed Johnson's suspension of Carl Mays, and Charles Comiskey broke ranks to side with the insurgents. There are numerous stories about why Comiskey, at one time a close friend of Johnson, no longer supported him. One tale had Comiskey angry over his failed attempt to purchase the minor league contract of pitcher Jim Quinn. He blamed his old friend for the screw-up, even though Garry Herrmann, not Johnson, had led the White Sox owner astray. Johnson and the five owners who were loyal to him—Jim Dunn included—traveled to New York to meet with their adversaries and iron things out. For the moment a shaky peace existed in the American League, but that would be only temporary.

Cleveland baseball fans were treated to a December 24 Christmas message from Tris Speaker and his boss. They both expressed a great deal of optimism about the 1920 campaign. Dunn happily announced that he had paid off Ban Johnson for the $100,000 loan back in 1916. Now he and his minority partners held 100 percent of the outstanding stock. He told the fans a new starting pitcher was his primary goal, but he would do his best to strengthen the team in any way possible.

Speaker, writing from Texas, had positive news to share with the faithful. Speaker wrote, "We have a good ball team. It is composed of hard working players who will try their best to win a pennant for Cleveland. I believe I have their co-operation, and I promise the fans to do my best to maintain such a spirit on the club." At the end of the message he reminded fans a pennant was never a sure thing, but he trusted that, come next October, the city of Cleveland would have much to enthuse about. These were not empty promises designed to drum up ticket sales or keep fans on the bandwagon. Both men were very sincere in what they said to the fans. Dunn worked diligently behind the scenes to give his new manager the talent needed for the team to excel. Speaker had a very strong desire to win, which he instilled in his players. Even though he had won two world championships with Boston, Tris was hungry for another. In 1920 he would show the Cleveland faithful what championship baseball was all about.

After the New Year Dunn, Speaker, and coach Jack McAllister met for a day of talks regarding the upcoming season. The consensus, which surprised nobody, was that they should add a left-handed starter to the staff. Speaker believed a few local boys should be signed and given tryouts in the spring. Two years ago they had found George Uhle on the Cleveland sandlots. Though the homegrown pitcher had not yet asserted himself, the club had much faith he would soon help the team as a starter or reliever. With all the great amateur clubs in town, there just might be a lefty who could help.

Several days later Dunn sent Fred Coumbe to St. Paul of the American Association in exchange for left-handed starter Dick Niehaus. After serving up the monstrous grand slam to Babe Ruth the previous July, Coumbe became number one on the expendable list. Niehaus had pitched briefly for the St. Louis Cardinals before going off to the service in 1918. He had won twenty-three games for St. Paul the previous season, which got Dunn's attention. Spring training would determine whether Niehaus had enough stuff to help a pennant contender. The move did show that the Cleveland owner meant what he said about acquiring pitching help.

The AL meetings were held in Chicago on February 10. Dunn and Speaker were unable to deal for the left-handed pitcher they sorely needed. The meetings did not yield any blockbuster trades, but the owners did agree to set a permanent trading deadline of July 1. This action was prompted by the Carl Mays fiasco of last July, which had caused an uproar of epic proportions. Another important issue centered on a grandfather clause allowing spitball pitchers currently on a major league roster to use the pitch at their discretion. A list would be submitted to the league office by each club before the start of the season. Any pitcher not appearing on the list would be prohibited from throwing the spitter. This rule would be of great help to the Cleveland club, which employed the master of the wet ball, Stan Coveleski.

Schedules were released the following day. The Indians would open the season at home on April 14 against the St. Louis Browns. However, for the third straight year the club would end the regular season on the road, this time with three games in Detroit. Of particular interest was a June road trip of twenty-three days covering seven different cities before returning home. The Indians would start in Chicago, move to St. Louis, travel to Detroit, and then visit Washington, Philadelphia, Boston, and New York before heading back. If they could survive that marathon journey, they would be in good shape for the rest of the season.

On the eve of spring training, Jim Dunn announced that plans were in motion to increase the seating capacity at League Park. A total of 3,500 seats were to be added in the left-field corner adjoining the lower stands on the third-base pavilion. This new construction would raise the total number of seats to near thirty thousand. The new stands were built to deter the practice of placing overflow crowds on the field. Dunn believed the extra seating would take care of the problem, though with a few more rivets and concrete, the densely packed park might just explode. In its early days League Park could seat about nine thousand fans. Now, some twenty-five years later, it had more than tripled in size. Adding any more seats would create a logistical dilemma for the enterprising owner.

On March 2, the infielders and outfielders left Cleveland for the long trek south to New Orleans. Already in camp was Tris Speaker, who as manager could no longer spend an extra couple of weeks in Texas before reporting well after everybody else. Now Spoke had to be there with the pitchers and catchers, who reported at the end of February.

The new manager introduced some extra wrinkles for the pitchers during their training. Speaker had his staff line up in front of the batting cage. Backup catcher Les Nunamaker took a bat and ball and proceeded to smash red-hot grounders at the hapless pitchers. Anybody who fanned on a grounder would take a seat until only one player was left standing. Jim Bagby took the first round, Speaker the second, and then Guy Morton two rounds in a row. There were no casualties during the drill. The boys ran several laps around the grounds, more than the customary one of previous years. Speaker definitely had things under his control.

After practice, some of the squad went to the nearby racetrack. In the sixth race, Speaker put down $100 on an 8–1 long shot. The horse, named Heavy Weapon, beat the field, giving Tris a whopping payout of $800. He did like the ponies, and this would cause serious problems between him and Ban Johnson in later years. The horses and the lopsided defeat in Detroit the previous August would be closely scrutinized by the AL office during the twilight of Speaker's career. A scandal involving Speaker, Ty Cobb, and Joe Wood came to light in the winter of 1926. Ban Johnson obtained a letter written by Wood that appeared to implicate the three ballplayers in fixing the September 25, 1919, game with Detroit. Johnson called Speaker "cute," meaning he flaunted the rules of baseball.

Commissioner Kenesaw Mountain Landis held an investigation but eventually cleared all three. Wood had retired several years prior, but Speaker and Cobb continued to play baseball. However, Speaker's days as a Cleveland Indian were finished. He signed with the Washington Senators for the 1927 season. Cobb played for Connie Mack and the Philadelphia Athletics.

In mid-March, Robert Maxwell, sports editor of the *Philadelphia Public Ledger*, picked the 1920 Indians to win the pennant. Maxwell did a circuit of the training camps and then decided which team had the best chance to win the flag. He wrote, "If there ever was a favorite in the American League, Cleveland fills the bill this year. This team is loaded to the water's edge with high-class playing talent and it is difficult to point out the weak spots."

The writer did a full-blown analysis of the team, breaking down the pitching staff, infielders, and outfielders for his syndicated column. He mentioned that Ray Caldwell had given up the after-hours partying, devoting all his time to repeating his triumphs of the previous season. In years past, Caldwell had been guilty of enjoying himself well into the early-morning hours and then reporting bleary eyed to the ballpark. This behavior nearly ended his career until Dunn and Speaker took a flyer on him. A dedicated Caldwell would be the dependable third starting pitcher the Indians needed.

In late March, Dunn journeyed to New Orleans to watch his club go through their workouts. He told reporters after a spirited practice that he had suffered a severe attack of baseball fever. The owner could not wait to see his team open the season and begin carving out victories. Tris Speaker's old outfield buddy Duffy Lewis stopped by training camp for a look. He told his friend the Indians looked like "a mighty fine ballclub."

The pressure was being placed squarely on the Indians to win it all. Even though Speaker had yet to manage a full season, reporters and players alike believed Cleveland had the inside track on the pennant. No matter what happened during the regular season, Tris would not get a pass from the writers or the fans. At this point, anything less than the pennant would be unacceptable in the local baseball community.

One of the interesting developments out of spring training was the play of Joe Evans and Charlie Jamieson. With Larry Gardner ready to play his usual 150 games at third base, Evans, with Speaker's encouragement, switched his position to left field. Dr. Joe had more than enough speed and agility to cover the ground, plus he batted right-handed. The outfield currently had four lefties in

Speaker, Smith, Jamieson, and Graney, while only Joe Wood hit from the opposite side. Evans smacked the ball extremely well throughout camp, giving himself an opportunity to see playing time on a regular basis.

Charlie Jamieson played some first base behind Doc Johnston, trying to
find a way to get on the field. He would not stick as a first baseman but
impressed everyone with his ability to hit the ball and run the bases. Manager
Speaker now had the luxury of deciding which of his six outfielders would get
the most playing time. Spoke had all the time he wanted in center field, while
Elmer Smith had to be in the lineup as the team's best power hitter. Joe Wood
had proven to be a capable outfielder who at times could reach the fences. Jack
Graney had done the job in left for many seasons, using his talents to draw
walks and get on base for the heavy hitters. Despite what these players brought
to the lineup, Speaker would find a way to get Evans and Jamieson on the field.

In early April, the bookies established Cleveland and New York as the 5–2
favorites to win the pennant. Chicago came in next at 4–1, with the Tigers listed
at 6–1. In the National League, both the Giants and the Reds were at 2–1 to finish first, while the Cubs were a 4–1 shot. Listed at 12–1 was the Brooklyn club,
expected to finish fifth in the standings. Robert Maxwell picked the Cincinnati
Reds to win the pennant but noted that Brooklyn looked the best of all the NL
clubs he visited. He believed the Robins (the Dodgers nickname did not officially take until the 1930s) pitching staff was excellent, and he praised the outfield, which featured Zack Wheat and Hy Myers. Maxwell thought the infield
was weak but in summary liked Brooklyn's chances to contend.

In the April 10 edition of the *Plain Dealer*, Henry Edwards picked Cleveland
and Detroit as the best clubs in the American League. The dean of the Cleveland
writers believed the time had come for the Indians to win their very first pennant. Edwards wrote that if the team found the left-handed pitcher they needed,
the pennant flag would fly over League Park. He continued, "The principal reasons for figuring Cleveland to have an even chance with Detroit for the pennant
are Tris Speaker and an improved pitching staff. Under Speaker's leadership the
tribe last year won more games than any other in the league during the same
period." Edwards thought the Tigers had the best chance to beat Cleveland due
to their strong pitching, plus the hitting of ageless Ty Cobb and Bobby Veach.

He did not believe the White Sox could repeat, and he considered the Yankees no threat due to their perceived lack of speed. Edwards was off the mark about the former and the latter, though appalling circumstances would remove Chicago from the race at the very end.

With a great amount of anticipation, the Indians took the field to start their twentieth season as members of the American League. They entered the field wearing brand-new wool sweaters made by Favorite Knitting Mills on West Sixth Street. A record crowd was expected, but very cool temperatures kept the total at twenty thousand. At times the sun broke through the heavy clouds, but it gave little warmth to the shivering crowd. Early in the game a number of fans behind the outfield ropes (the new left-field stands were not yet ready) gathered stray newspapers, scorecards, and peanut shells to light a bonfire. The groundskeepers were disgusted to see chunks of the outfield grass going up in smoke but made no move to put out the fire. At least no rain fell on the grounds while Cleveland turned back the Browns 5–0. The Indians collected thirteen hits, including doubles by Jack Graney and pitcher Stan Coveleski. A four-run second inning put the home team in front while Coveleski shut out St. Louis with only five hits.

In the stands for the opener were Jim Dunn's partners Pat McCarthy, Tom Walsh, and brothers Reed and Dick Lane. They had made the trip from Davenport, Iowa, to take part in the opening-day festivities and be on hand for what many believed would be a championship season. Dunn wanted his old friends and fellow stockholders to witness history in the making. Sunny Jim had been waiting for this moment since signing the papers designating him as owner of the Cleveland franchise. Four years later he stood on the brink, anticipating the hour when all his efforts would pay off and bring him what he had wanted for so long: a special flag reading "Champions of the American League" being raised in center field.

The annual luncheon held by the Cleveland Advertising Club introduced a new organization dedicated to the fortunes of the Indians. The "Stick to the Finish" club made their debut, announcing that they would follow the team until the last game of the season, regardless of the league standings. Tom Hendricks, an executive at White Motor Company, had founded the new club, with the motto of "Glue, Glue, Glue!" The purpose of the group was to show that Cleveland fans were not of the fair-weather kind and would stick to their team to the end. Dunn and Speaker heartily welcomed the new group of rooters, saying the words they wanted to hear: yes, they would bring home the pennant.

During spring training, Speaker had preached to his ball club that every game in April and May was just as important as the ones in September. He wanted the team to get off to a fast start and never look back. His players were listening and won three out of their first four games. With twenty-five thousand fans looking on, the Indians blasted Detroit 11–4. In the first inning, with Ray Chapman on first, Speaker launched a drive high over the right-field screen for a 2–0 lead. In the sixth inning, with the fans yelling for another, Tris belted a long drive, this time hitting the screen for a double that knocked in two more runs. One inning later, Spoke fielded a base hit and fired a strike to home plate to nail the Tiger base runner. The player-manager led by example and his team followed behind.

Usually when teams have a good run, everybody in the ball club contributes. The next day, Detroit had a 4–2 edge going into the bottom of the seventh. The Indians loaded the bases, which brought up Les Nunamaker. The backup catcher had entered the game as a pinch-hitter for Charlie Jamieson. Nunamaker fouled off six pitches and then lined a double to right center field that cleared the bases, giving Cleveland a 5–4 lead. Detroit fought back, tying the game at six with a run in the top of the ninth. Once again, Nunamaker came to the plate. This time he hit a slow roller but just beat the throw to first. Steve O'Neill tried to execute the hit and run but swung and missed. However, Nunamaker hustled as best he could, beating the throw to second. One pitch later, O'Neill hit safely past the infield, allowing the backup catcher to score the winning run. One day it was Speaker, one day someone else. With the season only a week old, the Indians seemed to have the magic that would carry them all season long.

After the Detroit series, Cleveland left home for the first road trip of the season. They spoiled the home opener for the Browns, bashing fourteen hits in an 11–4 romp. Larry Gardner started things off in the top of the first with a ringing double that scored Chapman and Speaker. In the fourth inning with the same two on base, Elmer Smith drove a triple to deep center field for two more runs. Stan Coveleski breezed through seven innings before Elmer Myers came on in relief.

At this early juncture of the season, thirty-four-year-old Larry Gardner was not hitting for a high batting average but had already driven in nine important runs. Gardner, like Speaker, was one of those players who needed very little time to get himself ready for the regular season. Speaker told curious reporters, "All Larry has to do [in spring training] to get in shape is for him to change his shirt, throw three balls to first, take two turns in batting practice and he's ready." Gardner, as was his routine, always came to camp two weeks late but rounded into shape well before his teammates. He had not missed a game the previous season. Aside from being an excellent hitter, Gardner was one of the most durable third basemen in the game. Only five foot eight and 165 pounds, he rarely missed a start. He had his share of bumps and bruises from opponents sliding hard into third base, but no matter how tough the collision, he managed to stay on the field. Gardner took to wearing knee pads to ward off the flying spikes hurled in his direction.

The Indians kept to their winning ways in April. Two wins over Chicago vaulted Cleveland into first place. Once again Larry Gardner proved he had quite a bit left in the tank, driving a triple to deep center field and then coming all the way around when shortstop Swede Risberg threw wildly to third. Late-inning heroics thrilled the hometown crowd when Charlie Jamieson lifted a fly ball to right field, scoring Joe Evans with the game winner. The highlight of the series was an acrobatic catch in deep center field by Tris Speaker. With two men on base and two out, Joe Jackson smacked a line drive far over Spoke's head, a sure double or triple. Speaker turned with the sound of the bat, racing to the deepest part of the outfield. Just steps away from the concrete wall, the Cleveland manager made a great leap, snagged the liner, and then crashed into the wall. Fans held their breath while Speaker bounced forward off the barrier. Despite the shock of the collision, he still had the baseball firmly tucked in his glove. White Sox manager Kid Gleason marveled at the catch: "I did not think it possible. I did not think any man could get that ball. . . . There was only one and he was on the job."

The wins just kept on coming. The Indians trekked to Chicago, where Stan Coveleski won his sixth straight game 3–2. A ninth-inning sacrifice fly by Jack Graney scored Steve O'Neill with the deciding run. The catcher lumbered home and, just as the throw arrived, barreled into Ray Schalk to jar the ball loose.

By mid-May, Cleveland had won seventeen of twenty-four ball games. Of those seventeen wins Jim Bagby and Stan Coveleski recorded fourteen between them. Both pitchers were on their way to spectacular seasons; however, the old problem of a third starter still hampered the Indians' fortunes. Ray Caldwell had not yet grabbed hold of the third position, while a fourth starter had yet to be chosen from among George Uhle, Guy Morton, and Elmer Myers. For the present, Cleveland displayed the timely hitting and exceptional defense that carried them to victory when their aces were unable to take the mound. To make it last an entire season would be a daunting task for Speaker and his club.

A game against the Yankees at the Polo Grounds drew a record crowd of 38,600. This beat the previous record of 38,281 at game 4 of the 1911 World Series. Though early in the season, a New York–Cleveland matchup got the undivided attention of the Yankee fans. Despite the turnstiles being closed, another ten thousand rooters showed up at the park but were turned away. The Indians scored five times in the first inning off the usually tough Carl Mays and then coasted to an 8–2 victory. Bill Wamby doubled in two runs, while Doc Johnston singled in two more. The team was playing great ball on the road, which kept them on top of the American League. For the first two months of the season it was all Cleveland.

Up to this point the Indians' front office had been quite silent. The newspapers speculated that Dunn was looking for another starting pitcher. Fans eagerly waited for an announcement, but nothing came. However, on May 29 Dunn revealed he had acquired first baseman George Burns from the Philadelphia Athletics. It was not enough that Connie Mack gave away Larry Gardner and Charlie Jamieson to Cleveland the previous season. Apparently Mack wanted to help even more by selling his big hitter to the Indians. Burns, who was a native of Ohio, had been in the American League since 1914. He started for the Tigers, banging out fifteen home runs over four seasons. The Athletics traded for Burns prior to the 1918 season, and he batted .352 for them, leading the American League with 178 hits. He batted below .300 the following year but still finished the season with eight home runs and nine triples. Why Mack unloaded a talent like Burns is mystifying, unless he really needed the money. Now Cleveland had a lefty-righty combination in Doc Johnston and George Burns. Johnston held his job for most of the season, with Burns in the role of pinch-hitter. The owners of the White Sox and Yankees had to be shaking their heads at Mack's recent moves. He had done his best to strengthen the Cleveland club while acquiring nothing more than a few thousand in cash.

While Cleveland could do no wrong, some off-the-field news brought the good times to a temporary halt. The wife of Stan Coveleski died unexpectedly at their home in Shamokin, Pennsylvania. She had been ill for several years, but her death came as a complete surprise to the family. Stan left the team to return home for the funeral and make arrangements for the care of his two young children. Jim Dunn sent several floral bouquets to the Coveleski family and had the center-field flag at League Park lowered to half mast. However, the job of winning a pennant could not be ignored. Coveleski returned to Cleveland only a week after his wife's death.

Several days later an ailing Jack Graney had to leave the lineup to have his tonsils removed. While he downed ice cream to ease the pain in his throat, an eager Joe Evans got his chance to play left field. Dr. Joe started against Detroit and rang up three doubles in a wild 11–10 loss. The Indians knocked out sixteen base hits, while Detroit had one more at seventeen. Ty Cobb, Bobby Veach, and Harry Heilmann accounted for nine hits between them. Manager Speaker had to use five pitchers to get through the game. The Tigers scored six runs in the second inning to seemingly give themselves a comfortable advantage. Cleveland erased that lead with seven runs in the bottom of the sixth. The Tigers scored again in the eighth to barely hang on for the win.

On June 12, the second-place Yankees came to League Park to open a four-game series. New York had pushed its way to half a game behind the Indians, thus creating the first key matchup of the season. Anticipating huge gate receipts, Jim Dunn had made sure the new left-field stands were now available for seating. In the opening contest, the teams battled to a 4–4 tie through seven innings. The break came in the bottom of the eighth when Ray Chapman walked, went to second on a ground out, and then scored on Larry Gardner's clutch base hit. Ray Caldwell held the Yankees in the ninth to get the win, 5–4.

The Sunday game brought a record crowd of thirty thousand spectators, jammed into every corner of the ballpark. Many of them lined up at 11:30 a.m. in hopes of getting a general admission seat. White shirts and straw hats were everywhere in the stands. Even with the new seating, fans still found their way to the outfield grass. This suited the Yankees just fine, as Bob Meusel and Wally Pipp lifted fly balls into the fan area for two ground-rule doubles. This ignited New York to a six-run first inning and an eventual 14–0 massacre. With Cleveland trailing 8–0 in the top of the sixth, Babe Ruth hit a tremendous blast over the right-field screen that cleared Lexington Avenue before it landed. The Indians fans roared their approval, reasoning that even if they could not win the game, they still wanted to see the Babe launch one. Did he ever!

After the ball game, Steve O'Neill received the happy news that his wife, May, had just given birth to twins, both girls, at their home in Minooka. He went to see best friend Johnny Kilbane to celebrate the arrival of his daughters. A few hours later, he received another message stating that May had become ill and he needed to come home immediately. O'Neill raced to the station, catching the first train going east. In a few days, all would be well with the family, allowing the Indians catcher to rejoin the club. He would not miss another game the rest of the season.

The series ended with Cleveland taking three out of four from the Yankees. In the final two games, Jim Bagby and Stan Coveleski allowed three runs between them to help put some distance between the first- and second-place teams. Les Nunamaker, getting a chance to actually catch, added four hits in two days, while Larry Gardner stroked a bases-loaded double to drive in three runs. The Indians now had a two-game lead over New York and six games over third-place Chicago. With a third of the season in the record books, pennant fever had taken over in northeast Ohio.

At the end of June, Cleveland went on the road to open a series in St. Louis. They were trailing 3–1 in the top of the fifth when Ray Caldwell reached first base with a walk. Joe Evans tapped a slow roller to second and beat the throw to first. Ray Chapman bunted back to the mound, but pitcher Urban Shocker threw late to third, loading the bases. Elmer Smith came to bat, driving a pitch into the right-field bleachers for a grand slam home run. For players other than Babe Ruth, home runs were still a somewhat rare feat. A number of them were inside-the-park jobs, but when Elmer Smith got hold of a fastball, he only needed to trot around the bases. The bases-loaded home run was an exceptional piece of hitting. However, Smith had a few more homers to go, one of which is still mentioned today.

With the Indians dropping a few ball games, the AL standings had tightened considerably by the end of June. They stacked up as follows:

Cleveland 43–22 (.662)
New York 44–23 (.657)
Chicago 38–26 (.594)

After the top three only Washington had a winning record. Boston and St. Louis were just below .500 while Detroit and Philadelphia were hopelessly behind, the Athletics with a miserable seventeen wins. Based on three months of play, it appeared that only Cleveland, New York, and Chicago were serious contenders. The Indians had recently seen Ray Caldwell emerge as a third starter, which took some pressure off Bagby and Coveleski. Joe Evans and Charlie Jamieson were handling left field while Elmer Smith and Joe Wood had right field taken care of. Tris Speaker had positioned himself for a good shot at another batting title. As manager he made all the right moves, platooning hitters and handling the pitching staff without any difficulty.

The Yankees had great hitting with Babe Ruth terrorizing every pitching staff he faced. The White Sox were beginning to demonstrate why they had finished first a year ago. They had four pitchers with a chance to win twenty games each, along with great batting from Joe Jackson, Happy Felsch, Buck Weaver, and Eddie Collins. None of these teams had any major weaknesses, meaning the three-team race would likely continue until the very end of the season. That was fine with the Cleveland fans as long as the standings did not change.

Pennant fever officially arrived in Cleveland on July 7. Fans who read the *Plain Dealer* noticed the Indians were now front-page news. Scores and highlights were listed under the headlines, something readers had not seen since September of 1908, when the Naps made their furious drive to reach first place. Even the most casual of fans could now glance at the first page to see what the Indians had done. The initial success of the 1920 club had brought a new confidence to the city that had proclaimed, no two ways about it, this was our year.

A review of the baseball statistics as of July 11 indicates the Indians were well on track to complete the mission. Each member of the starting lineup was hitting over .300. Tris Speaker led the way with an average of .396. Joe Evans came next with an average of .364, while Charlie Jamieson was having a career season, hitting .351. The rest of the starters, Doc Johnston, Elmer Smith, Larry Gardner, Ray Chapman, and Steve O'Neill, were clustered in the .300 category. In addition to batting nearly .400, Speaker had 112 base hits and 70 runs scored, both second in the league. The pitching staff had some gaudy numbers with Jim Bagby at 15–4, Stan Coveleski 13–6, and Ray Caldwell well above expectations at 10–4. At this pace, Jim Dunn could puff on his cigar and dream about World Series gate receipts.

Several days later, the Cleveland front office announced plans to accept reservations for World Series tickets as of August 15. Dunn and company were not trying to cash in early: hundreds of letters from fans requesting tickets had prompted the decision. Further plans disclosed the construction of a press box on the grandstand roof large enough to seat five hundred reporters and photographers. Clearly Dunn and Barnard were gambling a bit here, but after twenty years of waiting, they could not be blamed for their eagerness. To ensure there would be open dates on the schedule for any rainouts that might occur, all potential exhibition games were canceled. These games usually brought in some extra money, but with the exception of a July 25 game against Cincinnati, the Indians decided to keep all their open dates available in case they were needed.

In mid-July the Indians swept a doubleheader against the Boston Red Sox, winning both games 5–2. Joe Wood and Tris Speaker haunted their former teammates with spectacular plays on the field and at bat. In the fourth inning of game 1, Wood raced to right center field to haul down a long fly ball. Boston pitcher Sam Jones tagged up at third, seemingly a sure bet to cross the plate safely. However, Wood stopped his momentum, turned toward home, and fired a rope to catcher Steve O'Neill, who grabbed the throw, tagging out Jones as he slid across. Three innings later, Wood powered a home run to the center-field bleachers, scoring Speaker ahead of him. In game 2, Wood added three more hits—a double and two singles.

For his part, Speaker collected a total of five hits in ten at-bats, while scoring five runs. In game 2 the Red Sox had outfielder Fred Bailey on first base with nobody out. Harry Hooper laid down a sacrifice bunt, moving the runner to second. Speaker crept in from center field, and when Bailey made a brief move toward third, Tris raced to second, received the throw from Doc Johnston, and tagged out the startled Bailey. This was vintage Speaker, pulling off a neat double play that no other center fielder could manufacture in the heat of battle.

Near the end of July, Cleveland wound up its month-long road trip in New York. The team had already played a total of twenty-eight games on the road, winning a remarkable twenty contests. A successful finish with the Yankees would put Cleveland a comfortable distance in front. However, New York had a pretty fair idea how important the series was, taking three out of four to close the gap to only seven percentage points. To salvage the final game, the Indians scored twice in the eleventh inning to win 4–2. Jim Bagby went the distance, not allowing a run after the fourth inning. Larry Gardner provided the winning hit, a triple that scored Speaker and Wood. The attendance at the Polo Grounds reached nearly thirty-seven thousand, with over a thousand fans turned away at the gate. Plans to put the excess crowd on the field were canceled when the players objected to spectators sitting in center field, which put them in direct line with home plate and the view of the hitters. Although it was still late July, each game the Indians, Yankees, and White Sox played had postseason implications stamped all over it.

Throughout the season, Cleveland had been relatively injury free. Jack Graney's oversized tonsils were the most serious crisis the team had faced. During their stay in Washington, Joe Evans ate some tainted food, which made him violently ill. He traveled to Boston with the team but developed ptomaine poisoning, which sidelined him for the better part of a month. Evans had been having an outstanding season, his best as a pro to date. The platooning of

Jamieson and Evans gave the Indians a great combination in left field. Both players were hitting around .350 while handling the sun field with ease. Now it would be up to Jamieson to handle the job on his own. Jack Graney had been relegated to pinch-hitting duties, having tailed off a bit as a regular player. At this point in the season, losing anybody from the starting lineup would be a serious problem for Speaker and his team.

Back home at League Park to battle the White Sox, the players watched thousands of fans arrive early to welcome their club back to town. They yelled through batting practice and then again through much of fielding practice. In the bottom half of the first, the crowd rose to its feet when Tris Speaker drove a Lefty Williams pitch over the right-field wall. Three innings later, doubles by Gardner, O'Neill, and Coveleski added two more runs. Cleveland went on to win 7–2, keeping their slim lead over New York.

July came to a close with the Indians taking three straight from Boston. They scored a total of thirty runs in the series, backing that up with thirty-eight hits. Bagby, Caldwell, and Coveleski waltzed through the Red Sox lineup, yielding a total of nine runs in twenty-seven innings. The standings showed Cleveland two games ahead of the Yankees and four and a half in front of Chicago. With two months remaining in the AL season, the outlook appeared bright for the first-place team. However, the month of August would shock each member of the Cleveland Indians, enough to nearly derail the season.

12

A TURN FOR THE WORSE

The AL statistics through the end of July showed Tris Speaker with a remarkable batting average of .412. The hitter closest to him was the St. Louis Browns' George Sisler with a mark of .383. Speaker had collected 150 hits, 33 more than runner-up Babe Ruth. In the pitching department, Jim Bagby already had twenty-one victories against only five losses. Stan Coveleski had reached seventeen wins, while Ray Caldwell had accumulated twelve wins versus six losses. Most of the Cleveland regulars were still hitting well over .300, giving their pitchers the support they needed to rack up the victories. Ray Chapman was on his way to a terrific season with a batting average over .300 and eighty-nine runs scored, and topped the league with thirty-four sacrifices. His work at shortstop continued to be outstanding, making him one of the most valuable players in all of baseball. Statistics would not bring championships, but analyzing the Indians stats showed a team at its very best in every phase of the game.

James Lanyon, the sports editor of the *Plain Dealer*, weighed in on the strong possibility that a World Series would come to Cleveland. Lanyon wrote, "Winning the American League pennant will place Cleveland in a position it never held before. Such a thing would make our city the metropolis of the sport world. It would be a great thing for Cleveland." Lanyon realized the eyes of the sporting world would be focused on the city by the lake. He urged fans to behave like proper sportsmen regardless of the final outcome. In reality nobody had any inkling how the Indians fans would react if a pennant victory was finally realized. It is doubtful they would have rioted in the streets and burned down Euclid Avenue. However, the fans had a lot of pent-up frustration from the last twenty years. How they would manifest it was anybody's guess.

On August 7, Jim Dunn revealed he had obtained a permit to build a press box on the roof of the grandstand. He awarded the contract to Osborn Engineering Company, the firm that had originally built League Park in 1891. The project would cost $15,000, with construction scheduled to begin on August 16 when the Indians left town for another road trip. Dunn estimated that the press box could hold 480 baseball writers and telegraph operators.

The Cleveland owner had a lot to deal with as the season pushed into August. The Yankees were coming to town for a crucial four-game series for which tickets were at a premium. Earlier in the season, Dunn had set aside a total of sixteen thousand free tickets for schoolchildren living in the Cleveland area. Up to four thousand of the tickets were redeemable for each of the Yankees games. Realizing the potential revenue loss this could represent for such an important series, the Indians' front office announced that redemption of the free tickets was being moved to less significant dates. Dunn had been traveling for a few days, but when he returned to Cleveland he reversed the change of dates, declaring that the children should come and see the slugging Yankees. Dunn said, "I want the boys and girls that drew tickets to come to my park next week and see Babe Ruth. It may crowd us and force us to put a lot of fans on the field but when I gave those tickets to the school children there were no strings attached to the gifts." How many other baseball owners would have been as charitable as Dunn? Without hesitating, he potentially gave up thousands of dollars so that school kids could see Babe Ruth take his swats. But this was the same kind man who gave tickets to local orphanages and sent up bricks of free ice cream for the excited children when they took their seats at the ballpark. Even with a pennant at stake, Dunn made certain his kids were taken care of.

To get warmed up for the series with New York, Ray Caldwell tossed a six-hit shutout, beating Philadelphia 5–0. Tris Speaker developed some type of nerve problem that left him on the trainer's table and out of the game. Charlie Jamieson moved to center field, allowing Jack Graney to get a rare start in left. He made the most of his opportunity, getting a base hit and executing a nimble double steal with Ray Chapman. Though now a part-time player, Graney developed into a lethal pinch-hitter, which would help in the games ahead.

The New York Yankees rolled into town to begin the highly important series on Monday, August 9. The standings were as follows:

Cleveland 69–35 (.663)
New York 67–42 (.615)
Chicago 65–41 (.613)

Guy Morton took the mound for the Indians and got the leadoff batter to ground out to Chapman. Roger Peckinpaugh, a former Cleveland Naps shortstop and local resident, worked Morton for a walk. An instant later Morton tried the pickoff play but threw wildly, allowing "Peck" to race all the way to third. The Cleveland pitcher then walked Babe Ruth and Del Pratt in succession to load the bases. Duffy Lewis flied to Jamieson, which scored one run, and then Wally Pipp drove a pitch off the right-field wall to score Ruth. When the carnage ended, the Yankees had scored four times.

Cleveland tried to get the runs back in the bottom of the first. Charlie Jamieson led off with an infield single. Ray Chapman followed with another base hit. After two outs were made, Larry Gardner singled to right field, driving in two runs. In the bottom of the third inning, Elmer Smith hit a high-arching fly ball over the right-field wall to close the gap to 4–3. The Indians could not generate any more offense, however, losing the game 6–3.

Tuesday's game brought over twenty-one thousand fans to the ballpark. Due to the magnitude of the series, fans from all parts of Ohio and neighboring states were in the stands. Groups from Toledo and Youngstown made the trip along with diehards from Cincinnati and Dayton. Fans from Pittsburgh and Buffalo attended, as did J. M. Flanner, who hailed from Bridgeport, Connecticut.

Flanner told interested reporters, "Just on my vacation and I knew no better way to spend part of it than to come to Cleveland to see the best team in the American League and Babe Ruth." Unfortunately for Flanner and the other travelers, rain clouds formed around the second inning. The ominous clouds turned the field dark, forcing the umpires to wave the players off the field. Moments later heavy rains fell, soaking the field until it was unplayable.

The postponement of Tuesday's game brought a dilemma for the holders of the rain checks. All box and reserved seats for Wednesday's and Thursday's games were sold out, leaving them with no recourse to see the remaining two games. Prompt action by the Cleveland front office scheduled the makeup game for Friday, with all rain checks honored on that day. To ensure that the Tuesday seat holders could find similar seats, all general sales of box and reserved seats for Friday were being held until Friday morning. Anyone with a ticket from Tuesday had all day Wednesday and Thursday to exchange their seats. Those like Flanner who had come from out of town could mail in their tickets for a refund. Usually Friday was "Ladies' Day," but not on this occasion.

Game 2 saw twenty-seven thousand people in the stands hoping to see the Indians even the series. With Jim Bagby facing off against Carl Mays, it figured to be a low-scoring game. Neither team was able to score until the bottom of the third inning. Steve O'Neill lifted a pop fly into short left field that fell for a base hit. Charlie Jamieson followed with a single. After Ray Chapman flied out, Tris Speaker was hit by a pitch, loading the bases. Elmer Smith came to bat with the crowd yelling for a hit. Mays delivered a fastball that Smith nearly fell down trying to hit. Mays delivered another fastball, which Smith launched deep over the right-field wall. The Cleveland fans went wild, throwing hundreds of straw hats onto the field. Elmer crossed home plate only to be mobbed by his animated teammates. Smith had delivered another grand slam homer earlier in the season, but this one came at the most critical of times. Though only three innings had been played, fans believed victory was theirs, especially with Jim Bagby on the mound. The Yankees disappointed the League Park crowd, however, by scoring three times in the fifth inning and then tying the game in the sixth. Cleveland could not get anything more going against Mays, causing the game to go into extra innings. Carl Mays led off the top of the tenth inning with a double to center field. A single by Bob Meusel scored Mays with the go-ahead run. A throwing error and a single brought in two more runs to give the Yankees a 7–4 win.

Stan Coveleski pitched game 3, and New York jumped all over him in the first inning, scoring four times. The Indians had no answer for pitcher Jack Quinn, losing for the third straight time, 5–1. With the visitors on the verge of sweeping the series, only one-and-a-half games separated the two teams. The makeup game on Friday went again to the Yankees by the score of 4–3. At day's end the two teams were just one half game apart. The White Sox had pulled virtually even, trailing by only eight percentage points.

During the series, Cleveland pitchers walked Babe Ruth seven times in fourteen at-bats. Five of the walks resulted in runs scored by the Babe. On three occasions there was nobody on base when the Yankee slugger walked and eventually scored. Sportswriters questioned the strategy of all the walks, particularly when the bases were clear. Most of the walks were not intentional, but each Indians pitcher tried to get Ruth to chase pitches well off the plate. That may have worked a year earlier, but the Ruth of 1920 had become a more disciplined batter, holding off from pitches he could not reach. The tactic of not letting Ruth hit undoubtedly came from manager Speaker. This happened to be one of the few questionable moves he made all season long. Walking Ruth with men on base made perfect sense, but to give him a free pass with nobody on definitely backfired and probably cost the Indians at least a game of the series. The Cleveland pitchers had enough skill to throw strikes that were on the corners, lessening the chances of a blast over the right-field wall. They went the safe route, which only gave New York the advantage and a rapid turnaround in the standings.

Regardless of the poor showing against the Yankees at home, Dunn and associates announced on August 15 they would officially begin to accept applications for World Series tickets. Due to the limits on seating capacity at League Park, applications would be limited to two tickets per request. Each person had to make his or her own request for tickets and not send any money in advance as all checks would be returned to the sender. No applications would be processed from companies or groups. After the July announcement about accepting ticket requests the following month, the front office began to receive an overwhelming number of letters from northeast Ohio and around the country. Due to the heavy flow of paper, Dunn and Barnard had decided to stick with their original date of mid-August. They advised fans to be patient, as the estimated turnaround time would probably be several weeks at best. Though a tiresome process to get through, this one had to bring smiles to the front office. Most likely Jim Dunn reflected back to the February day in 1916 when he assumed ownership of the club. On that day he promised the fans that he would not stand for a tail-ender. It had taken some time, but the words Sunny Jim had spoken were about to come true.

The Indians left Cleveland for their last eastern road trip of the season. They would hit New York first to play three games there, then on to Boston for five more. Stops in Philadelphia and Washington would account for the remaining eight games of the trip. Of the forty-four games left on the schedule, Cleveland had to travel for twenty-four while playing twenty at home. The Yankees had a more favorable schedule with an even amount of games at home and away. If the race stayed tight, the Indians would likely have to clinch first place while away from home.

The eastern excursion began in New York on August 16. A light rain was falling at game time, and gray skies lingered throughout the afternoon. Not an ideal day to play baseball, but with so much at stake, a monsoon would have been necessary for any postponement. In the top of the first inning Charlie Jamieson led off with a base hit to left field. Ray Chapman, as he had done so many times in his sparkling career, laid down a perfect sacrifice bunt off Yankee pitcher Carl Mays. Both Speaker and Elmer Smith flied out, leaving Jamieson stranded at third. The rain continued through the second inning, but Steve O'Neill got a good look at a Mays delivery, planting a home run to the left-field stands. The score climbed to 3–0 in the fourth inning on an error and a sacrifice fly by Stan Coveleski.

The rain let up by the fifth inning, but the overcast skies still hovered over the Polo Grounds. Visibility became a factor for the players, who relied on their sharp eyesight to see the baseball and determine within an instant if a fastball or curve was coming toward them. To add a further handicap, the AL owners had recently whined to Ban Johnson that umpires were too liberal in tossing out damaged balls and distributing new ones to the players. This procedure forced the owners to keep a larger supply of new baseballs on hand, which threatened to create a severe financial crisis, with losses well into the tens of dollars. To help them pinch their pennies, Johnson sent a bulletin to all umpires advising them to keep balls in play as long as possible. The umpire could order a replacement brought in only if he believed that safety was becoming a factor.

With these conditions in place, Ray Chapman walked to the plate to start the top half of the fifth inning. In the third inning he had tried to sacrifice Jamieson to second but bunted the ball too hard, resulting in a double play. Now with nobody on base, he could swing away. Carl Mays looked at his catcher behind home plate. Behind Mays were dark skies, forcing Ray to concentrate harder. Mays gripped the scuffed, grass-stained baseball and delivered a fastball that sailed high and inside. Whether Chapman lost the baseball in the background or was fooled by the pitch is still open to conjecture. According to many players on the field and fans in the seats, he never moved as the ball struck him directly on the left temple. The ball landed with such force that it actually careened off the shortstop's head, rolling into fair territory. At first it appeared to those in attendance that the ball had been bunted. However, when Chapman slumped to the ground, most fans realized that the cracking noise they had heard was really the sound of the baseball smashing into Chapman's skull. The crowd of twenty-three thousand became completely silent while players from both teams rushed to the fallen shortstop. Moments went by while Chapman lay on the ground unconscious. At least two doctors jumped from the stands and onto the playing field to offer their assistance. After being given water and a dose of stimulants, Chapman opened his eyes, slowly stood up, and began walking gingerly to the center-field clubhouse. He staggered as far as second base, and then his rubbery legs collapsed underneath him. Two of Ray's teammates lifted him up in their arms, carrying him the rest of the way to the visitor's locker room. The game resumed with Harry Lunte, a light-hitting, good glove man replacing Chapman. Somehow, the Indians managed to keep their focus, winning the game 4–3.

While the game progressed, the Yankees' team doctor and another physician examined the semiconscious ballplayer. Soon it became obvious that an ambulance needed to be called to transport Chapman to nearby St. Lawrence Hospital. Jack Graney stood anxiously by his roommate, hoping to be of some help. He would later remark that Chapman turned toward him, attempting to speak. Graney realized the words were not coming, and with some quick thinking he grabbed a pencil and paper, holding them to Ray's hand. After a moment both the pencil and scrap of paper fell to the ground. Percy Smallwood, the Indians' trainer, thought he saw Ray motion to him. Smallwood rushed over to see the injured ballplayer pointing to his ring finger. A second later he heard the faint words, "Katy's ring, Perc, Katy's ring." Smallwood reached into his pocket to retrieve the diamond ring he had been holding for Ray. The ring in question was a gift from the bride to the groom shortly after their October wedding. Chapman usually gave the ring to the trainer before ball games for safe keeping. Now the ring was in its proper place.

The ambulance arrived, hurrying Chapman to the hospital, where X-rays would be taken to determine the extent of the damage to his skull. Based on the results doctors would decide whether or not to risk an operation. Initially the doctors at the ballpark feared that Chapman's skull had been fractured, but when he was examined by surgeons at St. Lawrence, they had differing opinions on whether there was actually a fracture. If at all possible, the surgeons wanted to avoid the very dangerous procedure.

Tris Speaker sent a message home to the newspapers saying the injury might not be as severe as first believed. It was possible that a fracture had not occurred and that operating wouldn't be necessary. He did take the time to phone Kathleen Chapman, however, advising her to catch a train to New York as soon as possible. To complicate matters, Chapman's young wife was pregnant with the couple's first child. Whatever Speaker said, he had to be very delicate so as not to startle the young bride and cause her any more alarm than necessary.

Before the newspapers went to press, they received a late bulletin from New York that said, "Surgeons at St. Lawrence Hospital tonight stated Ray Chapman has a severe fracture of the skull and would be operated on at once." All the worst fears were confirmed.

Shortly after midnight on the 17th, Dr. Thomas D. Merrigan, the surgical director of St. Lawrence, began the operation. He opened a three-and-one-half-inch incision at the left side of Chapman's skull, just below the left ear. Dr. Merrigan removed a piece of bone almost two inches long that had been shattered by the force of the pitch. He noted numerous blood clots that had already formed, due to the jarring of the brain on impact. The surgery lasted for just over an hour. Initial reports stated that the next forty-eight hours would be critical in Chapman's recovery.

For a brief period Speaker, Wood, and Graney noticed that Chapman began to breathe more easily. His pulse showed some improvement. While nobody smiled or shook hands, there appeared to be some prospect that their friend and teammate might recover. Unfortunately, during the early-morning hours, Chapman's pulse began to drop steadily, erasing any slim hope he could survive the trauma. At 4:40 a.m. Ray Chapman died. He had everything to live for: a pretty wife, a baby on the way, and a great opportunity to win a pennant for the very first time. His future after baseball had few limits. Now all of his hopes and dreams, along with those of his family, were gone forever.

Several hours later the body was moved to a funeral parlor on West 153rd Street and Amsterdam Avenue. The first to stop by and pay their respects were Ray's oldest friends in the ball club, Jack Graney and Steve O'Neill. For eight seasons they had been through the baseball wars together, traveling from city to city, laughing and joking, and sharing the ups and downs of professional ballplayers. Graney was the first to speak with reporters via the telephone. Very honest with his emotions, Graney said, "We feel as if we did not care if we ever played baseball again. We did not sleep last night and we cannot eat today. We have lost more than a fellow player, we have lost a real pal."

The shock among the Indians players had to be beyond measure. In the early part of the twentieth century, ballplayers spent a considerable amount of time together, forging very close relationships. To have one taken in death, in a calamity witnessed by every teammate on the club, surely would be a devastating blow. Fans would grieve in their own manner, but the players who knew Ray Chapman intimately had been dealt a wound that would take a substantial time to heal.

Kathleen Chapman, along with her best friend, Jane McMahon, arrived in the early-morning hours, traveling all night from Cleveland to New York City.

Speaker and others met her at the train station and then escorted her to the Hotel Ansonia, where the team had their rooms. Once inside her suite, Speaker broke the terrible news to her. According to *Baseball Magazine*, she said quietly, "I feared that something must happen. We have been too happy together and it couldn't last." Instead of having bright, joyous days ahead, she was now a widow with funeral arrangements to consider. Another all-night train ride, this time with the body of her husband, had to be an enormous ordeal for a young woman of twenty-six. Despite her great sorrow, she managed to hold up well, appearing very stoic at the funeral in Cleveland several days later.

The years to come would be filled with more tragedy, however, for both Kathleen Chapman and her soon-to-be-born daughter, Rae. Despite taking a second husband, Kathleen never recovered from the death of Ray, her one true love. In April of 1928, she drank a bottle of poison, ending her life at age thirty-four. Just a year later eight-year-old Rae Marie Chapman fell ill with measles and passed away. What began as a storybook romance between Ray and Kathleen ended in unthinkable sadness.

The New York owners canceled the Indians-Yankees game scheduled for the 17th. The Cleveland players now had a lot of time to reflect on yesterday's horrific incident. Some began to talk about Carl Mays with a great deal of anger and resentment. Stories circulated that Jack McAllister, the Indians' coach, had to talk both Steve O'Neill and Jack Graney out of attacking the Yankee pitcher moments after Chapman went down. Earlier in the season, Mays had hit Doc Johnston with a head-high pitch. This prompted talk that if the first baseman had not raised his arm in self-defense, he would have taken a severe blow to the head. To try and calm things down, Tris Speaker gave a statement to the press. He said, "It is the duty of all of us, of all the players not only for the good of the game, but also out of respect to the poor fellow who was killed to suppress our bitter feelings. We will do all in our power to avoid aggravating the unfortunate impression in any way."

The Indians' manager was commenting on reports from AL cities that players from both the Boston Red Sox and Detroit Tigers were drawing up a petition to have Carl Mays banned from baseball. Players from St. Louis and Washington met informally to discuss a possible strike to prohibit Mays from pitching any further. Pressed to comment on the situation, Ban Johnson said he would make no statement on the matter until he investigated the information available. Word circulated that several AL managers had complained to Johnson some years earlier that Mays had been scaring their young players by "dusting them off" at the plate.

For his part, a shaken Carl Mays turned himself in to the district attorney's office to give a statement. He explained the pitch had been an accident and that he did not intend to harm Chapman in any way. He had thrown a fastball for the inside part of the plate but unfortunately the pitch missed by several inches. The district attorney believed what he heard and sent the dazed pitcher home, exonerated of any criminal charges. F. C. Lane of *Baseball Magazine* was at the Polo Grounds when Chapman went down. After the game he visited the Yankees' locker room to interview Mays. At this point Mays did not know the seriousness of Chapman's injury. Lane found the pitcher sitting dejectedly in front of his locker, his face in his hands. When he did speak, Mays told the writer, "I was wild as a hawk. I always am when I am saved up for a special game. The ball was wet which didn't make it any easier to control." In his feature article, Lane would label Mays a man of mystery. In his commentary he unraveled a very sad tale of a man who had the misfortune of arousing the worst in players when he confronted them. Lane maintained he had never seen such a disliked ballplayer in the history of the game. The article went on to say that players with integrity called Mays a tricky ballplayer, that he was unscrupulous, and that he did indeed throw the beanball. Lane himself was puzzled that players he knew to be level-headed and forthright had the opinion that Mays actually was a headhunter.

In the same story, Lane relates a conversation with Mays about his alleged throwing-at-hitters activity. Mays responded, "I am sorry the fellows say such things about any pitcher. It is easy to make such statements and very hard to disprove them. Once you give a man that reputation it is likely to follow him." Apparently Mays accepted what players said about him and went about his business. If any other pitcher in the American League had thrown the pitch that fractured Ray Chapman's skull, the outcry would have been minimal. However it happened to be the one guy that had the bad reputation he could not shed.

Did Mays try and bean Ray Chapman? From all accounts studied the answer is
no. Carl Mays threw a high fastball toward the inside part of home plate. It
sailed somewhat, moving in on Chapman, who could not get out of the way.
Had Ray been able to duck just a few inches or straighten up, the pitch would
have either missed him or likely caused a glancing blow. In either instance,
Chapman would have survived to play baseball another day. An unsubstantiated
story in the New York World had John Henry, the former Washington Senators
catcher, attending the fateful game. Henry, a friend of Chapman, raced to the
clubhouse to be near his fallen comrade. Henry insisted that Chapman whis-
pered to him to tell Mays he would be all right. If true, the dying ballplayer had
no blame toward Mays for what had happened. The one man who could really
have set off fireworks was Tris Speaker. As a player once struck in the head by
the Yankee pitcher and mired in sadness for his best friend, Speaker had every
reason to demand justice. Instead he took the high road, never once casting
any responsibility on Carl Mays. If Speaker believed it was an accident, few people would doubt him.

The train carrying Chapman's body left New York's Grand Central Station
on the evening of the 17th. A large group of somber Yankees fans lined up by
the tracks, removing their hats while the casket was brought slowly to its car.
The traveling party consisted of Kathleen Chapman; her brother, Dan Daly;
Jane McMahon; Joe Wood; and Speaker. They would not arrive in Cleveland
until the next morning, which was Wednesday the 18th. Plans were made to
bring the body to the home of Martin Daly, where family members on both
sides and close friends could pay their respects. The family had decided not to
allow any viewing by the general public, opting to keep arrangements as
restricted as possible.

While the family grieved privately, Cleveland baseball fans walked the
downtown streets in utter silence. They swamped the local newspaper offices,
trying to get as much information as possible. Just two days earlier, the city had
vibrated with lively talk of winning a pennant and seeing the elusive World
Series finally come to town. Now all discussion of baseball virtually ceased. The
shock of Chapman's death had overcome the city that had been flush with pennant fever. It is hard to believe the town had been through similar circumstances

when pitcher Addie Joss died suddenly nine years earlier. Though Joss had passed away in his Toledo home, a victim of tubercular meningitis, both he and Chapman were Cleveland's adopted sons. They were close in age and were both pillars of the community, highly respected and great ambassadors for the game. Both men played to the best of their ability, were gentlemen on and off the field, and were adored by men and boys alike. They both possessed that rare quality that allowed them to make countless friends everywhere they went. Thousands mourned when Joss died; his funeral was one of the largest ever seen in Toledo. Based on the reaction to Ray Chapman's passing, his funeral likely would exceed Joss's in attendance. Though he was much closer to Chapman, Jack Graney had been with Cleveland when Addie Joss died. Larry Lajoie, still living in town, had played alongside both men. It is a very improbable circumstance for a team and a city to lose two of its brightest stars when both are still in the prime of their careers. Many who would attend Chapman's funeral had been to Toledo in April of 1911 to pay their last respects to Joss. Now they must do it a second time.

In the midst of all the sorrow, the Indians had to play a ball game on Wednesday. The Polo Grounds had all flags flying at half mast. Players on both teams wore black mourning bands on their left sleeves. The crowd of eighteen thousand stayed relatively quiet throughout the game. In the top of the third inning, the New York fans did a classy thing. When Cleveland shortstop Harry Lunte came to bat, he received a tremendous ovation from all in the stands. It was their way to pay their respects to Chapman, by encouraging his replacement. The Indians, behind Jim Bagby and an Elmer Smith home run, led 3–2 until the bottom of the ninth. Duffy Lewis singled for the Yankees, and then Wally Pipp homered to the grandstand for a last-ditch 4–3 win. Charlie Jamieson took Speaker's place in center field while Jack Graney started in left. The Indians had to be commended for just taking the field, let alone playing a very good game.

The series ended on Thursday with Cleveland winning 3–2. Ray Caldwell went the distance, although he gave up Babe Ruth's forty-third home run of the season. Elmer Smith came through again, crashing another home run deep into the grandstand. Caldwell blanked the Yankees through the final three innings, allowing only five hits for the game. The Indians players all showered, dressed, and quickly headed for Grand Central Station to catch a train for Cleveland. Friday's game with Boston had been postponed to allow the team to attend the Chapman funeral. Wally Pipp, Ernie Shore, and Duffy Lewis traveled with the Indians to represent the Yankees.

Back in Cleveland, tributes and floral arrangements were steadily flowing into the Daly home. Players, owners, umpires, politicians, and newspaper reporters were putting into words how much they had cared about Ray Chapman. All praised him as a great man as well as a superior athlete. His buddies from the navy, where Chapman had enlisted in 1918, commended him for his dedication to duty. They remarked that he expected no favors because of who he was. He wanted to earn his position the right way. Most were sure that if the war had continued, Chapman would undoubtedly have become an officer. Jim Dunn's wife was in Chicago caring for a sick niece; however, she planned to leave for Cleveland on Thursday to attend the funeral. Edith Dunn considered Chapman part of her family. She would join her husband and Ban Johnson on Friday.

Dunn, Speaker, and Wood gathered at the Hotel Winton to talk with reporters. Speaker tried to collect his thoughts about the tragedy. He said, "I presume I had more hopes of his recovery than some of the other boys. I suppose the fact I had been through a similar accident and had come through safely raised those false hopes that Chappie also would recover. I scarcely can realize yet that he is gone." Joe Wood added, "I never saw such expressions of grief before. There was not one of the team that was not almost prostrated by the terrible accident. The entire team wanted to come to Cleveland with us, but of course that could not be."

On Thursday the 19th, Martin Daly announced the funeral would be held at 10 a.m. the next day at St. John's Cathedral at East Ninth Street and Superior Avenue. Daly had been planning for the funeral to be held at St. Philomene Church, near the family home, where Ray and Kathleen were married. However, due to the thousands who wanted to attend, the venue needed to be changed. St. John's, one of Cleveland's oldest churches, had a very large seating capacity. Its location in the heart of downtown made it much easier to reach by trolley and automobile. The pallbearers were to be Speaker, Wood, Graney, O'Neill, the three Daly brothers, Tom Rafferty (a former Indian and close friend), and Howard Monks (another close friend of Chapman). For some reason, there were no members of the Chapman family designated as pallbearers. Ray's two uncles had arrived in Cleveland, as well as his parents and brother, Roy.

In honor of the fallen shortstop, all Friday major league and many minor league games would be halted for five minutes of silence. The "Flower from a Fan" fund, started earlier in the week by Cleveland businessmen, had raised $2,062.30. Each person who wanted to contribute had only to donate a dime for one flower. Children and adults alike came through with a vast number of dimes to buy a gigantic display of flowers for Chapman's burial site. Money left over would be contributed to a memorial fund to establish a monument at League Park. Books commemorating the funeral were printed for members of the ball club. Ray Chapman would receive heartfelt tributes that would be remembered for many years after his death.

As expected, thousands gathered inside and outside of St. John's Cathedral, waiting for the appearance of the funeral procession. At ten o'clock the hearse arrived carrying the coffin. The pallbearers surrounded the casket, lifting it up the steps of the cathedral and into the large sanctuary. Those in attendance may have not noticed, but Jack Graney and Tris Speaker were not among the pall-bearers. The rest of the team entered a moment later, but the two intimate friends of Chapman were not there. The next day the newspapers would say that both men were too grief-stricken to attend the funeral. Rumors soon circulated that a fight had taken place before the service, and that accounted for Speaker's absence. Graney's whereabouts were never explained except for a dubious story that he was so overcome with sadness that Larry Lajoie had to take him for a drive to the country to calm him down.

The requiem mass was conducted by Reverend William A. Scullen and the Reverend W. S. Nash of the Dalys' church, St. Philomene. The words were eloquent and the tribute grand. If there is such a thing as a good funeral, Ray Chapman certainly received one of the finest. After the mass concluded, the procession traveled east to Lake View Cemetery, where a brief service took place inside the chapel. The body was placed in a vault until burial arrangements could be made. Hundreds of floral displays were placed outside the chapel, one actually in the shape of a large baseball diamond. Newspaper photographs showed an enormous number of flowers, probably enough to fill a good-sized home.

Of all the tributes to Chapman, perhaps the best was a simple poem by a Cleveland woman. The *Cleveland News* published the lines written by Andrea Razafreriefo. By today's standards the poem appears to be somewhat silly. But in the context of its time, it really is a heartfelt rendering. The poem read in part:

> *Here is a flower from a fan*
> *To Ray, ballplayer and a man,*
> *Who played the game with all his heart*
> *And never failed to do his part.*
> *Oh, Chapman, though your work was done*
> *Before your team a pennant won,*
> *Your spirit flitted into space*
> *A winner of life's pennant race.*

A very large number of people had waited at Calvary Cemetery, where the burial originally had been planned. At the last moment the site was changed to Lake View Cemetery, which caught these mourners by surprise. No explanation was given for the change of locations. Reading between the lines, Lake View was a nondenominational cemetery, while Calvary happened to be a Catholic one. The Dalys were Catholic, while Chapman was not. The neutral location meant that Ray and Kathleen would not likely ever be buried in the same cemetery. Another unanswered question is why the Chapman family did not take their son back to Illinois. Did the parents of the deceased have any say in this decision? Ultimately, Ray Chapman's final resting place would leave him alone without any family buried near him.

Tris Speaker was born and raised in the small rural community of Hubbard, Texas. His uncles, James and Byron, were soldiers who fought for the Confederacy during the Civil War. While young Tris was growing up, the future leader of the Ku Klux Klan, Hiram Evans, had lived within the narrow confines of Hubbard. Given this environment, it would be difficult for anybody to learn about tolerance for those of different races and religions. When Speaker left home for a career in baseball, he had seen very little of the world outside of Texas.

It is mentioned that when Babe Ruth joined the Red Sox, he and Speaker had their differences. In a 1959 article in *Baseball Digest*, Tom Meany states that Speaker may have thrown some ethnic slurs at the Babe regarding his time at St. Mary's School. Author Robert W. Creamer in his excellent book, *Babe*, alludes to a 1914 argument between Joe Wood and Ruth. The result was Speaker, Wood's best friend, rarely speaking to Babe for many years.

At some point before 10 a.m., Steve O'Neill and Speaker had some strong words about the funeral; the specifics of their argument are unknown. It stands to reason that O'Neill and probably Graney, both Irish Catholics, took great offense at whatever Speaker said, and a physical confrontation seems to have followed. The only eyewitness to the alleged brawl, a young man of sixteen, claimed Speaker won a lopsided decision. However, his story is suspect: O'Neill stood with the pallbearers a short time later and helped carry the coffin inside St. John's. It is unlikely a bruised and battered O'Neill would have allowed himself to appear at the funeral in such a state.

The next day O'Neill went back to Boston with the team and caught as usual. In the first game of the doubleheader, O'Neill was replaced by Chet Thomas after his second at-bat. He did come back to catch all of game 2. The newspapers gave no reason why Thomas got in the game. Jack Graney played all of game 1 in left field, getting one of Cleveland's three hits. Joe Wood, filling in as manager, replaced Graney in the middle of game 2. The newspapers mentioned that the move took place because Jack was not hitting. For either of these players to be benched during a game was unusual. Steve O'Neill was one of the most durable catchers in all of baseball. It made no sense for him to be sitting on the bench when a fight for the pennant was taking place.

Ballplayers in the early days of the twentieth century rarely spoke about anything that occurred off the ball field. In his classic 1960s book *The Glory of Their Times*, author Lawrence Ritter interviewed old-timers such as Joe Wood, Sam Crawford, Davey Jones, Rube Marquard, and Chief Meyers. Most of the old ballplayers, then in their seventies and eighties, still had a sharp memory for the games they played and the incidents that happened on the field.

However, most of the interesting anecdotes and stories do not reveal any deep, dark secrets that may still be buried today. The baseball beat reporters of that time observed a rigid code of silence about off-the-field activities, reporting mostly those things that were too obvious to omit. Fights or arguments in the clubhouse were rarely if ever mentioned. A battle royal between Cleveland players hours before the Chapman funeral would get no space in any of the local papers. The papers did mention that Speaker was overcome with grief and exhaustion, which resulted in a nervous breakdown. This supposedly accounted for his absence at both the funeral and service at the cemetery. As player-manager, he had a tremendous burden on his shoulders, but his absence at Ray Chapman's funeral is very suspect.

Several years later sportswriter Joe Vila reported in his column for the *New York World* that a fight had taken place before the funeral, and O'Neill and Speaker were the participants. Vila reported that O'Neill had clocked Speaker in the eye, which kept him out of the regular lineup for days. Ed Bang of the *Cleveland News* denied the story, claiming Vila was "barking up the wrong tree." Decades later in Mike Sowell's outstanding book, *The Pitch That Killed*, Bill Wamby revealed to the author that the fight did actually happen, but even after some sixty years, the other surviving Indians would not discuss it. Wamby went on to say that Tris had some real problems with tolerance in 1920. A surviving member of the immediate O'Neill family clearly remembers talk of the fight and who won the struggle. A close friend of the O'Neills who lived in Minooka recalled that most of the town knew the details of the fight. Based on this evidence, it is fair to assert that the two men, both with frayed nerves and devastated by the loss of their close friend, did indeed lose their tempers and trade punches before the Chapman funeral. With all that had occurred, a very promising season looked to be headed in the worst possible direction.

13

DOWN THE STRETCH

"The Indians will fight harder than ever. They will not quit because Chapman is gone. They will battle more fiercely than before in memory of their departed colleague." These are the words of Henry Edwards, recorded in his "Comment on Sport" column shortly after the funeral. In the *Cleveland News*, Ed Bang countered with his slogan, "Do It For Chappie." The veteran writers were doing their best to boost the spirits of the forlorn players.

The Cleveland players surely wanted to win, but they had to deal with the effects of a grueling 1,400-mile round trip to Boston within twenty-four hours. The Red Sox management had done them a favor by canceling Friday's game, but the end result meant a doubleheader on Saturday. Even a well-rested team would feel the consequences of living on the rails for such a period. The Indians were completely spent emotionally and physically, losing both games 12–0 and 4–0. The Chicago White Sox now led the standings by ten percentage points over Cleveland, while the Yankees were close behind, trailing the Indians by only a game.

With the recent tragedy hovering over the club, the front office kept busy, trying to find an anchor for the reeling ship. Word came that a new left-handed pitcher would be joining the club in time for the series in Philadelphia. Walter "Duster" Mails had been acquired from Sacramento of the Pacific Coast League in exchange for two seldom-used pitchers and cash. Mails had a brief trial with Brooklyn in 1915 and 1916, pitching a total of twenty-two innings and being credited with two losses. He returned to the minors for the 1917 season, pitching in Portland, Oregon. Mails then enlisted in the army, missing the better part of two seasons. In 1919 he joined the Seattle club but later signed with Sacramento, from whom the Indians purchased his contract.

A native of San Quentin, California, Mails had the distinction of playing with an amateur team that visited the infamous penitentiary for several games with the inmates. He described the prison team as "tolerable" but fairly easy to beat. After finishing high school in 1914, Duster enrolled at St. Mary's College, the same school that produced Boston greats Harry Hooper and Duffy Lewis. In the winter, he worked at a candy factory owned by his brother-in-law Dan Dugdale. (A former major league catcher, Dugdale served as president and manager of Seattle, a member of the Northwestern League.) Mails left school when his relative offered him a chance to play in the Class-B league. By 1915 he had become a star, winning thirteen games in a row and at one point winning both games of a doubleheader. As his notoriety increased, so did his ego. Mails enjoyed staring into the grandstand to admire the pretty girls who gazed in his direction. After one game, he slyly remarked to reporters how much he loved eating chocolate cake. The next afternoon, Duster arrived in the clubhouse where a table full of cakes had been delivered to him. The identities of the bakers went unannounced.

His outstanding play resulted in a contract offer from the Brooklyn Robins, which led him to join the staff late in the 1915 season. According to Mails, he had frequent bouts of wildness. As he told *Baseball Magazine*, "Any batter who faced me then did so at his own risk. I was wild, not from choice, but because I couldn't help myself."

By age twenty-five Mails had overcome his erratic control, enabling him to once again attract the attention of major league scouts. The chance to sign a hard-throwing left-handed pitcher strongly appealed to Jim Dunn, who made the deal just in time for the stretch run of the season. Walter Mails boarded a

train for the coast-to-coast ride to Philadelphia, landing in the midst of a frantic race for the pennant.

On August 27, the Indians steamrolled the Philadelphia Athletics 15–3.
Harry Lunte had his biggest game, collecting three hits and knocking in three
more. The victory, only their fifth in their last seventeen games, showed the
Cleveland players regaining some signs of life. Trouncing the lowly Athletics
did not mean the club was all the way back, but the hustle and sharp play served
as an indicator that they were overcoming the loss of Ray Chapman. Time would
tell, but for the first occasion in nearly two weeks, the Indians sent a message
to Chicago and New York: the race for the pennant had yet to be determined.

The debut of Walter Mails lasted only one long inning. He started against
the Senators but gave up three runs and walked two batters in the opening
frame. Guy Morton took the mound for the second inning and silenced the
Washington batters, allowing only two runs the remainder of the game. The
Indian hitters, led by Larry Gardner's two doubles and a triple, easily overcame
the deficit with a 9–5 win. The road trip ended on a positive note, creating some
optimism after the tragedy in New York.

Jim Dunn took the central role in buoying the spirits of his ballplayers and
fans. Dunn commented for the press, "We have had our slump and are going
along nicely now while the White Sox have just started to go through what we
went through the last two weeks. I am not worrying about my boys. They have
recovered from the disaster that hit them and I expect them to come through
nicely for the Cleveland baseball public during the next few weeks." Dunn knew
his ballplayers would be enjoying a three-week home stand, which could not
have arrived at a better time. If Chicago or New York planned to grab the top
spot, they would have to go through the Indians at League Park to get it.

On September 2, Cleveland hosted the Detroit Tigers. Before the game
started, a brief memorial service was held for Ray Chapman. At 2:50 p.m. a bugler
from the Cleveland Naval Reserves sounded "Colors" while the flag was raised
to full staff and then slowly lowered to half. A total of fifteen thousand fans
stood at attention, hats at their sides. A choir backed by a full orchestra sang
"Lead, Kindly Light," followed by the bugler walking to the shortstop position
and playing "Taps." Everyone in attendance received an eight-page memorial

booklet, which featured the sermon from the funeral and a summary of Chapman's career. Jim Dunn ordered an additional thousand for himself, while Martin Daly ordered two thousand copies, presumably for his employees at the East Ohio Gas Company.

The two teams battled to a scoreless tie through eight innings. In the top of the ninth, Ty Cobb singled off Stan Coveleski to score the game's only run. In spite of the loss, Cleveland held on to first place by the tiniest of margins. Their lead over New York shrunk to three percentage points, with Chicago only two points behind the Yankees. The standings as of September 2:

Cleveland 77–49 (.611)
New York 79–51 (.608)
Chicago 77–50 (.606)

Though they had lost the first game back home, the mood of the team had brightened considerably. The beginning of September traditionally marked the time for gentlemen to discard the straw hats they had worn throughout the summer. Fans at the ballpark ripped their hats to shreds and then flung the remains on the playing field. When Jim Dunn entered the clubhouse, his boys grabbed their boss's expensive hat and tore it to pieces. Normally the Cleveland owner might have been a bit peeved at the players' antics; however, in this situation he had to smile, knowing his team had come full circle.

Several days later the St. Louis Browns came to League Park for a morning-afternoon doubleheader. The twenty-three thousand fans cheered loudly as Walter Mails won his first game as an Indian, going the distance for a 7–2 win. The second game saw the teams fight through eight innings, tied at four apiece going into the top of the ninth. Two singles by the Browns hitters put runners on first and third. At this point, seldom-used relief pitcher Bob Clark made way for Jim Bagby. Before the Indians ace could retire the side, one run had scored, giving St. Louis a 5–4 lead. Charlie Jamieson popped out to start the bottom of the ninth. Manager Speaker decided to make a change, batting Jack Graney for Bill Wamby. The move paid off when Graney drove an opposite field shot to right center and motored all the way to third. The animated Cleveland fans sailed several dozen hats on the field, causing a momentary delay while the hats were removed.

Up to bat came Speaker, who looked at a called strike and then lashed a single to center field to tie the game once more. Elmer Smith walked to the batter's box, having already hit a double and two singles. With the percentages against him, Smith connected on the second pitch, lining the ball to deep right center into the overflow crowd. Speaker circled the bases to score the winning run while hundreds of excited fans climbed out of the grandstand to celebrate. Unfortunately, they had forgotten that Smith's hit reached the overflow on the field, which called for a ground-rule double and for runners to advance only two bases. Speaker trotted back to third as Larry Gardner came to bat. For most of the season, Gardner had delivered in the clutch. This time was no exception as he smashed the ball to deep right center field for the game winner. Now the fans sprinted back on the field, destroying more straw hats and dancing about the infield. Some even turned handsprings, celebrating the dramatic ninth-inning rally. With slightly more than three weeks left in the season, Cleveland baseball fans were ready to tear down the ballpark should the home team win it all.

After a day off, the Indians readied themselves for a must-win series with the New York Yankees. The three scheduled games were vital to both teams' pennant hopes. At this time, Cleveland led New York by only eight percentage points. A sweep by either team would create some distance between the two, giving the victor the inside track. The Yankees arrived in town, leaving Carl Mays back home in New York. Co-owner Tillinghast Huston told reporters, "We are not taking Mays to Cleveland, not because we think there is danger of any trouble but out of respect to the feelings of the people there. We don't want to offend them." Nobody could predict what might have happened if Mays stepped out of the dugout and onto the field. Huston made a wise decision not to risk a potential ugly scene.

The same morning a very nervous twenty-one-year-old shortstop stepped off a train in downtown Cleveland, ready to join the big league club. Joe Sewell had been signed right off the campus of the University of Alabama and then sent to New Orleans for the 1920 season. When Ray Chapman went down, there was some talk of bringing up the college star, but Harry Lunte began to show progress at shortstop. After a few weeks, however, Lunte pulled a muscle in his leg, forcing Joe Evans to take over at short. Evans had been playing outfield all season, plus his best position in the infield was third base. Although Dr. Joe filled in admirably, his presence there had to be a stopgap measure. The Indians sent a scout to New Orleans to watch Sewell for a few days. He sent a good report to the front office, and Sewell, who was having a strong season for the Pelicans, was rushed to the Indians.

Joseph Wheeler Sewell grew up in the tiny farm community of Titus, Alabama, located in the southeastern part of the state. The population of Titus stood at approximately 100 residents, too small to be incorporated as a town or village. The farms had two basic crops to raise, cotton and corn. Joe's father, a country doctor, made the rounds of Elmore County on horse and buggy, later switching to a Ford Model T. Younger brothers Luke and Tommy were outstanding athletes in their own right. Luke would later join Cleveland as a catcher for many years, while Tommy had a brief trial with the Chicago White Sox.

After high school Sewell enrolled at the University of Alabama, intent on following the family tradition of studying medicine, but he got sidetracked playing varsity football and baseball, where he established himself as one of the Crimson Tide's better athletes. At 5'6" and weighing in the neighborhood of 150 pounds, Joe compensated for his lack of football size with speed, willpower, and a strong upper body. During Sewell's enrollment at Alabama, the school became a hotbed for professional baseball players and a talent pool for the Cleveland Indians. Catcher William Styles played briefly for Philadelphia and Cincinnati, and infielder Frank Pratt went to the Chicago White Sox. Riggs Stephenson, like Sewell a lifetime .300 hitter, would have an outstanding career, joining the Indians in 1921 and resurfacing later with the Chicago Cubs. Sewell's brother Luke enrolled in college two years after Joe but quickly caught the attention of Cleveland scouts, joining the Indians late in the 1921 season.

When Joe got the call to report to Cleveland, he had made few trips north of Alabama and had strong misgivings about settling in a city he knew nothing about, especially a big northern city where a fair amount of culture shock awaited him. He doubted his ability to jump to the major leagues, where the competition was much more intense than he had ever seen, let alone replace the great Ray Chapman on a team fighting for the pennant. Reluctantly, he boarded a train for Cleveland.

The New York Yankees arrived in Cleveland with much fanfare. The band from St. Mary's Industrial School, Babe Ruth's alma mater, traveled from Baltimore to perform each afternoon at the ballpark. The fifty boys ranged in age from six to sixteen. Each evening they were scheduled to appear at Grays Armory downtown to give a concert. During the show the Babe would join the band onstage to give a talk about his former school. The Orpheum Theatre advertised a showing of *Over the Fence*, a recent drama starring the renowned Hollywood actor Harold Lloyd. The ad touted the film as the "Greatest Swat Picture" ever made featuring the king of batters. The Cleveland fans had to hope that most of Ruth's swatting would be on screen.

Shortly after the Yankees were settled in Cleveland, a bizarre story circulated that a terrible auto accident had taken the lives of Babe Ruth, Bob Meusel, Del Pratt, and Duffy Lewis. The wild tale had been sent by telegraph to various brokerage houses in New York and the other AL cities. Cleveland police immediately got involved, tracing the wire to a nonexistent brokerage firm in the city. The actual wire read, "Meusel and Pratt, members of the New York American baseball team were killed in an automobile accident near here, (Cleveland). Babe Ruth who was also in the automobile had a leg and shoulder broken and three ribs crushed, and Lewis was badly injured." The police theorized that gamblers were behind the stunt, attempting to influence bettors to put their money on Cleveland to win. Fans in Cleveland and New York raced to the newspaper offices to get verification on the story. The culprits behind the scam were never found, but for several hours they caused a near panic within the baseball world.

Almost as an afterthought the two teams met on September 9 to open the series. The Indians worked over the Yankee pitchers for a 10–4 win. In the bottom of the eighth, behind timely hitting from George Burns and Larry Gardner, Cleveland scored four times to put the game away. Stan Coveleski allowed a homer by Ruth but otherwise pitched with just enough effectiveness to get the victory. The local fans were on their best behavior, giving a loud round of applause when Cleveland resident Roger Peckinpaugh came to bat in the first inning. When Ruth homered, the fans cheered once again as they usually did when the Babe put one in orbit. With the victory, the Indians now led Chicago by one full game, New York by a game and a half.

The next day, Yankees pitcher Bob Shawkey held the Indians to six hits in a 6–1 win. Once again Babe Ruth homered over the right-field wall, giving his team a two-run lead that Shawkey held for the rest of the game. The only run for the home team came in the seventh inning when Elmer Smith tripled and Doc Johnston doubled him home. The game marked the debut of shortstop Joe Sewell, who replaced Joe Evans in the top of the fifth inning. In two at-bats, he fouled out and grounded to first baseman Wally Pipp. One inning later Sewell uncorked a wild throw to first while attempting to complete a double play. He would later say that all the white shirts in the grandstand behind first base distracted his view of Doc Johnston. He may have had a valid point, as the stands were filled with twenty-three thousand spectators, causing a whiteout for anyone looking toward either baseline. The more experienced shortstops like Peckinpaugh had no problem finding their target to throw to, but Sewell had never played before a crowd so large. It is understandable that a rookie thrown into a pressure situation might get distracted and throw the ball away. Joe had a few more wild throws in him before he would settle down.

The final game between the two clubs brought a record crowd estimated at between thirty and thirty-two thousand eager fans. With Jim Bagby pitching against a very mediocre Hank Thormahlen, the edge went to Cleveland. However, at times the underdog comes through, and in this instance Thormahlen stopped the Indians with only seven scattered base hits. The Yankees knocked Bagby around, forcing him to the dugout with nobody out in the sixth inning. The visitors won the deciding game 6–2 to put them virtually even with the league leaders. The series presented Cleveland with an opportunity to take total command of first place. Instead, they inexplicitly failed to accomplish their goal; they actually let the race tighten considerably. Only a loss by the White Sox kept them in first place by one percentage point. Now with three weeks remaining in the season, the race was wide open between the three teams.

With the Yankees leaving town, Cleveland needed a break in the schedule. They got one in the form of the lowly Philadelphia Athletics, who were on their way to forty-eight wins for the season. The Indians took three out of four, winning the series finale 14–0. Before the last game, Connie Mack told interested reporters, "I showed you two pretty fair pitchers in [Rollie] Naylor and [Eddie] Rommel. I'll show you another just as good today. Just keep your eyes on Keefe." The writers had trouble watching Dave Keefe, as he lasted two innings and then left for the clubhouse, giving up five runs and eight hits. For the next six innings, Mack used a relief pitcher who held the Indians to nine runs and fourteen more hits. Larry Gardner had a double and a home run, while Tris Speaker banged out a double and three singles.

James Lanyon of the *Plain Dealer* expressed his frustration with the Cleveland fans, who were not satisfied with winning three out of four from the AL cellar dwellers. Apparently there were a number of frontrunners in the stands who were critical after the Indians lost the third game of the series. In his editorial, Lanyon urged everybody to "Put the muffler on the old 'Take 'im out' yapping, the 'Put in a pinch hitter' clamor and 'We ain't got a chance' chat." Lanyon went on to say, "Go out today and tomorrow and the next day and the next and pull for the Cleveland club. Don't quit 'em cold." Nobody quit the following day when Walter Mails threw a four-hit shutout, beating Washington 1–0. The only run of the game took place in the eighth inning when Joe Sewell singled with two out. Steve O'Neill lined a double to the left-field corner that looked like the game winner. However, the Senators' third baseman decoyed Sewell by crouching next to the bag and reaching for a nonexistent throw. Joe took the bait, sliding hard into third, only to realize he had been fooled. Before he could scramble to his feet, the throw came in to the plate, forcing the mortified rookie to stay put. While the fans shook their heads in disbelief, they soon cheered when pitcher Tom Zachary uncorked a wild pitch, allowing Sewell to jog home with the go-ahead run. Mails set Washington down in the top of the ninth, and with the victory the Indians moved back into first place. Chicago beat New York 8–3, sending Cleveland to the top spot by three big percentage points. With a little more than two weeks left in the season, the standings showed:

Cleveland 86–52 (.623)
New York 88–54 (.620)
Chicago 86–55 (.610)

On September 17, Cleveland scored nine runs against two Washington pitchers, winning by a wide margin of 9–3. Bill Wamby homered; Joe Evans had three hits while Stan Coveleski helped his own cause with a double and a triple. The White Sox trimmed the Yankees again, allowing the Indians' lead to expand to one full game. Cleveland had now won five of their last six games, but the tense battle for first place continued without any breathing room. None of the three teams displayed any signs of fading yet, which meant the race was destined to continue into October.

The Indians' front office had spent several weeks sorting through ticket requests for the World Series. They carefully organized the thousands of applications that would have required double the seating capacity of League Park. Many of the requests came from out of town, but Dunn and company announced that those living outside of Cleveland who had attended games throughout the year would get the same consideration as the local fans. Plans called for the allotment of tickets to begin the last week of September. The only other step to take was for the Indians to win it all and validate the tickets.

The balance of power shifted within the next week, as the Yankees began to drop back in the standings while the White Sox kept pace with Cleveland. The Chicago club was playing great ball in September, making a run for another World Series appearance. They were building momentum for the decisive trip to Cleveland, which would begin on the 23rd. The three-game matchup could conceivably determine who had the upper hand for the postseason. Both teams were tied at ninety-one victories apiece, while Cleveland had fifty-two losses and Chicago fifty-five. A sweep by either team would put the other in dire straits. The Indians warmed up for the pending series by taking three straight from the Boston Red Sox by a combined score of 22–4. Jim Bagby won his twenty-ninth game of the season, shutting out the Sox in game 1, 2–0. The hitting of Smith, Gardner, and Speaker powered Cleveland to wins in games 2 and 3. The fans hoped the players had not spent themselves in the thrashing given to Boston.

While the Indians prepared for the most important series of the year, a major story broke out of Chicago that the 1919 World Series was not on the square. A grand jury in Cook County had evidence that at least seven White Sox players had thrown the series. Ban Johnson acknowledged that he had proof that games were tainted. He appeared before the court to testify along with Chicago owner Charles Comiskey. Subpoenas were issued for a host of people, from ballplayers to league officials. The timing of the announcement, on the eve of the Cleveland-Chicago series, could not have been worse. If there were guilty players on the White Sox team, they had to be looking over the shoulders for fear of an indictment or a man in a suit with a subpoena.

The opening game had Jim Bagby seeking his thirtieth win of the year against Dickie Kerr, who was having a fine season himself. Going into the top of the sixth inning, both pitchers were in control, holding each team to one run. To the disbelief of the Cleveland fans, Chicago unloaded on Bagby over the next two innings, scoring four times to take a 5–1 lead. Joe Jackson, Happy Felsch, and Ray Schalk did most of the damage, finishing with nine hits between them. The final score stood at 10–3 for the White Sox. If any of the visiting team had worries about the investigation back home, they certainly did not show it on the playing field. The attendance for the game totaled twenty-four thousand, most of who expected Bagby to breeze to another win. Now the gap between the two teams closed to just a half game.

The pitching assignment for game 2 featured Walter Mails versus Urban "Red" Faber. Manager Speaker had several options in this situation, but he chose his newly acquired pitcher to face the powerful White Sox hitters. In the bottom of the first, Charlie Jamieson led off with an infield single. Bill Wamby laid down a perfect bunt, advancing Jamieson to second. Tris Speaker bounced out, but Elmer Smith singled to center, scoring the game's first run. One inning later Joe Sewell singled and stole second. That brought Steve O'Neill to bat, and he responded with a base hit to score run number two. Walter Mails pitched the game of his life, holding Chicago to only three singles and throwing his second shutout of the month.

In the top of the fifth inning, he put on a tremendous display of pitching, getting himself out of a bases-loaded jam with only one out. Mails started the inning striking out Swede Risberg. He then walked catcher Ray Schalk and pitcher Red Faber in succession. He continued the wildness, throwing two straight balls to Amos Strunk. The lack of strikes caused Speaker to call time and jog to the mound for a chat with Mails. It proved to be an animated discussion, with Speaker waving both arms while he talked. Three Cleveland pitchers started warming up in the bullpen, putting the fans in a most fearful state. The meeting on the mound did not help matters, as Mails threw two more balls to load the bases. Buck Weaver dug in at the plate, watching the first pitch go wide of the strike zone.

While the fans roared, Mails put one over the plate to even the count. Weaver swung at the next offering, fouling it off to the third-base side. With the count at one ball and two strikes, Mails delivered a scorching fastball that Weaver swung at and missed. That brought the very dangerous Eddie Collins to the batter's box, looking for a pitch he could drive to the outfield. With the count at two balls and two strikes, Collins bashed the next pitch down the left-field line. It barely curved foul, dropping into the overflow crowd standing behind the line. Silence descended over the field as Mails wound up once more. He threw another fastball on the inside corner, which Collins flailed at for strike three. A tremendous wall of noise came from the twenty-four thousand fans in the park. Ladies jumped up and down on their seats while the men tossed their hats high in the air and slapped one another on the back. There were still four more innings to play, but Mails bore down and blanked the White Sox the rest of the game, displaying remarkable poise throughout the afternoon. The outstanding performance earned Mails a fancy new suit of clothes from B. R. Baker men's clothing store. Before the game started, the store manager approached Mails, offering him the pick of the best suits available if he won the ball game. The next morning the winning pitcher stood outside the stylish men's store, waiting for the doors to open.

The final game of the series proved to be a disappointment as Lefty Williams, one of the alleged conspirators, stopped Cleveland on just five hits. The White Sox scored five runs to easily win the rubber game, 5–1. They left town trailing the leader by just one half game. The Indians still had eight games to play, all of them on the road, while Chicago had only five left, with two of them at Comiskey Park. The standings:

Cleveland 92–54 (.630)
Chicago 93–56 (.624)
New York 91–59 (.607)

While the Indians and the White Sox scuffled for league honors, Cleveland mayor William Fitzgerald paid Jim Dunn a visit at team headquarters. The mayor had some concerns regarding betting pools and ticket scalping in the area around League Park. He wanted to make certain the illegal activities would be brought under control by the time of the World Series. The mayor did not issue an order to the chief of police but wanted detectives and police officers to step up their efforts to shut down the gamblers and scalpers. The cleanup initiative came at the same time as the allegations concerning the 1919 World Series. Whether the mayor acted on his own initiative or had orders from above is not certain. At any rate he urged the police force to crack down on the ticket scalpers and gambling houses. Within a day three men were arrested for attempting to make a profit from their baseball tickets. One was busted for selling an extra ticket at forty cents above face value, while another got nabbed at the Hotel Winton when he sold a one-dollar ticket for six dollars. This got the attention of the Internal Revenue Service (IRS), who stationed field operatives around League Park to gather evidence. The current law stated that any baseball or theater tickets sold above cost were subject to a 50 percent tax, and if they went unreported, the seller was eligible for a fine of $10,000 or one year in prison. Surely the man who made forty cents did not have to worry about prison, but a message to the hard-core scalpers rang loud and clear. The Cleveland director of the IRS, Harry Weiss, warned the offenders, "We are determined to break up ticket scalping and we shall be especially vigilant from now on, particularly if part of the World Series should be played in Cleveland." As for the gambling houses, the chief of police indicated that most of his men were well known to the crooks. On many occasions a lookout would spot the officers approaching the houses and send out an alarm, and everybody scattered. The chief related that he might assign new officers unfamiliar to the gamblers in an effort to shut down the known houses. All this activity indicated something big was about to come down from the grand jury in Chicago.

The Indians arrived in St. Louis, clinging to their half-game lead. They got off to a poor start, spotting the Browns a 5–3 lead. Today's hero would be Joe Sewell, who knocked in four runs, including a bases-loaded double in the third to put Cleveland in front. Relief pitcher George Uhle singled home a run in the seventh and then yielded to Stan Coveleski, who finished the game. Uhle pitched seven strong innings, holding St. Louis scoreless while his team charged ahead. The final score: Cleveland 7, St. Louis 5. Chicago kept on winning, trouncing Detroit 8–1.

The following day saw no change in the standings. Walter Mails won his sixth game in a row, beating the Browns 8–4. Charlie Jamieson launched a three-run homer in the top of the eighth inning to put the game out of reach. Each day a different player stepped up to lead the Indians. For most seasons the trio of Speaker, Smith, and Gardner carried the team each time out. Now Joe Sewell, Charlie Jamieson, Steve O'Neill, and Joe Evans were coming through with the timely hits. On the mound, Walter Mails made an immediate impact while George Uhle proved to be very effective in relief. This was a team effort in every sense of the word.

With six games remaining on the schedule, Jim Dunn decided to take a calculated risk by signing off on a project to add six thousand more seats to League Park. The plan called for two thousand seats to be built in the right-field area while an additional four thousand would be raised outside, just above the right-field wall. To accomplish the job, men were hired to work double shifts until the stands were completed. Dunn estimated he had about a week before the series to get the work finished. If progress proved to be slow, he would get the two thousand seats completed and forget about the larger addition.

On September 28, Jim Bagby won his thirtieth game of the season, staggering to a 9–5 win. His pitching was not up to par, but his two doubles in four trips helped the Indians win three straight against St. Louis. Joe Evans added three hits and two runs batted in while scoring twice. Evans had a number of friends in the stands who knew him from medical school at the local Washington University. In just a few weeks, he was headed back to St. Louis to begin his practice. His patients would have to wait a while longer to see the doctor.

That same day, seven members of the Chicago White Sox were indicted for allegedly fixing the 1919 World Series. Charles Comiskey immediately suspended all seven players, including Joe Jackson, Happy Felsch, Buck Weaver, Eddie Cicotte, Lefty Williams, Swede Risberg, and Fred McMullin. Chick

Gandil, the alleged ringleader, was no longer in the major leagues, as he stayed home in California due to a salary dispute. This action effectively destroyed the club's chances of overtaking the Indians. Chicago lost four starters in the field and two pitchers who had each won twenty games. Joe Jackson had put up spectacular numbers for the season, batting. 382 with 12 home runs and 121 runs batted in. He had over 200 hits, as did Buck Weaver. Center fielder Happy Felsch was hitting.338 with 14 homers and 115 RBIs. Losing these players from the lineup left the White Sox climbing a steep mountain without any rope.

The timing of the suspensions leads one to speculate on what might have happened if the Chicago players had not been indicted. They were playing superb baseball, keeping pace with Cleveland all through September. Their abrupt withdrawal from the game with one week left in the season eased the way for the Indians to triumph. However, the Indians were playing their most inspired ball of the season. They had overcome the death of Ray Chapman to play exceptionally game after game. They came from behind numerous times, got clutch pitching from Walter Mails, and did everything necessary to win. Tris Speaker had done an excellent job of keeping the team together, not to mention his fine season at the plate. The Cleveland players were hungry for a pennant, many playing their career best to accomplish their goal. They had no quit in them, playing hard each and every game. Even if the White Sox had not been shattered by the grand jury indictments, the Indians had showed no signs of letting up on the accelerator.

The Indians completed their four-game sweep of St. Louis, clobbering the Browns 10–2. An early fall chill kept attendance below a thousand fans. However, the dropping temperatures had little effect on the Cleveland batters, who collected twelve hits. Joe Wood rapped out three hits and drove in two runs. Steve O'Neill added three more hits, while Stan Coveleski scattered eight hits over nine innings. The White Sox were idle, allowing the Indians to add a half game to their lead. With four more days left in the season the standings were:

Cleveland 96–54 (.640)
Chicago 95–56 (.629)
New York 95–59 (.617)

The Yankees were finished in every sense of the word. They had no games left on the schedule and could not claim the pennant even if Cleveland lost all four remaining games. Chicago still had a slim chance to reach first place, but with a patched-together lineup, their outlook appeared quite dismal. The time to uncork the champagne had not arrived yet for the Indians, but the bottles were being chilled in great anticipation.

The hometown heroes left St. Louis bound for the city of Detroit, where the final series of the year would be played. On October 1, the two clubs squared off for a doubleheader. In game 1, Cleveland jumped out to a 4–0 lead behind Walter Mails. The lefty mowed down the Tigers for seven innings, holding Ty Cobb and his teammates in check. Things got dicey in the bottom of the eighth inning when two Detroit hitters singled with one out. Donie Bush tapped a roller to Larry Gardner, who uncharacteristically fumbled the ball to load the bases. That brought up Ty Cobb, who lashed a double to left field. Two runs scored on the hit, and then Bobby Veach lined a shot toward Charlie Jamieson. The usually sure-handed left fielder came in on the run and grabbed the ball but could not hold on, allowing Bush to score from third. Harry Heilmann singled to center, scoring Cobb with the tying run. The game went to extra innings, where the Tigers won it 5–4 on a two-base error by Joe Sewell and a single from Babe Pinelli. Credit Detroit with a fine comeback, but crucial errors by Gardner and Jamieson opened the door.

In the second game the Indians took no chances, scoring in eight of the nine innings for a 10–3 win. Ray Caldwell stepped up and pitched a pretty fair game, not allowing any runs after the sixth inning. Chicago had lost, giving Cleveland a two-game lead with two more games to play. The Detroit fans cheered for the visitors throughout both games, no doubt expressing their opinion about what had occurred in Chicago just days before. For the good of the American League, few fans wanted to see the White Sox back in the World Series. The guilty had been suspended; however, a stigma remained on the ball club, even on those who had nothing to do with the scandal.

On October 2, twenty long years of waiting ended when Jim Bagby won his thirty-first game, leading the Cleveland Indians to their first-ever pennant, 10–1. They would play Brooklyn in the World Series. Bagby completed a spectacular season, leading the American League in wins, games pitched, complete games, innings pitched, and winning percentage. He dominated the league from Opening Day to the end of the season. He pitched at times with two days' rest, came on in relief when needed, and did not miss a turn. His performance in 1920 ranks as one of the greatest in the history of Cleveland baseball. Of all the players in the ball club, one can point to him as the most valuable player. Almost overlooked were his contributions as a hitter: he finished the year with a batting average of .258, a home run, and thirty-three hits. While holding the Tigers to one run during the pennant clincher, Bagby managed to belt a triple and score a run. Whenever he pitched, the Indians had nine hitters in the lineup.

During the locker room celebration, Jim Dunn sent a telegram to Tris Speaker. It read: "My sincere congratulations to you and all members of the Cleveland ball team. I am sharpening the tomahawks and I am sure we will scalp the Dodgers. You fought fairly and squarely and deserve the championship." The players certainly deserved the pennant, but so did their owner. He spent thousands of dollars to put the right team in the field. He made astute deals by trading for Gardner and Jamieson, and then shelling out the money for Caldwell, Burns, and Mails. He got lucky with Joe Wood and gave one of his scouts the green light to sign Joe Sewell when the Indians had little need for a shortstop. Dunn made all the right moves, resulting in a glorious pennant for the city of Cleveland. The long, frustrating wait was over; Sunny Jim had fulfilled his pledge.

14

BRING ON BROOKLYN

Before the Indians clinched the pennant, Jim Dunn petitioned the National Commission to open the World Series in Brooklyn. Dunn needed several more days for his bleacher project to be completed. The commission met in Chicago to discuss the situation and to decide on umpires and official scorers for the postseason. After some deliberation, it was decided that the best-of-nine series would start at Ebbets Field, with games on October 5, 6, and 7. October 8 was designated as a travel day for both teams. The series resumed on October 9 in Cleveland, where four games would be played on successive days. If games 8 and 9 were needed, the two ball clubs would travel back to Brooklyn to play on October 14 and 15. For the second straight year, league officials decided to play the nine games instead of seven. The extended play allowed more fans the opportunity to experience a World Series. More fans equaled more revenue, making everybody happy. With the schedule complete, the commission selected the umpires. Chosen were Bill Klem and Hank O'Day from the National League and Bill Dinneen and Tommy Connolly from the American League. The commission designated J. G. Taylor Spink of *The Sporting News* to be one official scorer, along with Joe McCready, the current secretary of the Baseball Writers

Association of America (BBWAA). The remaining two scorers would be picked by the local chapters of the BBWAA in Cleveland and Brooklyn.

Another important issue was the eligibility of shortstop Joe Sewell. The laws of the National Commission stated that for a player to appear in a World Series, he must be on the team roster by August 30. Dunn telegraphed Charles Ebbets asking for permission to add Sewell to the player list. Ebbets wired back his approval, allowing the Indians to keep their lineup intact. Now, with less than a month's experience in the major leagues, the young man from Alabama would be asked to man the shortstop position in front of capacity crowds every game.

When the Indians locked up first place, the front office announced elaborate plans for the ticket distribution, designed to keep scalpers from getting their hands on tickets and gouging fans who were shut out at the box office. A total of 16,624 tickets per game were set aside for those who had mailed in their applications before the deadline of September 21. Each successful purchaser would receive eight tickets, two each for the four games to be played at League Park. No fan could receive more than the eight-ticket allotment or any number of tickets less than eight. The office announced that nine thousand general admission tickets would be sold at the gates each day of the series on a first come, first served basis. The number of available tickets for each game totaled 25,624. Fans mailed in forty thousand applications, and an additional five thousand after the deadline. The team could only fill about 20 percent of all the mail requests.

The method for obtaining the reserved seats proved to be quite efficient. Each of the lucky applicants received an identification card in the mail with a serial number and space for the fan's name and address. A specific time for the applicant to visit the ticket office appeared on the card. When the fan arrived at one of the eight ticket windows, the card would be compared to the original application to verify that the serial number, signatures, and addresses matched. If all seemed to be in order, the tickets had to be paid for in full on the spot. Only cash or certified checks would be accepted. The allotment of 1,987 field boxes went for a price of $52.80 each, including the war tax still in effect. Prices varied depending on where your reserved seats were located—either in the

upper or lower stands or down the foul lines. This system did not block scalping completely, but it promised to curtail the activity as much as possible. All
applications were thoroughly examined, and any that looked suspicious were
tossed out. Any request on hotel stationary was rejected, as well as any that had
a typewritten signature. Each application had to be checked by four different
workers before it could be approved. This measure was put in place to avoid
overlooking anyone who bought tickets on a regular basis or had a prominent
name. The Cleveland postal workers were of great assistance, delivering identification cards only if they were addressed to a person they knew lived at the
corresponding address. As a result, a number of cards were returned to the front
office to be canceled. More applications were then pulled by the staff and sent
to people who had lost out in the first allotment. The front office really did its
homework, trying to make certain that legitimate ticket buyers would be the
ones who filled the grandstands beginning October 9.

At midnight on October 3, the Indians returned home from Detroit to a
large welcoming committee at Union Station. The fans were courteous, allowing the tired ballplayers to get to their rooms for a good night's sleep. Tris
Speaker went directly to the Hollenden Hotel to meet with owner Dunn in his
suite of rooms. The two discussed plans for the series, just forty-eight hours
away. They now had to concentrate their efforts on a ball club they had seen very
little, if anything, of during the season. Speaker had to decide on his pitching
rotation and on who would play in the outfield, and think through what little
he knew about the Brooklyn pitchers and hitters.

The NL champs were no stranger to World Series play. They had won the
pennant in 1916, facing off against the Boston Red Sox. However, they managed
to win only one game, the victim of some outstanding pitching by Ernie Shore,
Dutch Leonard, and a very young Babe Ruth. Coincidentally, Larry Gardner had
hit the three-run homer in game 4 that gave the Red Sox the lead in a 6–2 win.
The Brooklyn club of 1920 had some veterans left over from 1916, along with
some new talent that had pulled away from Cincinnati in the final month of
the season. They were led by manager Wilbert Robinson, who began his major
league career back in 1886 with Philadelphia. As a catcher, Robinson played regularly for seventeen seasons. Much of his time was spent with the Baltimore

Orioles, one of the roughest ball clubs of the National League. Robinson's teammates included John McGraw, Willie Keeler, Hughie Jennings, and a host of
others who outplayed and intimidated the rest of the league. The Orioles set the
standard for dirty play by tripping opposing base runners as they sped by or
grabbing their belts, and they fought with anybody and everybody. Their reign
of terror lasted through most of the 1890s. When his playing days were over
Robinson became the pitching coach for the New York Giants but left in 1914
to manage Brooklyn. Now in his sixth season, "Uncle Robbie" had led his ball
club to its second World Series appearance.

The players managed by Robinson were a solid if not spectacular bunch.
The pitching staff had a twenty-three-game winner in Burleigh Grimes. A master of the spitball, Grimes led the National League in winning percentage while
placing third in strikeouts, wins, and ERA. Edward "Jeff" Pfeffer was in his
eighth season as a starter for Brooklyn. The 6'3" right-hander won twenty-three
games in 1914 and twenty-five more in 1916. The remainder of the staff featured Leon Cadore, a fifteen-game winner; Al Mamaux; Sherry Smith; and
favorite son Richard "Rube" Marquard. Cleveland baseball fans were quite familiar with Rube, as he had spent his formative years in their city.

Back in 1906, several well-respected Clevelanders had pounded on Charlie
Somers's door, urging him to take a look at a tall left-handed pitcher. Marquard
had been attracting notice in the amateur leagues, prompting the locals to barge
in on Somers and urge him to sign Rube. The owner refused to do anything,
which became a major misstep by the Naps organization. The following year,
Rube had a great season pitching for nearby Canton, causing another parade to
Somers's door. This time Larry Lajoie journeyed south of the city limits to watch
Marquard throw. When he returned to Cleveland he advised Somers that he did
not like the way Rube fielded his position. Many years later the left-hander would
claim that Somers had asked to see him at the owner's League Park office just
months after Lajoie's scouting report. According to Rube, Somers and his partner, John Kilfoyl, then made an ill-advised lowball attempt, offering Marquard
the same salary he was earning working for Tellings Ice Cream. Marquard refused
the token offer and then signed with Indianapolis. He had a great season there
in 1908, which sent him on his way east to McGraw and the New York Giants.

The Naps had made a colossal error in not signing Rube when they had no competition. Twelve years later, the local boy still pitched in the majors, eventually racking up two hundred wins and three twenty-game seasons.

The only Cleveland player with real knowledge of the Brooklyn pitchers was third baseman Larry Gardner. While a member of the Red Sox, he had faced Smith, Marquard, and Pfeffer in the 1916 World Series. Gardner powered two home runs, the second a three-run blast to deep center field off Marquard. Both Speaker and Gardner batted against Marquard in the 1912 World Series, when the left-hander pitched for the New York Giants. Doc Johnston had probably seen the Brooklyn pitchers while a member of the Pittsburgh Pirates in 1915 and 1916. The rest of the Indians would be facing these pitchers for the first time. Gardner remained confident, telling reporters, "I've batted against most of the Brooklyn hurlers and I'd back our four first stringers against their much boasted seven any time we meet them in a series."

The Brooklyn infield did not match up well with their counterparts in Cleveland, but the players had experience, some speed, and power. At first base, the veteran Ed Konetchy had the big bat; however, at age thirty-five he was a liability running the bases. The Robins were the fifth team in Big Ed's career, following stops in St. Louis, Pittsburgh, and Boston, all in the National League. In between his NL years, Konetchy jumped to the Federal League in 1915, where he recorded a career high of ten home runs. In 1919 he joined the Robins, where he batted a respectable .298.

Pete Kilduff handled second base. He entered the National League in 1917 with New York, moved to the Chicago Cubs, and then came to Brooklyn during the 1919 season. He became a starter in 1920, playing in 140 games. Shortstop Ivy Olson began his career with none other than the Cleveland Naps in 1911. Two years later Olson lost his job to Ray Chapman but played a number of games at third base and a few at first. Olson had troubles with Naps manager Joe Birmingham, which resulted in his release after the 1914 season. The newspapers called him a "scrappy" ballplayer, doing anything he could to help his team win. He became the regular shortstop for the Robins in 1916.

At third base was Jimmy Johnston, the younger brother of Doc. The local and national newspapers would feature photos and stories about the two brothers competing against each other for the first time in a World Series. A smaller version of his older brother, Jimmy could hit and had speed on the bases. He originally started in the outfield but found a home at third base with the Robins. With a strong arm and good fielding skills, the younger of the Johnston boys won a starting job in the 1917 season. *Baseball Magazine* noted that the Brooklyn infield, while not a well-oiled machine, was a competent outfit that fought hard.

The biggest deficiency in the National League champs was to be found behind the plate. Otto Miller had been in the club since 1910. After a couple of seasons on the bench, Miller joined the regulars, catching the majority of the games. He had no power and only adequate skills as a catcher. For the 1920 season, Otto had nine doubles, two triples, and no home runs in 301 at-bats. By comparison, Steve O'Neill rang up huge numbers, with thirty-nine doubles, five triples, and three home runs. At catcher, the Indians had a decided advantage.

The Brooklyn outfield, with stars Zack Wheat and Hy Myers, compared favorably with any other club in the National League. Both players could do it all: hit with power, play great defense, and run the bases with great skill. Ironically, Cleveland had a chance to buy Wheat during spring training of 1909. That year the Naps trained in Mobile, Alabama, where they heard about an outfield prospect on the local squad. A Cleveland scout watched Zack for several days, concluding he would not be able to hit major league pitching. Brooklyn saw things differently, signing Wheat that same year. By 1910 he became a starter, enjoying one outstanding season after another. For the current championship season, he had batted .328 with 191 hits.

Although Henry "Hy" Myers, the Robins center fielder, had no connections to Cleveland, his birthplace happened to be in East Liverpool, Ohio. At the age of twenty, Myers played briefly for Brooklyn in 1909 but spent the better part of the next three years in the minors, putting in only a brief appearance with the Robins in 1911 before being demoted to Mobile in the Southern League. An injury to one of the Robins outfielders in 1914 prompted manager Wilbert Robinson to give Myers another chance. This time he took advantage of his opportunity, winning the outfield job for years to come. In 1920 he had a career season, leading both leagues in triples with 22. An excellent defensive player,

Myers could cover a lot of ground in the outfield, and he had a strong, accurate throwing arm.

The weather forecast for October 5 called for fair skies with moderate winds. All else had been taken care of: the playing field was in great shape, all seats at Ebbets Field were sold, and approximately four hundred reporters had arrived. As of Monday, the only thing missing was a team to play the Robins. For some unknown reason, manager Speaker had scheduled his team to arrive in Brooklyn on Tuesday, just hours before game time. The Indians would not have a workout the day before the opener, as was the custom for a team unfamiliar with the opponent's field. The *Cleveland News* reported that Speaker had actually held a secret workout on Monday morning. The players spent several hours practicing bunting and defending against double steals. The outfielders put in time throwing to the bases and home plate. On the long ride to New York, the players would discuss strategy and pool any information they had on the Brooklyn team. Speaker took a new approach, the first manager to do so in World Series history.

During the overnight trip, Doc Johnston led the boys in a rendition of "Dear Old Girl." It was the first time the team had done any singing since Ray Chapman passed away. The song was a favorite of the late shortstop, who usually took the lead on the vocals. As Jim Bagby remarked, "The tightness that has gripped our muscles and nerves and minds for weeks is all gone now. We are feeling easy again." The Indians were ready to play ball.

While marking time in the press headquarters, a group of writers made their predictions as to who would be the hero of the postseason. Many chose Tris Speaker. Some votes went to Burleigh Grimes, Stan Coveleski, and Hy Myers. Henry Edwards believed Steve O'Neill would be the player to capture top honors. However, the longtime reporter thought that another player might be the one to lead the Indians to victory. Edwards wrote, "And do not be surprised if Elmer Smith covers himself with glory. He is not given to worrying except when he fails to get his hits and that has been decidedly infrequent this season. I positively believe he will take down as good a reputation as any player." Edwards did not have a crystal ball or read palms, but his prediction would be right on the money when the teams returned to Cleveland.

The *Plain Dealer* went overboard lining up celebrities and sports figures to cover the games for them. Damon Runyon, one of the country's outstanding sportswriters, would give his unique analysis of each game. Billy Evans, the umpire and syndicated columnist, had been signed to contribute, along with Brooklyn outfielder Zack Wheat. Between Henry Edwards's slightly biased stories and the commentary of a player from the rival team, one could now expect some balanced coverage. In addition the newspaper announced that the sports page would include the best stories from the Associated Press and Universal Service as part of the coverage. Readers would also be seeing the best work of selected news photographers, including local staffer Andy Kraffert. Known for stalking the League Park foul lines in his long black coat, smoking a cigar, Kraffert had the skills and technique to catch ballplayers in action. Given the limitations of the available camera equipment, action shots were a difficult proposition, one that few photographers could master. To offer a completely different perspective, the William Taylor Son & Company Department Store announced that Ann Sawyer, their clothing buyer, would add her World Series commentary to the sports page. The popular downtown store advertised heavily in the *Plain Dealer*. Combining those ads with Ms. Sawyer's opinion on the games was a clever stunt to increase their visibility. Husbands might actually pay attention to the fabulous sales available, even the ones for their wives.

At 6:15 p.m. on the evening of October 4, the train carrying the Cleveland Indians left Union Station, bound for New York. Packed in the equipment trunks were sparkling new blue uniforms with black socks. Each jersey had a black armband to be worn on the left sleeve throughout the series. The players had not forgotten their pal. In addition to wearing the armbands, the team had already voted to give Mrs. Chapman a full share of the player receipts. The travel plans called for an early arrival in the morning and a trip to the team's hotel for a final meeting, after which they would proceed to Brooklyn for a quick workout. Speaker told the press he would not determine his starting pitcher until close to game time. The candidates were Jim Bagby, Stan Coveleski, and Walter Mails. Of the three, Coveleski had had the most rest, while the odds of starting an inexperienced pitcher such as Mails seemed remote. If Speaker went with the percentages, his choice would be Coveleski.

The weather forecast proved to be unreliable. Opening Day of the 1920 World Series saw gray skies with strong wind gusts coming from the north. The wind swirled around the ballpark, giving notice that fly balls were going to be an interesting adventure for all concerned. Fans shivered in the stands, trying their best to stay warm in the football-like conditions. At 2 p.m. the Brooklyn players took the field with Rube Marquard on the mound. The selection of the veteran left-hander may have surprised the home crowd, but Wilbert Robinson likely thought the smarts and experience of Marquard just might throw the Cleveland hitters off. For an inning, that was the case. Joe Evans led off with a ground ball to shortstop Olson for the first out. Bill Wamby flied to Zack Wheat and to the delight of the anxious crowd, Rube fanned Tris Speaker.

Stan Coveleski did indeed start the game for the Indians. His first pitch to Ivy Olson resulted in a fly ball to Joe Wood. Jimmy Johnston struck out, then Tommy Griffith grounded out to Joe Sewell. In the top of the second inning, the wind really became a factor. Lead-off batter George Burns lifted a towering fly ball behind first base. Ed Konetchy lumbered after the ball with Pete Kilduff right behind him. Neither could judge the path of the baseball, and it dropped for a base hit. Burns rounded first base, but when he noticed shortstop Olson not covering second, he dashed for the extra base. Konetchy picked up the ball in short right field, heaving it in the general direction of second. With only Burns near the bag, the ball continued into left field while the Cleveland first baseman came all the way around for the first run off the series. A bizarre play, but nevertheless a run for the good guys. Larry Gardner grounded out, but Joe Wood walked, and Joe Sewell singled off a distracted Marquard. The next hitter, Steve O'Neill, ran the count to two balls, two strikes. The Brooklyn pitcher delivered a strike across the plate that O'Neill sent to the left-field corner, scoring Wood.

In the fourth inning Cleveland tallied another run when Joe Wood drove a pitch to the front of the left-field fence, just missing a home run. After Joe Sewell flied out, Steve O'Neill came through again, ripping his second double of the game to score Wood. The Indians would not get another base hit the remainder of the ball game, but with Coveleski hurling his lively spitball at the Robins hitters, the outcome was never in doubt. In the eighth inning, Speaker showed the Brooklyn fans how to play center field by hauling down Tommy Griffith's drive to deep left center field. As he had done so many times in his career, Speaker ran like a gazelle, spearing the ball at the last possible second. The sold-out crowd rose to their feet in anticipation, only to have their collective hope gone in seconds. For most of the afternoon, the loudest noise originated from a Cleveland fan who brought a megaphone to the game, bellowing out encouragement to the visiting team. The final: Cleveland 3, Brooklyn 1.

After the game, a large group of sportswriters hovered around Speaker to get his thoughts on the game. The manager had only praise for Coveleski, saying, "With the wind blowing as hard as it was, he worked under a handicap but he delivered in the pinches and that is what counts. It was just a ball game with him. He pitched a typical Coveleski game." Speaker went on to compliment Joe Sewell, telling the reporters his shortstop had the makings of a great player and that he expected Sewell to keep playing well. He told the writers that he firmly believed American League pitching did not have to take a backseat to the National League. The World Series had barely begun, but the Indians had proved they were up to the task. They took care of business quickly, taking the crowd right out of the game. Brooklyn had to regroup in a hurry or the series would be a brief one.

Back home in Cleveland a boisterous crowd gathered outside the *Plain Dealer* offices to watch the electronic scoreboard. William O'Connell, an elderly gentleman in his seventies, grabbed hold of a lamp pole and held on throughout the game. Despite the surging mob around him, O'Connell clung to the light pole, refusing to be moved. After the game when the mass of people began to file away, O'Connell told reporters he had watched every World Series since the scoreboard became available. He said, "I've tried again and again to get a ticket so I could see just one game. I'm over 70 and I can't stand in line all night for a bleacher seat. I am not as young as I used to be." He could only hope Jim Dunn would read the next day's paper and send a ticket to his most loyal of fans.

The celebrations went all the way from Cleveland to Minooka, Pennsylvania. There was a parade and a bonfire, and speeches were delivered in honor of favorite son Steve O'Neill. Virtually every family in the small mining community came out for the celebration, which lasted well into the night. Jack O'Neill, one of Steve's older brothers, greeted the crowd and took part in the spur-of-the-moment festivities. If the Indians went on to win the series, no doubt all of eastern Pennsylvania would hear the noise.

In his first newspaper column, Zack Wheat claimed Cleveland had gotten all the luck. He noted that both teams had an equal number of hits, but the Indians made theirs count while the Robins did not. He cited a major slipup when his team elected to pitch to Steve O'Neill in the fourth inning with Joe Wood on second. In hindsight, Wheat thought O'Neill should have been intentionally walked, allowing Marquard to pitch to Stan Coveleski. For the most part, the Brooklyn outfielder praised the efforts of his opponents, citing Speaker for his phenomenal running catch in the eighth inning. Wheat ended his column by pointing out that the series had just begun and that tomorrow another game would be played.

The most compelling game summary came from the pen of Ann Sawyer, the William Taylor Department Store buyer. Ms. Sawyer admitted she had not gone to Brooklyn for the game, but she revealed that with a sharp pair of binoculars she could see one of the downtown scoreboards from her office window. She noted in her report, "The game was 14–12 in favor of Brooklyn. In the number of men that played, I mean. And that's funny because I thought it only took nine men to play baseball." She disagreed with the sportswriters who claimed Steve O'Neill was the game's most valuable player. She nominated Taylor's, which had once turned down a teenage Rube Marquard for a job as a floorwalker. According to her logic, if Rube had gotten the job he would still be working in Cleveland and not on the mound for Brooklyn. She asked, "Where would Cleveland be without their three Rube runs?" Ms. Sawyer admired home-plate umpire Bill Klem for his conventional blue serge suit. She then reminded her readers to watch for the two pantsuits now available for only $60 to $90 at Taylor's. Of all the assorted writers with their differing viewpoints, Ann Sawyer stood alone.

Game 2 began with less wind, and temperatures were a bit improved from the previous day. However, the megaphone announcer had caught a fierce cold, prompting the Cleveland writers to report they could not understand a word he said. Jim Bagby got the assignment for Cleveland against Brooklyn's best pitcher,

Burleigh Grimes. Manager Speaker decided to use his left-handed lineup against the Robins right-hander. Charlie Jamieson replaced Joe Evans in left field, Elmer Smith took over for Joe Wood in right, and Doc Johnston started at first base for George Burns. In this game the lefty-righty theory would not have any effect on the outcome. Burleigh Grimes had his spitball breaking sharply, baffling the Indians hitters from the first inning on. Tris Speaker rapped a single off Grimes in the top of the first inning but remained on first while Elmer Smith struck out. The anxious hometown fans got something to cheer about in the bottom of the first. After Ivy Olson popped out, Jimmy Johnston singled to deep short. Joe Sewell made a play on the ball, but Jimmy Johnston beat the high throw to his brother Doc. On the first pitch Jimmy took off for second, sliding in ahead of the throw. Tommy Griffith grounded out, but Zack Wheat lined a double past Speaker to score Johnston.

Cleveland threatened in the top of the second when Larry Gardner led off with a double to left field. Doc Johnston tried to sacrifice, but Grimes hustled to the ball and fired to third, catching Gardner in a rundown. After Joe Sewell popped out to short, Doc tried to equal his brother by stealing second. A good throw from Otto Miller cut down Johnston to end the inning.

Bagby retired the side in order to end the second inning but found himself in trouble by the bottom of the third. Grimes led off with a base hit to center field. Olson bunted near the mound, where Bagby grabbed the ball and threw wildly to second. In reaching for the throw, Sewell collided with the sliding Grimes, who twisted his knee while trying to get out of the way. Time was called, allowing the injured pitcher to walk around the infield to stretch out his leg. Al Mamaux started throwing in the bullpen, waiting for manager Robinson to wave him on. Several minutes went by, and then Grimes limped back to second, indicating he could stay in the game. Bagby got Jimmy Johnston to foul out, but Tommy Griffith lined a double to score the hobbling Grimes, Olson taking third. In a curious move, Speaker had Wheat intentionally walked so Bagby could pitch to Hy Myers with the bases loaded. Setting up a force at any base might be good strategy; however, in this case, the batter had been one of the Robins' best hitters throughout the season. If Myers came through, the second-guessers would be all over Speaker, at least through the series. The Indians' manager proved himself right as Myers bounced to Gardner. The throw went to O'Neill for one out, then the catcher relayed to first trying to complete the double play. The throw went slightly off line, striking Myers in the back. Griffith raced for the plate, but Doc Johnston alertly retrieved the baseball and pegged it home in time for an unusual double play that ended the rally. The Robins got their first indication of what trying to slide past O'Neill was like. Griffith approached the plate only to find his path securely blocked by the Indians catcher. He never got close, setting off a tirade from Wilbert Robinson, who demanded umpire Tommy Connolly call interference. Uncle Robbie's face turned bright red as he argued in vain, inspiring Damon Runyon to write, "Robinson's face is aflame as he talks to Connolly, but the umpire merely shakes his head. Then Robinson waddles back to the bench, a picture of indignation."

Brooklyn got its final run in the fifth inning when Olson singled, went to second on a ground ball from J. Johnston to Doc Johnston, and then scored on another hit from Tommy Griffith. Burleigh Grimes, with his sore knee, retired the Cleveland batters without any problem until the top of the seventh. Larry Gardner singled for his second hit of the game. Doc Johnston forced Gardner at second to bring up Joe Sewell. While the Brooklyn crowd yelled, Sewell tagged one to deep right field. Tommy Griffith raced back to the wall, leaped, and snagged the would-be double. Game 2 belonged to Griffith, with his clutch hitting and tremendous catch, robbing Sewell of extra bases. Next batter O'Neill singled, which made the right fielder's grab all the more significant. Speaker called in Jack Graney to hit for Bagby. Grimes wasted no time, fanning the pinch-hitter on three pitches. The Indians threatened again in the eighth when Grimes walked Charlie Jamieson and pinch-hitter George Burns. Tris Speaker rolled a ground ball to Pete Kilduff, who threw to first, with both runners advancing. Elmer Smith came to bat, hitless in three trips. The several hundred Cleveland fans in the bleachers yelled for Elmer to put one over the wall. Grimes pitched carefully, getting Smith to pop out weakly behind home plate. With two out, Gardner walked to load the bases, sending the older Johnston brother to the plate. Once again Grimes got tough, getting Doc to ground out to second. The Indians managed a base hit in the ninth inning, but the game ended with Jamieson hitting a fly ball to Wheat. Brooklyn evened the series, taking game 2, 3–0.

In his postgame comments Speaker came right to the point. Tris remarked, "We could not hit with men on bases and Brooklyn had two batters who could. I think that is the best reason I know for explaining why we lost." Game 2 mirrored the opening game, except that Grimes had the good spitball instead of Coveleski, and the Robins hit when men were on base. Tommy Griffith repeated the performance of Steve O'Neill by knocking in two of the three runs. After two ball games the teams were even in all aspects. Both clubs showed similar talents: good pitching and timely hitting. From what fans and reporters witnessed, it appeared this series might be headed to nine games. Thursday's game in Brooklyn had added importance as the next four contests were scheduled in Cleveland. Back home the Indians fans were circling League Park like vultures.

Now that the Robins had evened the series, their fans came out to Ebbets Field in great force. Several thousand had to be turned away after the last general admission ticket was sold. The fans were loud and rowdy throughout the game, drowning out the Cleveland crowd, which still numbered several hundred. There were cowbells ringing throughout the stands and an automobile horn piercing the air every minute. Ray Caldwell got the start for the Indians, winning the nod from manager Speaker over newcomer Walter Mails. Caldwell, with his many years of experience, seemed to be a good choice. "Slim," as they sometimes called him, had his finest season in 1920, winning twenty games in thirty-three starts. Like most of his teammates, Caldwell was making his first appearance in a World Series. Now that he was on the national stage, the pitcher certainly wanted to show the country he still had the goods.

Opposing Caldwell would be hard-throwing left-hander Sherrod Smith. Throughout the regular season Smith had split his time starting and relieving. He had pitched well for both assignments, winning eleven games while recording a superb ERA of 1.85. The game opened with Joe Evans from the righty brigade grounding out to Olson. Bill Wamby drew a walk, bringing up Speaker with a chance to do some early damage. Tris grounded out, with Wamby taking second. George Burns, who had circled the bases on a pop fly in game 1, came to the plate. This time there was no strong breeze to help him as he grounded out to end the inning.

With a strong ovation from the Brooklyn rooters, Ivy Olson led off the bottom of the first with a walk. Jimmy Johnston laid down the sacrifice bunt, moving the runner to second. Yesterday's hero Tommy Griffith grounded to Sewell, who fumbled the ball for an error. Up to this point in the series the Indians shortstop had played like a veteran, but in today's game he would not be of much help. Runners stood at first and third, resulting in Speaker moving his infield in to cut off the run at the plate. His strategy backfired when Zack Wheat lined a single just past the reach of Larry Gardner. Olson scored the game's first run while Brooklyn still had runners on second and first. The second-guessers would claim that Speaker did the wrong thing in bringing his infield in. Had he not chosen to do so, Gardner may have caught Wheat's liner, thus saving a run. In his defense, Speaker had probably noticed Caldwell did not have good command of his pitches. His decision to bring in the infield was done to prevent a big inning for the Robins. The point became moot when Hy Myers singled to right field, scoring Griffith from second. Speaker called time, motioning to the bullpen for Walter Mails to relieve Ray Caldwell. This turned out to be the starting pitcher's one and only chance in a World Series. He had lasted just a third of an inning, allowing two runs and two hits. Statistics would show that of the twenty pitches thrown by Caldwell, ten of those were balls. In addition to the wildness, the error by Sewell played a big role in Caldwell's departure. Had the ball been fielded cleanly, the Indians might have survived the inning with no runs scored. However, that is all conjecture; the score stood at 2–0.

Most Brooklyn fans recognized the new Cleveland pitcher as one of their own from 1915 and 1916. Mails pitched very little in those two seasons, but his nine walks in seventeen total innings probably jogged the memories of those in the grandstand. Regardless of his checkered past, Mails got the next two batters to fly out to end the inning. Mails put on a terrific performance, not yielding another run during his stint. Inevitably, this would lead to discussions of why Speaker did not start Mails in the first place. He had an exceptional September, winning several crucial games down the stretch. He kept pace with Bagby and Coveleski all through the drive to the pennant. Had Caldwell managed to right himself and finish the game, it is likely Mails would not have pitched at all in the series. However, when the opportunity came along, Walter Mails seized the moment in a very big way.

The game moved to the top of the fourth inning, when Bill Wamby slapped an apparent base hit past Johnston at third. Shortstop Olson moved far to his right to backhand the ball on the outfield grass. He stumbled for a moment, righted himself, and then fired a strike to first base to barely get Wamby. The importance of the play was amplified a moment later when Speaker lined a shot down the left-field line. Wheat raced over to get in front of the ball, but somehow it eluded him, rolling all the way to the corner. Speaker turned on the speed, rounding third and crossing home plate with Cleveland's first run. Wheat got charged with a two-base error on the play. The situation could have been worse if Olson had not made his spectacular stop of Wamby's grounder and thrown him out. Using the great support behind him, Sherrod Smith went on to pitch an outstanding game, yielding only three hits and winning 2–1. In the last four innings Smith faced just twelve batters, giving the Indians no chance to tie the game or go ahead. The series now had the Robins in the lead, two games to one.

Traveling to Cleveland with two games in the win column left Brooklyn in good shape for the remainder of the series. They needed to win only one out of four games there to bring the contest back to Brooklyn. If they could salvage a split, game 8 in New York would have them with an advantage of four games to three. So far the pitching of Burleigh Grimes and Sherrod Smith had yielded one run in eighteen innings. At that pace, the Robins' chances looked pretty good for the games at League Park. The oddsmakers now had the series at even money, where the Indians were 6–5 favorites going in.

The composite box score for the three games showed Brooklyn with eighteen hits in eighty-seven at-bats for an average of .209. The Indians' totals were even worse, with fifteen hits in ninety-one at-bats for a dismal average of .165. Bill Wamby had not gotten a hit in nine at-bats, while the left-field platoon of Evans and Jamieson had gone one for eleven. Steve O'Neill led all Cleveland hitters with a .500 average, going five for ten. That represented a third of all the Indians' base hits. On the Brooklyn side Zack Wheat played as advertised with an average of .455. Ivy Olson was having a great series to date, hitting .444

while performing like an all-star at shortstop. Tommy Griffith surprised everyone by batting .333 with three big hits in nine trips to the plate. As the numbers indicated, Cleveland had dug itself a medium-sized hole that it needed to get out of.

Zack Wheat wrote an upbeat column for the Friday *Plain Dealer*, stating his team simply outplayed the visitors. He wrote, "There's no reason why we shouldn't keep up this winning brand of baseball in Cleveland. We started now and I don't think they can head us. We've seen all their most vaunted pitchers already, while we still have got some good ones that haven't started." Wheat had every right to be confident of his team's prospects for the remainder of the series. They had held their own at home against the AL champs, so why couldn't they at least split the four games? Wheat believed they could, ending his column with his prediction that game 4 would be a peach of a game.

Thursday evening the Indians hustled to Grand Central Station, where five railroads cars waited to start the journey home. Besides the players, there were the Cleveland writers and the delegation of fans who had witnessed the first three games. Manager Speaker had not lost any confidence in his boys, telling reporters they would still win the series. Speaker remarked, "The Brooklyn players were up on their toes and certainly played great baseball. Our men in the field did not do so well today." He had positive things to say about Joe Sewell, still believing his shortstop would soon be one of the best. Spoke used some psychology there, propping up the young kid trying to fill Ray Chapman's shoes. The pressure on Sewell had to be enormous, aside from the fact that he had the least amount of experience of any player on either team. A sold-out crowd was watching every game. No fewer than four hundred newspapermen were scrutinizing every play he made. Sewell displayed a lot of guts just by showing up for the games. His play in the field could be debated, but certainly not his courage.

15

STANDING ROOM ONLY

"This is the red hot end of the World's Series. This town knows something is going on." These were the colorful first observations of Damon Runyon in his Saturday column. He had arrived in Cleveland on Friday, studying the fans who were gathered in the streets talking baseball. He noticed whistles blowing all around him and observed crowds forming in the hotel lobbies where reporters and the baseball hierarchy met to talk about the next day's game. Runyon likely had a room at the crowded Hollenden Hotel, the place to be to get an insider's prospective on all the pre-game action. He watched Wilbert Robinson greet friends with a healthy slap on the back that the writer likened to the cordial kick of a mule. He described Jim Dunn as a bluff man, well met. Runyon admired Dunn for buying a baseball club with little promise and upgrading it to an organization returning fat dividends.

While the Hollenden proved to be the social hub of the Series, just about every street within the city limits was buzzing with anticipation. An estimated three thousand out-of-towners arrived throughout the day, looking for tickets and a place to stay. The hotels filled up quickly, leaving many visitors scrambling to find a place with four walls, a roof, and a bed. Cleveland police sent extra details around the streets of Public Square, hoping to maintain as much law and order as possible. For the most part the celebrants behaved themselves, content to march through the town, raising their voices for the gallant Indians. Frank Menke, a local reporter for the *Plain Dealer*, summed up the situation by writing, "Often it has been said that if a collection of Cleveland athletes ever figured in a blue ribbon diamond event, the populace would go insane. The prophecy has come true, for tonight everything else is forgotten in the city save one thing—and one thing alone."

A detail of police officers marched to Linwood Avenue to keep a close eye on the fans lining up to buy the general admission seats. The League Park ticket windows did not open until 10 a.m. on game day; nevertheless, fans began arriving by 2 p.m. on Friday, some twenty hours early. The first person in line, Edward Fox, told the press he had traveled from Proctor, Vermont, carrying with him a large box containing his dinner, midnight snack, breakfast, and Saturday lunch. Every few minutes new fans joined the line in front of the ticket windows. Along with the locals were ticket buyers from Pittsburgh, Detroit, Denver, and St. Louis. Some of the people in line were acting as agents for those who had no desire to stand, naming their price for the service provided. Photographers got several images of the long line, showing men with suits and caps while the ladies wore long coats with fashionable hats. The one relevant question that went unasked: what did these folks do when nature called? If Edward Fox waited out the entire twenty hours, he deserved a front-row seat.

The effort to put the clamps on ticket scalping intensified as throngs of people milled around downtown. The Indians' front office hired fifty workers to patrol the hotels, cigar shops, and any place of business where the scalping might take place. The police believed most of the actual ticket selling was done by individuals and not any organization. No arrests were made on Friday, but word was reported of individual seats going for $15 to $40. Blocks of four tickets were being offered at $150 to $250. Eyebrows were raised when Brooklyn's Zack Wheat reported that a stranger had approached him offering four tickets for $100. Reporters found a café on Superior Avenue where the soft-drink clerk had a block of seats he believed would sell for $260. A survey of cigar stores indicated that single seats were available for $25, or $50 a pair. Field agents from the IRS met with E. S. Barnard to discuss their plans for arrests and con-fiscation of any tickets sold illegally.

Many of the ticket holders for the next four games lived outside of Cuyahoga County, and not everybody had a reliable automobile that could take them thirty or forty miles to the ballpark and get them home. The city of Akron developed an original plan for hauling fans to League Park and returning them home in the early evening. The Northern Ohio Traction & Light Company pro-duced a nine-car trolley train that would get fans to 66th and Lexington in ninety minutes. The train consisted of three motor cars and six trailers, allow-ing it to split into three separate sections if necessary. The nine-car total repre-sented the largest interurban train running in the country. Prices were not listed, but the trains were more than likely filled to capacity.

Ann Sawyer of Taylor's reported a storewide rush on ninety-foot stepladders. She believed that from the outside, the outfield walls would resemble a glori-fied toboggan slide with fans trying to peek over the top. Her insightful col-umn ended by reminding the men who planned to throw their hats in the air to fling a handsome new velour one from Taylor's, at only $20.

All the anticipation Clevelanders had been feeling vanished promptly at 2 p.m. on Saturday afternoon. Twenty-seven thousand fans filled the ballpark, sitting and standing anywhere they could. Each corner of the park had a flag fly-ing with just a hint of a breeze circulating around the field. As an added bonus, temperatures peaked at a warm seventy-one degrees, allowing the spectators to remove their overcoats and roll up their sleeves as if it were July. As soon as the Indians trotted onto the diamond for batting practice wearing their brand-new white uniforms, the fans erupted in noise. Everything the Indians did produced a clamor from the stands, along with pennants and scorecards waving from every angle. The racket did not cease for the entire afternoon. The fans even cheered the boy raking the dirt around the bases and the peanut vendors. Overhead an airplane made numerous passes over the park—a unique alterna-tive to having a ticket.

Outside the grounds, activity was just as lively. Young boys volunteered to park cars for a nominal fee. Most of the homes in the vicinity had signs on their lawns offering parking at twenty-five cents. People stood on the rooftops of warehouses around the ballpark, able to get a fair view of the action below. The Andrews Storage Company had space for fifty people but chose to allow only its employees a free view of the game. A fan from out of town offered to pay thirty-five dollars for a place on the Andrews rooftop. The owner politely declined the money, explaining that his workers would be getting the prime space. The man then asked for a job.

Trees and telephone poles were filled with boys and men who had claimed their spots hours before. Among the tree climbers was Martin Tilow, an eleven-year-old from the neighborhood. Martin settled in his roost, biding his time until the game started. While he waited, several men approached the owner of the property. Bids as high as $30 were made to dislodge Martin from his spot. The owner turned down all offers, allowing Martin to keep his elevated seat for free. Kate Carter, the only female reporter on the scene, filed the story in the *Cleveland Press*. The next day Martin received a free grandstand seat courtesy of the newspaper. Several locals had rented empty stores in the neighborhood, hoping to make some extra money serving food before and after the game. Delivery trucks dropped off roast beef and other foods at 3:30 a.m. By morning sandwiches and coffee were prepared and then hustled to the line of fans arriving at the ballpark. All these temporary entrepreneurs stood a good chance of profiting from their efforts, although they were destined to go out of business within a week.

The usual pregame ceremonies were conducted shortly before 2 p.m. The crowd looked on as a dazzling lavender-colored automobile arrived on the grounds. The Templar Motor Company, devoted followers of Doc Johnston, presented the gift to the startled ballplayer. A number of motion picture cameras trailed behind Tris Speaker as he received a large floral arrangement paid for by friends in Hubbard, Texas. After the game, he had the flowers sent to Lake View Cemetery to be placed at Ray Chapman's vault.

Unknown to most of the crowd in the stands, the U.S. Naval Radio Station was preparing its wireless operators to broadcast the game. With assistance from the *Cleveland Press*, the station, located off Lake Erie, would send a continuous message to wireless operators within a 750-mile radius. This included ships sailing the Great Lakes as well as stations throughout Canada. The transmissions were sent in code and then translated for baseball fans across a wide area. Though no words were spoken, it was a revolutionary idea that would pave the way for announcers and live broadcasts of baseball.

With all the ceremonies completed, the Indians took their positions. Stan Coveleski walked to the mound for his warm-up throws. According to reports, he told his teammates to get him two runs and that would be enough for him to win. Usually a quiet, unassuming man, Coveleski had his adrenaline flowing. Ivy Olson led off with a ground ball to Larry Gardner for out number one. Jimmy Johnston did the same to Joe Sewell, while Tommy Griffith popped out to end the quick inning.

Charlie Jamieson opened the bottom half of the first by lining a bullet right back at Leon Cadore, the Robins starter. The pitcher grabbed the ball in self-defense. Bill Wamby worked Cadore for a walk, jogging to first base with one out. Speaker singled to center field with Wamby holding at second. The fans shook the foundations of the park, screaming for Elmer Smith to belt one. The cleanup hitter responded by driving a pitch to center field for a base hit. Wamby came around to score, while Speaker hustled to third. Gardner flied out deep enough to Myers to allow Tris to tag and score well ahead of the throw in. Cadore struck out new car owner Doc Johnston to end the inning.

In the bottom of the second both Joe Sewell and Steve O'Neill singled, chasing Cadore from the hill. Al Mamaux came on in relief, doing a fine job to strike out Coveleski and getting Jamieson to fly out. When Joe Sewell strayed too far off second, he was doubled off by an alert peg from Hy Myers to end the inning. Brooklyn could do nothing in their half of the third inning, going out in order. Wamby started the home half with a base hit. Speaker got his second hit of the day, another single to center. Wamby challenged the throwing arm of Myers, beating the throw to third base. On the play, Speaker raced to second, wisely getting himself in scoring position. Once again Wilbert Robinson elected to change pitchers, bringing in lefty Rube Marquard to face Smith. Speaker used his righty-lefty theory, sending George Burns to bat for Smith. Spoke could do no wrong as Burns singled to left, driving in both runs and extending the lead to 4–0. The Indians had doubled Coveleski's request to give him two runs to work with.

Brooklyn scored a run in the top of the fifth on J. Johnston's single and a double by the hot-hitting Griffith. Cleveland answered in the bottom of the sixth off the Robins' fourth pitcher of the day, Jeff Pfeffer. Consecutive singles by Coveleski, Joe Evans, and Wamby, all with two outs, gave the Indians their fifth run of the game. The final score: Cleveland 5, Brooklyn 1. The series stood at two games apiece, switching the momentum back to the home town. As might be expected, Speaker expressed his thanks to Coveleski after the game. He said, "He is not only the best spitball pitcher in the country but he also is one of the best pitchers in the land. He was like an iceberg on the rubber today. I don't believe he realized there were 27,000 crazy fans here this afternoon." For his second win in four days, Coveleski gave up five hits and struck out four while walking only one batter. He had distanced himself from the other pitchers on both staffs, winning two important games and surely ready to pitch again if needed.

Before the conclusion of game 4, another crowd assembled at the ballpark ticket windows. Much like the previous day, the eager rooters were prepared to wait out the twenty hours until the windows opened up. Enterprising boys from the neighborhood gathered up empty soap boxes and sold them to those desperate for a seat. The wooden containers were going for twenty-five cents a pop. A young girl named Emma brought cups of hot coffee from her home just across the street, methodically collected change from the buyers, and then walked back to her house, where she gathered more coffee from her mother. Emma served her customers for several hours and then retired to her home with enough money to buy a new dress.

When the early-morning sun first appeared, a group of men broke out the playing cards, and games of poker began. They continued until the ticket windows opened. Mysterious bottles of an unknown liquid began to surface, but after close examination the contents turned out to be hot coffee or tea. A number of veterans from World War I were among the all-night crowd. According to the *Cleveland News*, an ex-soldier shouted out, "Remember the Argonne? Well this is a joy compared to that. All we have to do is wait, not for the zero hour, but for the gates to open. Say, ain't it a pipe?"

The after-hours crowd included Esther Manning of Cleveland, a young woman in line alone. She told interested reporters that she had seen game 1 and had tickets for the remaining three. Her reason for standing in line? Two friends had bet her $50 she would not have the nerve to hold her position in line all night long surrounded by men. Ms. Manning represented a new generation of American women who were throwing off the old taboos on the eve of the Jazz Age. Some, like Esther Manning, came to baseball games without the traditional escorts. Female attendance at the last eight Ladies' Day games at League Park had totaled 11,471. The September 17 game, right in the middle of the pennant race, had 2,650 women in the stands, a new record. Women were now a force to be reckoned with, at the ballpark and outside it.

Late Saturday evening through early Sunday, the downtown streets were mostly deserted, save for a small number of drunken celebrants weaving their away across the sidewalks. Visitors slept soundly at the packed hotels, getting their rest for Sunday's game. At approximately 6:15 a.m., four guests were awakened by a loud rapping at their hotel door. One of the sleepy guests stumbled to the door to find four men armed with revolvers demanding all the cash and valuables in the room. Several minutes later they escaped with money and diamonds in the neighborhood of $3,500. The police arrived at the Hollenden within minutes, arresting three men who were in a room near the site of the robbery. The detectives did not find the loot there, but they found several pairs of dice along with an electric drill and mercury, commonly used to load the dice for the purpose of cheating. The victims immediately identified two of the crooks, sending them to jail for a morning of questioning. One of the victims, who had come from Pennsylvania to watch the games, had lost $800 in cash plus a three-and-one-quarter-carat diamond ring during the heist. It is not known if the stolen property was ever located.

On the heels of the robbery at the Hollenden, the newspapers reported a number of busts by undercover agents, primarily for scalping tickets. One of those nabbed in the process turned out to be none other than Rube Marquard. The appalling details named the former Clevelander as the man attempting to sell four box seats for $350. The police took Marquard into custody but agreed to release him in time for Saturday's game. Marquard appealed to the Cleveland chief of police for a temporary release, which Chief Frank Smith agreed to. The last thing the Brooklyn team needed was a distraction off the field. Whether or not he was guilty, Marquard had created one, and it was ridiculous. So far it had been a less than joyous homecoming for the pitcher: first he gave up a key single in a losing effort, and then he grabbed headlines for the scalping incident. His fiancée, Naomi Malone, who watched Saturday's game in manager Robinson's box, claimed her man was innocent. She said, "There is absolutely nothing to this story they are telling about Richard scalping tickets. How could he have had all those tickets? It's all nonsense."

Nonsense or not, a municipal court judge set the arraignment for Monday morning on a charge of "violation of the exhibition ordinance." A total of ten arrests were made throughout the city over the weekend. One of those busted was Fred Wagner of the Colonial Smoke Shop on Superior Avenue. He had sold his eight reserved tickets to a fan from Columbus, Ohio, for $120, a profit of nearly $85. The Cleveland front office voided all eight tickets, offering the Columbus buyer a refund at the gate. Justice would indeed be served, to ballplayers and all others.

Shortly before game time on Sunday, the six members of the League Park ground crew began to work on the infield. Two of the men dragged what looked like doormats around the baselines to smooth out the dirt. Another group pulled a heavy iron roller around the pitcher's mound to flatten it down, while the remaining two used a pail and brush to whiten the baselines. When the crew finished the maintenance, another man brought out a garden hose to wet down the infield. Cleveland now had a fast track for the ball club's speedy runners. There were quite a few, including Jamieson, Speaker, Evans, Johnston, and Sewell, who could sprint around the bases when needed. For most of the season the team used the hit-and-run quite often instead of stealing. Now, in the midst of the World Series, the grounds crew made certain to keep the infield fast to give their club every advantage possible.

Cy Young made an appearance on the diamond, stopping by the dugout to wish the Indians good luck. The old Cleveland Spider with a record 511 wins came up from his farm in southern Ohio, where he concentrated on raising sheep. Along with the former pitcher were Billy Coveleski and Roger Johnston, the young sons of the Cleveland pitcher and first baseman. Six-year-old Roger had on an authentic Cleveland uniform, which his father no doubt pulled a few strings to get. Seated in the stands was Mrs. James Bagby, seeing a major league game for the very first time. She did not know it, but she was in for an amazing experience.

For today's game, which featured another day of perfect weather, Jim Bagby would match pitches with Burleigh Grimes. They had already faced each other in game 2, with Grimes throwing his splendid shutout. Based on the year-long accomplishments of both pitchers, it figured to be another low-scoring contest. Ivy Olson got things going with a base hit to left field. He would advance to second but no further as a ground out and fly ball ended the inning. In the bottom of the first, Charlie Jamieson walked to the batter's box with cowbells and auto horns blasting away. He added to the commotion by lining a single to right field. Bill Wamby fouled off a number of pitches before grounding a single past third base. As Tris Speaker walked to the plate, the Brooklyn infielders had a conference near the mound. Likely they were discussing the possibility of a bunt, and which base to throw to should Speaker drop one down. Sure enough, Spoke did roll a bunt to the right of the pitcher's mound. Grimes reacted quickly, but as he reached to glove the baseball, his feet went out from under him. Sitting on his rear end, Grimes threw off balance to first, much too late to make a play.

Now the crowd was in a frenzy as Elmer Smith stepped in to hit. The powerful lefty had already homered twice with the bases full during the regular season. Could it possibly happen again? Grimes threw a spitball that Smith swung at and missed badly. Grimes threw another with the same result. A third offering came over the plate but a bit too low, and umpire Bill Klem signaled for ball one. Grimes looked in for the sign and then delivered a fast one right down the middle. Smith, always a good fastball hitter, met the pitch square on the nose. The screaming liner rose steadily, clearing the screen over the right-field wall and then sailing high over Lexington Avenue before landing on the adjacent street. The crowd in the stands let out a roar that could be heard all the way across Lake Erie. Elmer Smith had just hit the first grand slam in World Series history. Years later an elderly Smith, living in the suburbs of Cleveland, recalled the event. He had expected nothing but spitballs from Grimes. After he had seen several of them, the fourth pitch came in nice and straight right over the plate. Smith swung from the heels, launching a tape-measure home run that ended up being the turning point of the World Series. After the game Smith would tell reporters he could feel the excitement in the stands when he came to bat. He said, "That home run pitch was just what the doctor ordered. I hit it as squarely in the nose as I ever hit any ball and I could feel it was destined to travel from the way it cracked off my bat." Some fifty years later, Smith still wondered why Grimes did not throw him another spitball. In game 2 Grimes had easily disposed of him with a steady dose of the wet ball. At the most crucial moment, Grimes either decided to change strategy or simply threw a spit ball that did not break. The result went a long way toward dashing the Robins' hopes for the championship. Now the Indians led the game 4–0, putting the Robins in a big hole.

With one out in the top of the second, Ed Konetchy belted a triple to deep center field, his first hit of the series. Pete Kilduff followed with a line drive to left field. Jamieson raced in, snagged the ball on the run, and threw a strike to home plate. The slow-footed Konetchy tagged up at third, plodding toward home. Steve O'Neill took the throw and dropped to his knees on the third-base line, several feet in front of home plate. Big Ed slid hard, but the wall of granite never moved, completing the double play. The auto horns blared again as the Indians trotted off the field, their 4–0 lead well protected.

Doc Johnston singled off Grimes's knee to start the bottom of the fourth inning. He took second on a passed ball and then moved to third when Joe Sewell grounded out. The Robins decided to intentionally walk O'Neill to send pitcher Jim Bagby to the plate. Most teams in the American League knew the Indians pitcher was no easy out. Evidently Brooklyn did not. Bagby looked over one pitch and swung at the second, launching the baseball far into the new right-field stands for a three-run home run. Pandemonium reigned at League Park. Never before had the fans seen such a display of power in a ball game—and in a World Series, no less. In just two mighty swings, seven Indians base runners had crossed home plate. The Brooklyn players, including their pitcher, were shell-shocked watching the parade around the bases. Even if nothing else happened, this game would be remembered for many, many years. However, the action was far from over. A terribly shaken Grimes gave up another single to Jamieson, prompting Uncle Robbie to change pitchers. Seldom-used Clarence

Mitchell jogged in from the bullpen, trying to stop the onslaught. He managed to retire the side, getting Wamby to fly out, followed by Jamieson's unsuccessful attempt to steal second.

To their credit, the Brooklyn Robins did not quit. Kilduff started the fifth inning with a single. Catcher Otto Miller got a rare base hit to center field. That brought to the plate Clarence Mitchell, a good hitting pitcher who sometimes took a turn playing first base. The Cleveland infielders moved back, looking for a chance to turn a double play. Wamby, knowing that Mitchell could swing the bat, took an extra two or three steps back. Bagby delivered, and Mitchell smoked a rising line drive just to the right of second base. Wamby took another step and then made a tremendous leap, reaching his glove as high as he possibly could. Frozen in midair, he caught the liner, moving his right hand quickly to trap the ball in his glove as he landed near second. With the crack of the bat both runners had taken off, each thinking to advance two bases. Wamby easily stepped on the bag for out number two. Joe Sewell yelled, "Tag him, Bill, Tag him!" Wamby turned toward first, seeing the startled Miller standing motionless just a few feet away. The catcher had no chance to get back to first. His feet seemed to be anchored in the dirt as the Cleveland second baseman applied the tag for out number three. The entire play happened in a matter of seconds. The spirited crowd became silent, not certain of what they had seen. It took about a minute for the realization to set in that an unassisted triple play had just taken place. A deafening roar burst from the stands, this time probably reaching Detroit. Only one of the many photographers on the field was quick enough to get a shot of the play. The sole cameraman had the swift reflexes to capture the image of Wamby tagging Miller out. It is an amazing photo, showing Kilduff turning around at third base as if to say "What happened?" This spectacular feat signaled the end for the Robins. They might have survived a grand slam, but a three-run homer from the opposing pitcher along with a lightning-fast unassisted triple play indicated the show might be over for the guys from Brooklyn.

Wamby later described the play for the large group of reporters eager for a prime story. He said, "When I started after the liner of Mitchell's, I hadn't any idea there was a triple play in sight. I would have taken a double play and called it quits. I took the ball with my gloved hand and stepped on second base for the second putout. But I still didn't dream of a third out until I turned and saw Miller dashing right at me down the baseline." Wamby downplayed his leaping grab of Mitchell's line drive, explaining it was no difficult stunt. One can argue that Wamby was simply in the right place at the right time. However, his sharp instincts killed any momentum the Robins were building.

The Indians scored again in the sixth inning when base hits by Smith and Gardner brought Speaker home with the eighth run. Jim Bagby cruised through the rest of the ball game, allowing a single run in the ninth inning. The game ended appropriately with a pop fly to Bill Wamby. The 8–1 win gave Cleveland the advantage, with three games to two, and brought them that much closer to a world championship.

The happiest man in the grandstand was none other than Jim Dunn. He glanced around his ballpark, noting that almost every seat was taken, including those in the new right-field bleachers just installed days before. He jumped from his seat when Elmer Smith's blast cleared the right-field wall, waving his hat while four of his boys circled the bases. He rose again, smiling broadly, while Jim Bagby sent a drive into the bleachers. He stayed seated along with the other twenty-seven thousand fans while his second baseman completed the miraculous triple play. Like the others it took him a moment to sort out what had just happened. Dunn had seen a remarkable game, one that would stand alone in baseball history. Everything he hoped for from his team was about to come true. Folks heard Sunny Jim say, "That sure is a ball club. The baseball writers will have something to send their papers tonight." Probably the understatement of the year.

Wilbert Robinson remarked after the game, "Those Indians are savage hitters when once they get going. That I always knew." Robinson's motivational skills would be sorely tested before his team took the field for game 6. His players had to shake off the effects of a crushing defeat or soon the series would be over.

The receipts after game 5 totaled $397,931 with attendance at 123,628, just a fraction under twenty-five thousand per game. The players' share totaled $214,870.74, with members of the winning team slated to receive an estimated payout of roughly $4,300 apiece. Losers would receive approximately $2,900.

All additional receipts from the remaining games would go directly to the owners. Locally the vendors at League Park were doing record business. The ice-
cream sellers gave up dishing out individual servings, instead selling boxes of the
tasty desserts for one dollar. They had little problem moving their inventory. As
might be expected, the scorecard printers could not keep up with the thousands
who wanted them. Several downtown businesses had mounted electric scoreboards in front of their buildings, and fans swarmed to get a good spot where
they could follow the action inning by inning. Crowds estimated at seven thousand pushed and shoved to get the best vantage point possible as police officers
on horseback tried to clear lanes among the keyed-up throngs of people.

The Indians' front office had done an admirable job of planning for all the
contingencies that went with hosting a World Series. They came up with an
innovative ticket plan to keep ticket scalping to a minimum. They saw to it that
the hundreds of newspapermen had lodgings and transportation at one of the
best hotels. The office hired a large number of college students from nearby
Case and Western Reserve Universities to work as ushers in an effort to handle
crowd control. The young men were paid $2 per game, plus a chance to see a
good part of the action. One thing that went unaccounted for was the mess left
behind by the thousands who stood in line to buy general admission seats. A
one-block area near the ticket windows was strewn with crumpled newspapers,
torn boxes, half-eaten food, and cigar butts. People from the neighborhood
picked through the rubble, taking away paper and boxes for kindling. However,
the ugly clutter would remain until the series ended or moved back to Brooklyn.

Game 6 of the series would be the first contest in Cleveland to be played
on a regular work or school day. The Cleveland city schools placed twenty-eight
truant officers in and around League Park to nab any children who had ducked
out of class. The chances of boys and girls sneaking away from school and making a dash for League Park seemed very high. The principal of Akron Central
High School, L. W. MacKinnon, developed a novel strategy to keep his students
from disappearing. He set up blackboards in the classroom with mini-scoreboards
on them. He relayed the score inning by inning to each teacher, who updated
the results. The students in French class were instructed to create presentations
on baseball without speaking any English. The math classes devoted their lessons

to computing baseball statistics on batting, fielding, and pitching averages. The strategy worked well, with few students attempting to leave the classroom. As far as the other schools, it was anybody's guess.

A Cleveland newspaper ran an editorial with the simple headline "Wow!" It went on to say, "Cleveland is in a frenzy. The old town is skipping about like a colt in springtime. Will Cleveland win? What a question! Will the sun rise? Will a Bolshevik dodge soap?" With a lead of three games to two, expectations were running high that the Indians would claim the world championship. After so many years of disappointment, fans, and now the newspapers, abandoned all caution. The question now was no longer if we would win but how quickly we would do it.

Preparations for game 6 began at 9:30 a.m. Monday morning when the box-office windows opened for business. By 10 a.m. the bleachers had begun to fill, nearly four hours before the throwing of the first pitch. A half hour later, boys started climbing the trees around the ballpark that had the best views. Before 11 a.m. the rooftops on Lexington Avenue were packed with energetic fans. Reporters and photographers arrived around noon, along with the head usher, who yelled to his employees to man their positions and quit smoking! At 12:30 p.m. the Indians appeared on the field, ready to take batting practice. Several hundred fans moved to the front railing of bleachers, poised to grab any baseballs that came their way. The secretary of war, Newton Baker, and the U.S. ambassador to France, Myron Herrick, found their seats in the grandstand. The Robins arrived on the field about an hour before game time. A round of cheers erupted when a bold teenage girl jumped over the outfield bleacher railing with fountain pen and base-ball in hand. Mickey Gleason raced over to Brooklyn's Al Mamaux to plead for an autograph. The amused pitcher signed the ball and then watched with the crowd while Mickey ran back to the bleachers, hauled herself over the railing, and, with a huge grin, took her seat. The news photographers followed the infatuated Ms. Gleason back to her seat, snapping pictures of the excited young girl holding her treasured baseball. Unknowingly, she had now set a precedent for future genera-tions to run onto the baseball field and raise havoc with ushers and policeman.

Moments before the game began, Elmer Smith and Bill Wamby stepped out of the dugout to receive gold watch fobs sprinkled with diamonds. The expensive gifts were a display of gratitude for their extraordinary feats on Sunday. Cleveland fans were not about to let good deeds go unrewarded. The movie cameras were rolling as the two stars waved to the stands and headed back to the dugout. A minute or two later, the Indians charged onto the field amidst a huge welcoming from the twenty-seven thousand fans in attendance. Walter Mails took the mound for Cleveland, getting the start ahead of veteran Ray Caldwell. One has to wonder if Mails had any thoughts about his brief time on the Brooklyn squad back in 1916, when he was released without much of a chance to prove himself. This time he had earned the trust of manager Speaker, who decided to go with his hot pitcher instead of the one who had finished with a twenty-win season. Mails got the side out in order, striking out Jack Sheehan, who had played a total of three regular-season games. An injury to Jimmy Johnston forced a change at third base, which certainly did not help Brooklyn. The Indians came to bat facing another left-handed pitcher in Sherrod Smith. Joe Evans singled to left field, the first hit of the ball game. The Robins guessed correctly that Bill Wamby would be bunting and called for a pitch out. Evans took off with the pitch but was easily thrown out at second. Wamby flied out, and then Speaker fouled to Miller to end the inning.

Both teams had opportunities to score in the second inning. With two out, Konetchy singled to right field. Joe Sewell added to his series error total, bobbling a ground ball from Kilduff. Otto Miller grounded to Gardner, who uncharacteristically could not make a play, loading the bases. That brought Sherrod Smith to the plate, lifting a fly to Speaker to end the inning. George Burns walked to start the Cleveland half of the inning. Gardner forced him at second, but Joe Wood singled to left. Zack Wheat made a nice play on the ball, throwing to third and nearly getting Gardner. Wood took second on the throw, putting two runners in scoring position. Joe Sewell hit one on the ground to second. Kilduff fielded the ball and threw a strike home to get the sliding Gardner. Steve O'Neill had a chance to drive in a run but grounded out to Kilduff for the third out.

The game moved along rapidly, with both pitchers taking firm control. Neither side did much at the plate until the sixth inning. Brooklyn right fielder Bernie Neis walked on four pitches, bringing up Zack Wheat. Mails delivered to the plate, where O'Neill fired to first base, picking off the Robins base runner. The throw came to the wrong side of the bag, but George Burns made the long reach and smartly put the tag on Neis. Wheat smacked a hard ground ball to Sewell, who made a nice stop and a quick throw to get Wheat at first. Hy Myers bounced one behind second, but again Sewell made a good play, fielding the ball and then throwing to Burns in time.

As the Indians came to bat in the bottom of the sixth, the fans became eager for some action. The day before, they had had much to cheer about, but thus far the blaring from auto horns and megaphones was mostly sporadic. Sherrod Smith got Evans and Wamby for the first two outs. Speaker, in his customary ritual, swung three bats, discarded two, and stepped to the plate. The crowd woke up when Spoke drove a single to left field. While George Burns stood in the batter's box, Smith threw over to first several times, trying to keep Speaker close to the bag. Facing toward home, Smith fired a pitch across the plate. Burns met it squarely, lining the ball to deep left center. Both Wheat and Myers took off like jackrabbits, speeding as fast as they could to cut the ball off. Speaker rounded second, switching into high gear for a dash all the way home. The fans screamed while the ball landed just in front of the bleachers, where Myers picked it up and threw toward the infield. When the ball arrived, Speaker had already scored, while Burns stopped at second. Before Myers reached the baseball, a young boy leaned over the railing, trying to grab a souvenir. Fortunately he could not get hold the ball, which would have meant a ground-rule double and sent Speaker back to third. The play stood; Cleveland had broken the scoreless tie. While Burns rested at second base, the crowd kept on yelling, really letting go for the first time in the afternoon. At this juncture, one run looked awfully big.

Walter Mails continued his dazzling pitching, setting down Brooklyn without a hit in the top of the seventh. Sherrod Smith was equally brilliant, doing the same to the Indians hitters. In the top of the eighth with one out, Ivy Olson doubled to left field. Mails refused to yield, getting the next two hitters without the ball leaving the infield. Joe Evans singled in the bottom of the eighth, his third hit of the game, but Smith kept the Indians from scoring. The Robins had one last chance with one out in the ninth inning when Joe Sewell made his second

error of the game, allowing Myers to reach first. Mails showed no signs of frustration, calmly getting Konetchy to force Myers at second. Kilduff, the last hope,
lifted a routine fly ball to left field. Evans got in position and then tightly
squeezed the ball for the final out. Walter Mails had pitched a spectacular game,
holding Brooklyn to three hits while not allowing a single run. His teammates
could not give him much support, but Mails put on an unwavering display of
nerve, topping his recent efforts in September. His counterpart had pitched
nearly as well, but the double by George Burns gave Sherrod Smith a disheart-
ening loss.

An obviously pleased Speaker had high praise for Mails and Burns after
the game. He said about Mails, "It was a tough spot he was in this afternoon,
the toughest of the series. He was given the acid test if ever a young player was
and proved 18 carats fine." He lauded Burns for his great play as a substitute
during the summer, adding, "He never rose to the occasion any more successfully than he did today when he rapped one of Sherrod Smith's best offerings
to the center field bleachers for two bases and scored me all the way from first."
So far it had been a great series for two unheralded ballplayers that few expected
to contribute much. Even with Speaker's platoon system, Doc Johnston usually
played against left-handed pitchers. For some reason, the manager decided to
use Burns against the Brooklyn lefties. The tactic paid dividends in game 1 and
now in game 6. Mails probably would not have seen any action if Ray Caldwell
had pitched like he did during the regular season. When Caldwell faltered in
game 3, Mails pitched six and two-thirds innings without giving up a run. He
continued that streak in game 6, adding a complete game shutout to his total.
His ERA for the World Series was 0.00. Regardless of the outcome, Mails had
earned himself a full share of the player receipts.

On the brink of elimination, the Brooklyn club put on a brave face for the
reporters gathered in the Hotel Winton lobby. The players paced back and forth,
boldly promising to send the series back to New York. Zack Wheat told
reporters, "We'll hit from now on. If Coveleski pitches tomorrow we'll drive
him out of the box." Manager Robinson assured the writers his team was not
beat and would prove it the next afternoon. Uncle Robbie planned to start either
Marquard or Grimes on Tuesday, confident either one could slam the door on

the Indians. In the three games played at League Park, the Robins had scored a grand total of two runs. The composite score of the games was 14–2. To steal a victory and continue the series at Ebbets Field, the Brooklyn players needed a complete turnaround.

Ann Sawyer, in her final column for Taylor's Department Store, had little doubt the World Series would end in Cleveland. She wrote, "Once upon a time Brooklyn was famous for three things: its nearness to New York, its big bridge and its baseball team. Today Brooklyn is still famous—for its nearness to New York and its big bridge." Ms. Sawyer urged the men who were going to stand in line all night at the Indians' ticket office to wait outside Taylor's instead for the start of the 20-percent-off sale on men's suits. Throughout the series, America's best sportswriters were covering the games, among them Ring Lardner, Hugh Fullerton, Damon Runyon, and Cleveland's own Ed Bang and Henry Edwards. While Ann Sawyer did not possess their wealth of knowledge concerning the game of baseball, her observations gave readers a breather from all the scores and statistics.

Those familiar with the weather in northeast Ohio know that October can be a miserable time. Winds sweeping off Lake Erie are commonplace, along with heavy rainfall. Perhaps the weather gods, who had never seen Cleveland baseball this late in the fall, decided to be kind for a change. Game 7 approached with another day of clear skies and warm temperatures hovering around seventy-two degrees. Damon Runyon marveled at the summer-like conditions, writing that he had never seen such nice weather in a World Series. He noted the thousands of men in shirtsleeves who were a blur of white when the sun shined in their direction. Runyon observed that the crowd was still red hot with enthusiasm, as if it were the first game of the home stand. He wrote about the all-night vigil at the ticket windows, the boys and men on rooftops, the fans clinging to trees, and the bleachers filled to capacity by noon. In other cities, fans cooled down a bit after several games, but not in Cleveland, where the fans showed the same kind of mania they had three days ago. Runyon had a lot of material to work with.

More presentations and awards were made just before 2 p.m. Another automobile stood on the infield, this time a gift to Elmer Smith for his bases-loaded home run. A delegation from Niles, Ohio, the birthplace of George Burns, carried with them a fancy gold watch for the Indians first baseman. A local jeweler had gold watches for O'Neill and Coveleski as well. It had been a bountiful series for the Cleveland players, who received gifts by the boatload. If they could take one more ball game, no doubt their contracts for 1921 would include some higher figures.

Despite having only two days' rest, Stan Coveleski started the game for Cleveland. Speaker and Dunn had no yearning to play any more games in Brooklyn, hence their choice of the spitballing right-hander to finish things at home. Wilbert Robinson decided to counter with Burleigh Grimes over Rube Marquard. Grimes had pitched two days earlier but lasted only three innings during the Indians' seven-run onslaught against him. Robinson could only hope his number one starter had something left to keep the series alive.

Both pitchers appeared razor sharp from the onset. No base hits were recorded until the third inning, when with one out Grimes beat out a high chopper to Joe Sewell. Olson grounded to short, but Sewell could not handle the ball, leaving both runners safe. Sheehan hit one on the ground, which skimmed off Olson's leg for an interference call and out number two. Grimes had to return to second but was stranded there when Griffith flied out.

Cleveland managed to collect its first hit in the bottom of the third when Bill Wamby legged out an infield single. With two outs, Grimes got Speaker to ground out to end the inning. At this point the crowd remained somewhat quiet, waiting for something to stand up and cheer about. They got their first chance in the fourth inning when Zack Wheat lifted a drive off the right-field wall. Elmer Smith played the bounce flawlessly, wheeled around and rifled a strike to second. Wheat slid hard, but Wamby applied the tag, putting out the Robins left fielder. Coveleski retired the next two batters to move to the Indians' half of the fourth. After Smith grounded out, Gardner singled to right field. The hit-and-run was on as Gardner took off with the pitch. Doc Johnston slapped the ball to right field, sending the lead runner to third. Joe Sewell flied out to Wheat with neither runner able to advance. Catcher Otto Miler motioned for time out, jogging to the mound to confer with Grimes. The problem at hand was whether or not to pitch to Steve O'Neill. If they walked him, the bases would be loaded for Coveleski. A base hit from the pitcher would likely be good for two runs, which the Robins could not afford. Wilbert Robinson signaled from the dugout to go ahead and pitch to O'Neill. Several reporters in the press box called out to watch for a double steal. On the first pitch Grimes threw a strike down the middle. A split second later Johnston dashed for second, anticipating a throw across that would give Gardner a chance to sprint for the plate. Miller recognized the play, throwing the ball back to Grimes. The pitcher turned to second, where Johnston stopped dead in his tracks about three feet from the bag. In the heat of the moment, Grimes lost his cool, throwing wildly to second base, and allowing Gardner to walk home with the game's first run. Johnston had baited Grimes into making a throw, where the smart play would have been to hold the ball and let the runner reach second. The Brooklyn bench had to be gnashing their teeth when O'Neill flied out harmlessly to right field to end the inning.

The game was far from over, but with Coveleski pitching another outstanding game, the Cleveland fans sensed the ultimate victory could not be far away. In the bottom of the fifth with one out, Charlie Jamieson topped a slow roller down the third-base line for an infield hit. After Wamby flied to left field, Tris Speaker belted a long drive to the exit sign in right center. Jamieson scored the game's second run while Speaker pulled into third with a triple. Now the fans were on their feet, cheering mightily for their player-manager. The trees outside the park shook, but the boys and men perched there managed to hold on to the branches while yelling at the top of their lungs.

The sixth inning went by without either team able to get a base runner. The top of the seventh caused some heart tremors when with two out Joe Sewell lapsed into his erratic play. He knocked down a hard ground ball from Ed Konetchy but could not make a throw. The official scorers ruled the play a base hit. Pete Kilduff shot another grounder in Sewell's direction that he botched for his second error of the game. Robinson decided to roll the dice, sending up Bill Lamar to pinch-hit for Miller. Lamar, a reserve outfielder, had made only forty-four trips to the plate during the entire season. This would be his third at-bat in the series, in which he had gone hitless so far. Lamar, as rusty as he was, served as Brooklyn's last gasp at staying alive. He gave it a good try, bouncing the ball near second. Bill Wamby fielded the baseball cleanly and then threw to first to end the rally. In the bottom of the seventh, O'Neill drove a double to left center field. Coveleski attempted to sacrifice, but this time Grimes made an alert play, throwing to third to catch O'Neill in a rundown. Charlie Jamieson swatted a double to right field, scoring Coveleski with the Indians' third run.

Though two innings remained, it was time to get the champagne and cigars ready. The Robins went down in order in the eighth inning, unable to do anything with Coveleski's pitches. Al Mamaux replaced Grimes on the mound, retiring the Indians in order. That brought the ninth inning, which the population of Cleveland had been waiting to see since April of 1901. They had been charter members of the American League for twenty years but not a single pennant or World Series win to brag about. A certain a number of fans in attendance had been with the club since the launch of the franchise, wondering when their turn would come. Now they stood, their eyes on the great Coveleski, praying he could turn back the Robins just one more time.

The leadoff hitter in the top of the ninth was Tommy Griffith, who had played well early in the series. He popped a fly ball to Jamieson for out number one. Zack Wheat refused to go away quietly, lining a base hit to center. Hy Myers grounded to Sewell, who flipped to Wamby for the force at second. Fans began climbing out of the grandstand, edging as close to the field as they dared. The scoreboard clock showed three minutes before 4 p.m. when Coveleski delivered to Ed Konetchy. The big first baseman swung hard but grounded to Sewell, who again tossed to Wamby to end the ball game. The Cleveland Indians were champions of the world. They had taken four games in a row to defeat Brooklyn, five games to two. Thousands of delirious fans raced around the field while the Indians sprinted hard for the safety of the clubhouse. These were moments of pure joy that could never be recaptured.

An elated Jim Dunn stood smiling in his field box, accepting congratulations from friends and foes alike. Charles Ebbets, the Brooklyn owner, stopped by to offer his best wishes. Excited fans crowded around, demanding a speech. Dunn slowly removed his hat and spoke from the heart. He said, "I am the happiest man in the world today. I know you are happy too, after all it is your team. It is Cleveland's team more than it is mine. I thank you for your enthusiasm and for your loyalty." Before he could make any attempt to reach the clubhouse, a small boy handed him a scorecard and pencil. For ten minutes, Dunn signed hundreds of autographs for his devoted fans. When the line thinned, he walked toward the locker room while his entourage followed, slapping him on the back and offering more congratulations. Countless times over the last five seasons, Dunn had made the very same walk to center field and then on to the clubhouse to see his boys. With sunny skies around him, this walk was the sweetest of them all.

16

A SEASON TO REMEMBER

There were multiple players on the Cleveland club who deserved accolades for their play in the World Series. Although Bill Wamby did not hit well, his extraordinary unassisted triple play still has not been duplicated in ninety years of post-season play. Elmer Smith's grand slam was not equaled until 1936, many years after the baseball became much livelier. Walter Mails's shutout in game 6 took place at a crucial time when Brooklyn desperately needed a win. Jim Bagby won only a single game but had to his credit a three-run homer, the first ever by a pitcher in a World Series. George Burns and Charlie Jamieson came through with clutch hits, while Tris Speaker played his usual excellent brand of baseball. Steve O'Neill gave a clinic on how to block home plate, along with a series average of .333. But however great these accomplishments, the one player who stood above everybody else was the coal miner from Shamokin, Pennsylvania, Stan Coveleski. Using his spitball to set up his other pitches, Coveleski won three games, allowed two runs in twenty-seven innings, and issued only two walks. His earned run average came in at 0.67. He pitched game 7 after only two days' rest. In that effort, statistics revealed he threw just ninety pitches throughout the game. There were others before him who had won three games in a World Series, Christy Mathewson and Joe Wood among them. However, Coveleski achieved this for a team that had never won a pennant and for a city that was starving for a chance to experience the thrill of a world championship. And he did it after losing his wife during the early part of the season. He survived that tragedy to have one of his finest years. Without a doubt he was the most valuable player in the World Series.

Hours after the final game, telegrams of congratulation came to the League Park office. Outgoing president Woodrow Wilson sent his best wishes. James Cox, the governor of Ohio and candidate for president, wired his thoughts on behalf of all Ohioans. Eddie Collins sent Speaker a telegram stating, "Courage and co-operation will tell." Messages came from all parts of Texas congratulating its favorite son. Speaker got an invitation to be the special guest at the Texas state fair beginning in mid-October. There would be banquets and dinners for just about everybody connected with the ball club.

Before the Brooklyn players could get away from Cleveland, Rube Marquard appeared before a judge on the ticket-scalping charge. On the witness stand, Marquard explained that he had purchased the tickets for his brother, who was arriving from Youngstown to watch the games. He further explained that a man he knew from Brooklyn approached him asking for tickets. Marquard claimed he had pulled the tickets from his pocket as a joke when the police nabbed him. The arresting officer told a completely different story, telling the judge he had witnessed Marquard attempting to sell the tickets on two occasions. According to the policeman, the clerk at the cigar counter tipped off the defendant, who quickly put the tickets away. The judge found Marquard guilty but fined him only a dollar plus court costs. After the trial, Charles Ebbets announced that the pitcher had played his last game for Brooklyn. Ban Johnson added that Marquard would be barred from trying to sign with any team in the American League. Very harsh treatment for a petty crime, but this action came on the heels of the Black Sox scandal. Any ballplayer who committed even the slightest indiscretion stood to be penalized severely. Rube Marquard had the misfortune to get caught red-handed during the shocking revelations of a crooked World Series the previous year. His trip back home to Cleveland, where family and friends awaited him, turned out to be a very unwelcome one.

The evening after the Cleveland victory, a last-minute celebration was organized to honor the heroes one more time. The event took place at Wade Oval, a park-like setting with a lagoon and brook. City officials had a platform constructed for the players, along with a row of chairs in front for family and friends. Police put up ropes about fifty feet from the seating area to keep the happy revelers a safe distance away. When the players arrived, it seemed the entire crowd from League Park had followed them. A band played "Hail, Hail, the Gang's All Here." Numerous requests were made for the team to sing "Take Me Out to the Ball Game," which they did in loud voices for all to hear. Mayor Fitzgerald stood up to speak, but firecrackers and skyrockets drowned out any words he had to say. The thousands of fans began pushing forward, crossing the brook and trampling the ropes holding them back from the players. The celebration became a mob scene, with chairs broken and the platform surrounded by the still excited fans. In hindsight a parade scheduled later in the week might have been a wiser course to pursue. Nevertheless, there were no injuries and few reports of anybody falling into the lagoon.

Within several days, most of the players were on their way home for a nice, comfortable winter. This time they did not need to work. Each player's share of the World Series money came to $3,986.84. A pool of $5,000 was divided equally among the front office people, trainer, and head groundskeeper. The team made certain that Edna Jamieson, the woman who dutifully answered the busy League Park office phones, got her fair share of the pool. Tris Speaker would do some fishing and hunting, and then spend most of his time in Texas. George Burns left for Philadelphia, where he worked at a sporting goods store. Larry Gardner returned to Vermont to work at his auto repair and sales shop. Jim Bagby decided to continue selling autos back home in Georgia. Dr. Joe Evans traveled to St. Louis, where he was on staff at a city hospital. Joe Sewell returned to the University of Alabama to finish his education. He was honored at several banquets that featured fish fries, crackers, and dill pickles. After dinner the boys adjourned to the veranda to smoke cigars and drink some good southern coffee. Others decided to take it easy over the winter months, living well with their championship money. Joe Wood spent time hunting and fishing with Stan Coveleski. Charlie Jamieson bought a house in New Jersey and then went to work selling groceries.

Six of the players remained in Cleveland. Bill Wamby, George Uhle, Jack Graney, and Elmer Smith usually stayed in town most of the year. Steve O'Neill had decided to raise his family in the Cleveland area, while Doc Johnston took a job running a downtown pool hall. Hopefully Doc kept a low profile whenever Ban Johnson stopped in the neighborhood. Walter Mails rode a train west to Seattle, where he planned to leave his bachelor days behind him. It had been a storybook year for Mails, who in a period of less than two months had helped win the pennant and World Series for the Indians. He received a full share of the player receipts, as did Joe Sewell.

Before the players disappeared around the country, the O. R. Rust Company presented each member of the team with a black leather belt complete with a silver buckle. The player's initials had been engraved on the pure silver, a fitting gift for the world's champions. There would no more pennants in Cleveland for another twenty-eight years. The team finished second to the Yankees in 1921. Jim Dunn passed away during the early part of the 1922 season, leaving a large hole in the organization that would take years to fill. However, this group of ballplayers could always hold their heads high. They were the ones who broke the string and brought to life an entire city in the most unforgettable summer in Cleveland baseball history.

SOURCES

Books

The Baseball Encyclopedia. New York: Macmillan, 1979.
Creamer, Robert W. *Babe: The Legend Comes to Life*. New York: Simon &
    Schuster, 1974.
Lewis, Franklin. *The Cleveland Indians*. New York: Putnam, 1949.
Ritter, Lawrence. *The Glory of Their Times*. New York: Macmillan, 1966.
Rose, George. *Cleveland: The Making of a City*. Cleveland, OH: World
    Publishing Company, 1950.
Sowell, Mike. *The Pitch That Killed*. Chicago: Ivan R. Dee, 1989.

Periodicals

Baseball Magazine (1912–1921)
Boston Daily Globe (1916, 1917)
Cleveland Leader (1916–1917)
Cleveland News (1916, 1917, 1920)
Cleveland Plain Dealer (1914–1920)
Cleveland Press (1916, 1917, 1920)
New York Times (1920)
The Sporting News (1912–1920)

Libraries and Archives

Chattanooga-Hamilton County Public Library (Local History Department),
Chattanooga, Tennessee.

Cleveland Public Library (Eugene Murdock Collection), Cleveland, Ohio.

Cobb County Public Library (Georgia Room), Marietta, Georgia.

Department of Intercollegiate Athletics, University of Mississippi, Oxford,
Mississippi (player files).

Dorothy Alling Memorial Library, Williston, Vermont.

Enosburg Falls Historical Society, Enosburg Falls, Vermont.

Herrin City Library, Herrin, Illinois.

J. D. Williams Library (Archives & Special Collections), University of
Mississippi, Oxford, Mississippi.

Mayfield Regional Library, Mayfield Heights, Ohio.

National Baseball Hall of Fame Library (player files, Charles Somers file),
Cooperstown, New York.

Pennsylvania Anthracite Heritage Museum, Scranton, Pennsylvania.

Sandusky Public Library, Sandusky, Ohio.

Society for American Baseball Research, Cleveland, Ohio.

Wetumpka, Alabama, Chamber of Commerce.

Personal Communications

Family of James C. Dunn, e-mail correspondence, 2009–2010.

Family of Steve O'Neill, interviews, 2006, 2009–2010.

Family of Bill Wambsganss, interviews, 2009–2010.

INDEX

ABOUT THE AUTHOR

Scott H. Longert is the author of *Addie Joss: King of the Pitchers* (1999). He lives in Beachwood, Ohio, with his wife, Vicki, and their golden retriever, Blair. Longert is patiently waiting for another World Series victory by the Cleveland Indians.